DOCTOR WHO

THE THIRTEENTH DOCTOR

"As the Doctor would say, brilliant!"
BIG COMIC PAGE

"I can't say enough good things about this. It's everything that *Doctor Who* does best."
BUT WHY THO?

"This is one book newcomers and old fans alike are sure to enjoy. 9/10!"
EXPLORE THE MULTIVERSE

"This comic captures the energy and dramatic elements of the recent *Doctor Who* series. All of the creative team work together to produce a solid adventure which is sure to win the hearts of the fans."
MONKEYS FIGHTING ROBOTS

"Perfectly captures the look and voices of the characters!"
ADVENTURES IN POOR TASTE

"If you're a fan overflowing with love for the new Doctor, this is a great place to get an extra dose of *Doctor Who*."
COMICBOOK.COM

"Highly recommended... Bold, sassy, intelligent, and accessible to new fans. 5 out of 5!"
GEEK SYNDICATE

"A perfect continuation of what we've come to love about Series 11. 5 out of 5!"
KABOOOOOM

"A radical romp through time and space!"
NERDIST

"Houser nails it."
NEWSARAMA

"The art team continues to excel!"
SCIFI PULSE

Editor
Jonathan Stevenson

Senior Designer
Andrew Leung

Titan Comics

Managing Editor **Martin Eden**	Sales & Circulation Manager **Steve Tothill**	Head Of Rights **Jenny Boyce**
Production Assistant **Rhiannon Roy**	Publicist **Imogen Harris**	Publishing Director **Darryl Tothill**
Production Controller **Peter James**	Direct Marketing Officer **Charlie Raspin**	Operations Director **Leigh Baulch**
Senior Production Controller **Jackie Flook**	Ads & Marketing Assistant **Bella Hoy**	Executive Director **Vivian Cheung**
Art Director **Oz Browne**	Commercial Manager **Michelle Fairlamb**	Publisher **Nick Landau**

For rights information contact Jenny Boyce
jenny.boyce@titanemail.com

Special thanks to Chris Chibnall, Matt Strevens, Sam Hoyle, Mandy Thwaites,
Suzy L. Raia, Gabby De Matteis, Ross McGlinchey, David Wilson-Nunn,
Kirsty Mullan and Kate Bush for their invaluable assistance.

BBC Worldwide

Director Of Editorial Governance
Nicolas Brett

Director Of Consumer Products And Publishing
Andrew Moultrie

Head Of UK Publishing
Chris Kerwin

Publisher
Mandy Thwaites

Publishing Co-Ordinator
Eva Abramik

DOCTOR WHO: THE THIRTEENTH DOCTOR VOL. 2: HIDDEN HUMAN HISTORY
ISBN: 9781785866913

Published by Titan Comics, a division of Titan Publishing Group, Ltd. 144 Southwark Street, London, SE1 0UP.
Titan Comics is a registered trademark. All rights reserved.

BBC, DOCTOR WHO and TARDIS (word marks and logos) are trade marks of the British Broadcasting Corporation and are used under licence. BBC logo © BBC 1996. Doctor Who logo and WHO insignia © BBC 2018. Thirteenth Doctor images © BBC Studios 2018. Licensed by BBC Studios.

A CIP catalogue record for this title is available from the British Library.
First edition: August 2019.

10 9 8 7 6 5 4 3 2 1

Printed in Spain

Titan Comics does not read or accept unsolicited DOCTOR WHO submissions of ideas, stories or artwork.

BBC

DOCTOR WHO

THE THIRTEENTH DOCTOR

WRITER
JODY HOUSER

ARTISTS
ROBERTA INGRANATA
RACHAEL STOTT

COLORIST
ENRICA EREN ANGIOLINI

COLOR ASSISTANT
VIVIANA SPINELLI

LETTERERS
COMICRAFT'S SARAH JACOBS
AND JOHN ROSHELL

TITAN®
COMICS

BBC

BBC

DOCTOR WHO

THE THIRTEENTH DOCTOR

PREVIOUSLY...

The Doctor, Graham, Yaz, and Ryan came up against the nefarious Hoarder - a greedy and manipulative monster intent on getting anything and everything he wants... whatever the cost. With the help of new friends, and fellow time travellers, Perkins and Schulz, the gang made sure the Hoarder won't be bothering anyone ever again. Now, the Fam are ready to begin a new adventure across time and space...

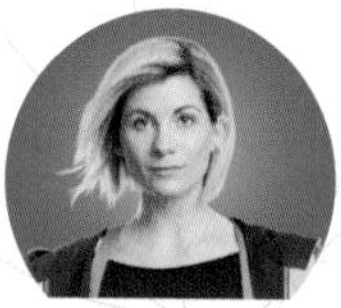

The **Doctor**

The Thirteenth Doctor is a live wire, full of energy and fizzing with excitement and wit! The Doctor is a charismatic and confident explorer, dedicated to seeing all the wonders of the universe, championing fairness and kindness wherever she can. Brave and selfless, this Doctor loves to be surrounded by friends!

-

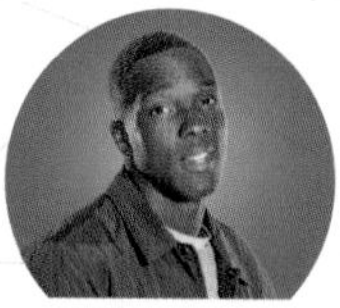

Ryan Sinclair

Ryan is 19 years old, born and bred in Sheffield. He works in a warehouse while studying to become a mechanic. He likes video games and is great with technology! Ryan is dyspraxic, which means he sometimes finds physical co-ordination tricky – but his curiosity and energy always win out over fear.

-

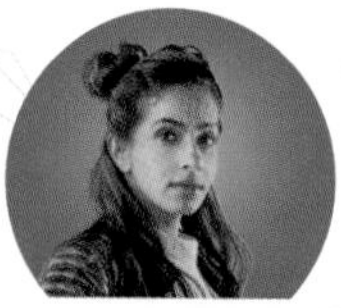

Yasmin 'Yaz' Khan

Yaz is a 19-year-old Sheffielder, friendly and self-assured, a quick logical thinker and a natural leader – the perfect person to have around in a crisis! Yaz loves her job as a probationary police officer, but wants more – not because she's bored, but because she loves adventure and the thrill of the new!

-

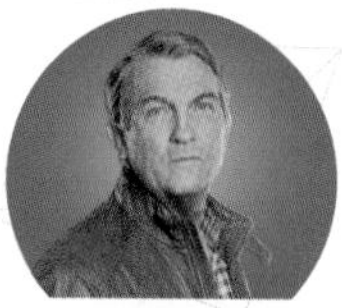

Graham O'Brien

Graham is a funny, charming and cheeky chap from Essex – he's a family man and an ex-bus driver, with a sharp sense of humor and a caring, warm nature. He might be of a different generation (and might sometimes move at a slower pace than Yaz and Ryan), but he's brave, selfless, and wise too – just like the Doctor.

-

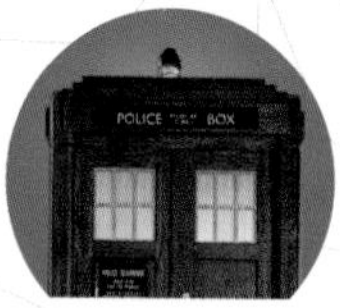

The **TARDIS**

'Time and Relative Dimension in Space'. Bigger on the inside, this unassuming blue police box is your ticket to amazing adventures across time and space! The Doctor likes to think she's in control of her temporal jaunts, but more often than not, the temperamental TARDIS takes her and her friends to where and when they need to be...

-

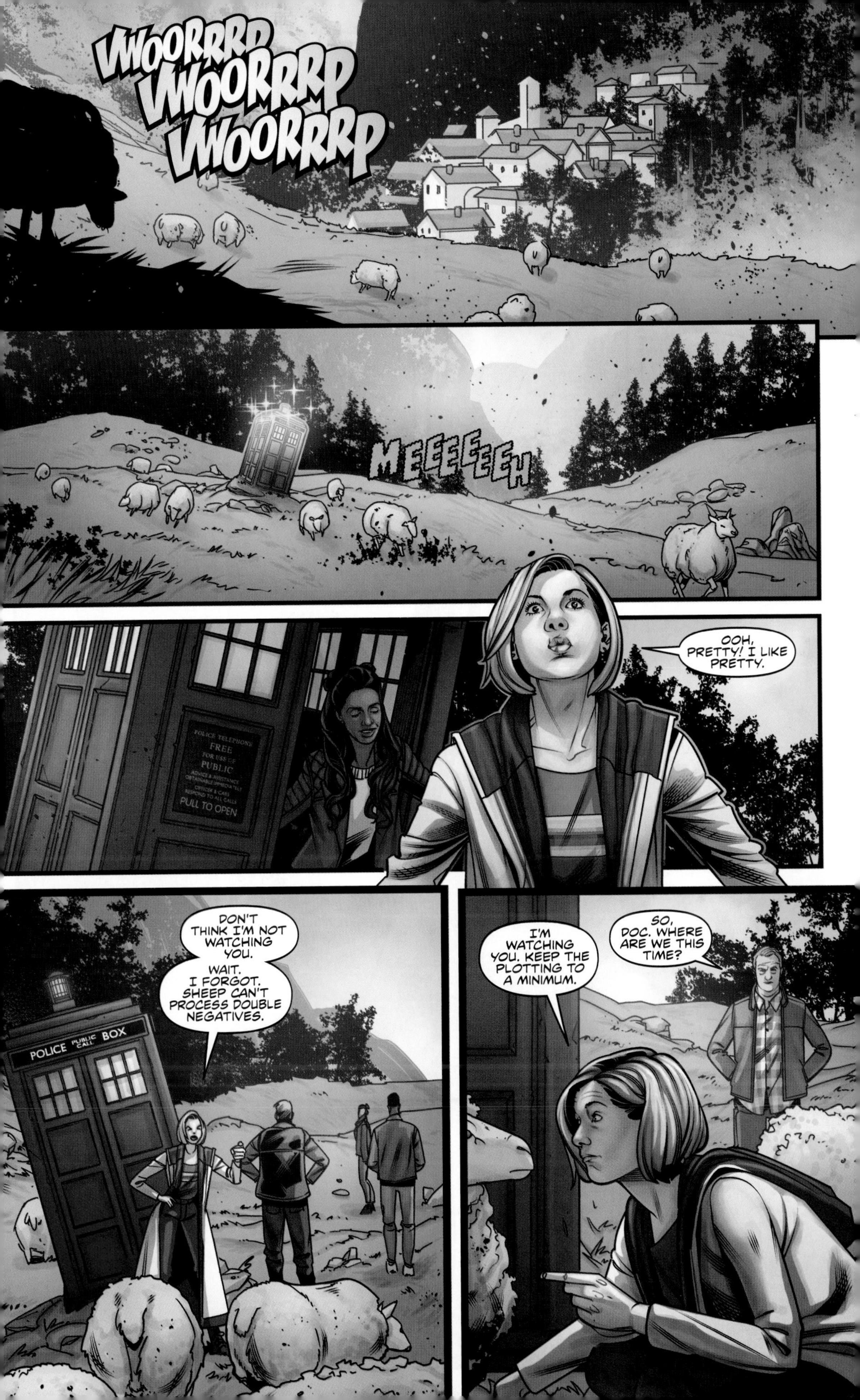

VWOORRRP VWOORRRP VWOORRRP
MEEEEEEH
POLICE TELEPHONE FREE FOR USE OF PUBLIC
PULL TO OPEN
OOH, PRETTY! I LIKE PRETTY.
POLICE PUBLIC CALL BOX
DON'T THINK I'M NOT WATCHING YOU.
WAIT. I FORGOT. SHEEP CAN'T PROCESS DOUBLE NEGATIVES.
SO, DOC. WHERE ARE WE THIS TIME?
I'M WATCHING YOU. KEEP THE PLOTTING TO A MINIMUM.

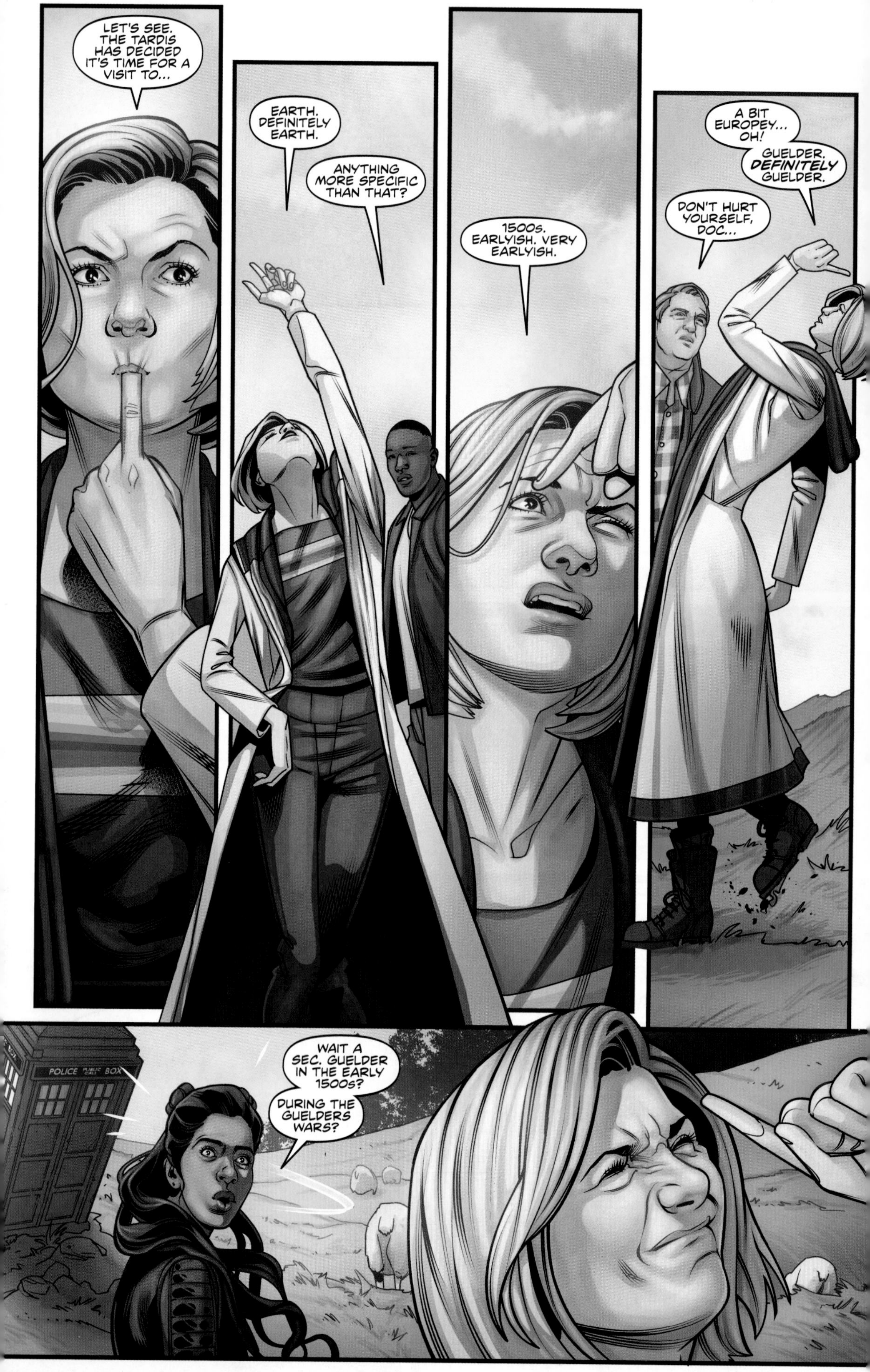
LET'S SEE. THE TARDIS HAS DECIDED IT'S TIME FOR A VISIT TO...
EARTH. DEFINITELY EARTH.
ANYTHING MORE SPECIFIC THAN THAT?
1500s. EARLYISH. VERY EARLYISH.
A BIT EUROPEY... OH!
GUELDER. DEFINITELY GUELDER.
DON'T HURT YOURSELF, DOC...
POLICE PUBLIC CALL BOX
WAIT A SEC. GUELDER IN THE EARLY 1500s?
DURING THE GUELDERS WARS?

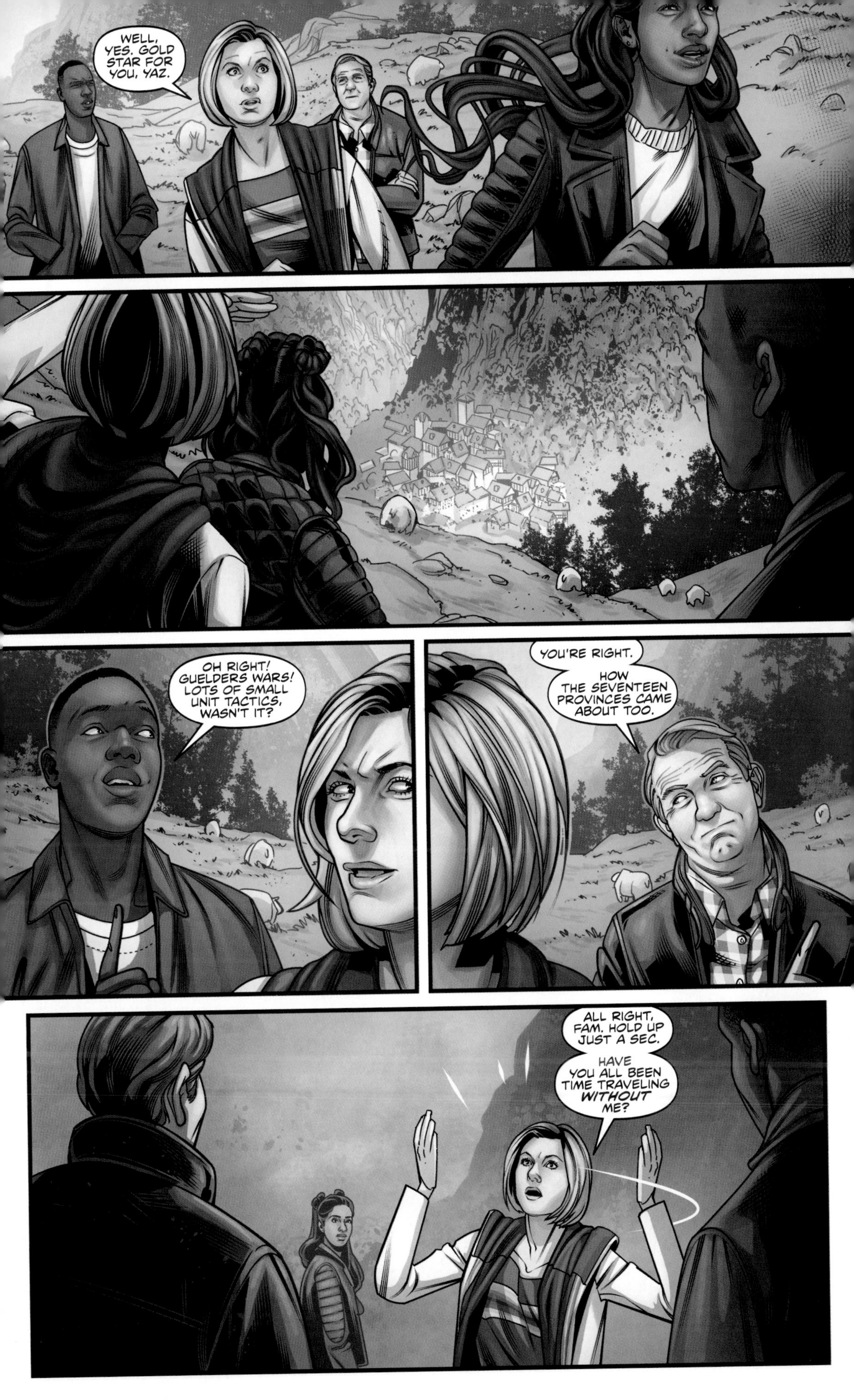
WELL, YES. GOLD STAR FOR YOU, YAZ.
OH RIGHT! GUELDERS WARS! LOTS OF SMALL UNIT TACTICS, WASN'T IT?
YOU'RE RIGHT.
HOW THE SEVENTEEN PROVINCES CAME ABOUT TOO.
ALL RIGHT, FAM. HOLD UP JUST A SEC.
HAVE YOU ALL BEEN TIME TRAVELING *WITHOUT* ME?

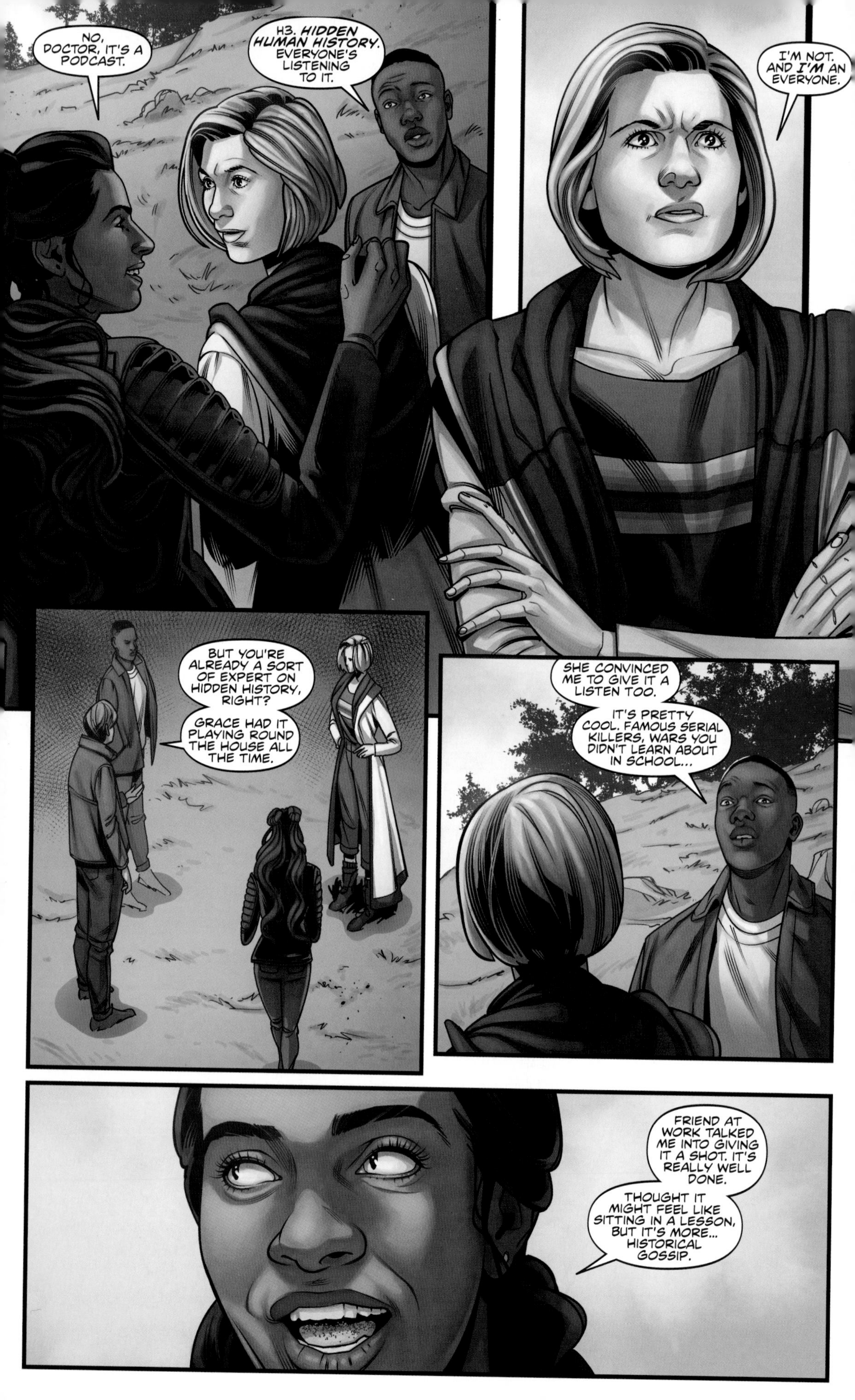
NO, DOCTOR, IT'S A PODCAST.
H3. HIDDEN HUMAN HISTORY. EVERYONE'S LISTENING TO IT.
I'M NOT. AND I'M AN EVERYONE.
BUT YOU'RE ALREADY A SORT OF EXPERT ON HIDDEN HISTORY, RIGHT?
GRACE HAD IT PLAYING ROUND THE HOUSE ALL THE TIME.
SHE CONVINCED ME TO GIVE IT A LISTEN TOO.
IT'S PRETTY COOL. FAMOUS SERIAL KILLERS, WARS YOU DIDN'T LEARN ABOUT IN SCHOOL...
FRIEND AT WORK TALKED ME INTO GIVING IT A SHOT. IT'S REALLY WELL DONE.
THOUGHT IT MIGHT FEEL LIKE SITTING IN A LESSON, BUT IT'S MORE... HISTORICAL GOSSIP.

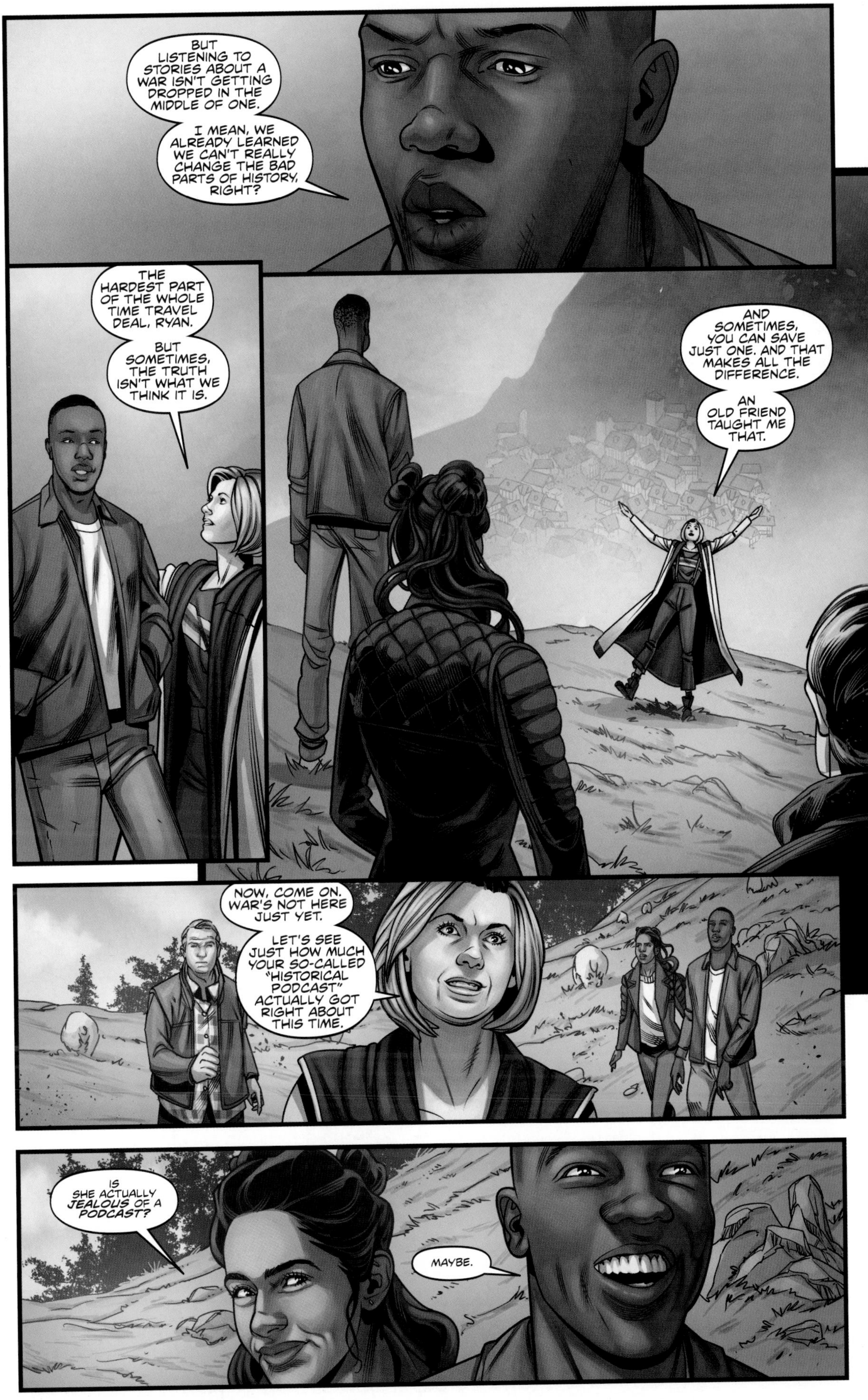

BUT LISTENING TO STORIES ABOUT A WAR ISN'T GETTING DROPPED IN THE MIDDLE OF ONE.
I MEAN, WE ALREADY LEARNED WE CAN'T REALLY CHANGE THE BAD PARTS OF HISTORY, RIGHT?
THE HARDEST PART OF THE WHOLE TIME TRAVEL DEAL, RYAN.
BUT SOMETIMES, THE TRUTH ISN'T WHAT WE THINK IT IS.
AND SOMETIMES, YOU CAN SAVE JUST ONE. AND THAT MAKES ALL THE DIFFERENCE.
AN OLD FRIEND TAUGHT ME THAT.
NOW, COME ON. WAR'S NOT HERE JUST YET.
LET'S SEE JUST HOW MUCH YOUR SO-CALLED "HISTORICAL PODCAST" ACTUALLY GOT RIGHT ABOUT THIS TIME.
IS SHE ACTUALLY *JEALOUS* OF A *PODCAST*?
MAYBE.

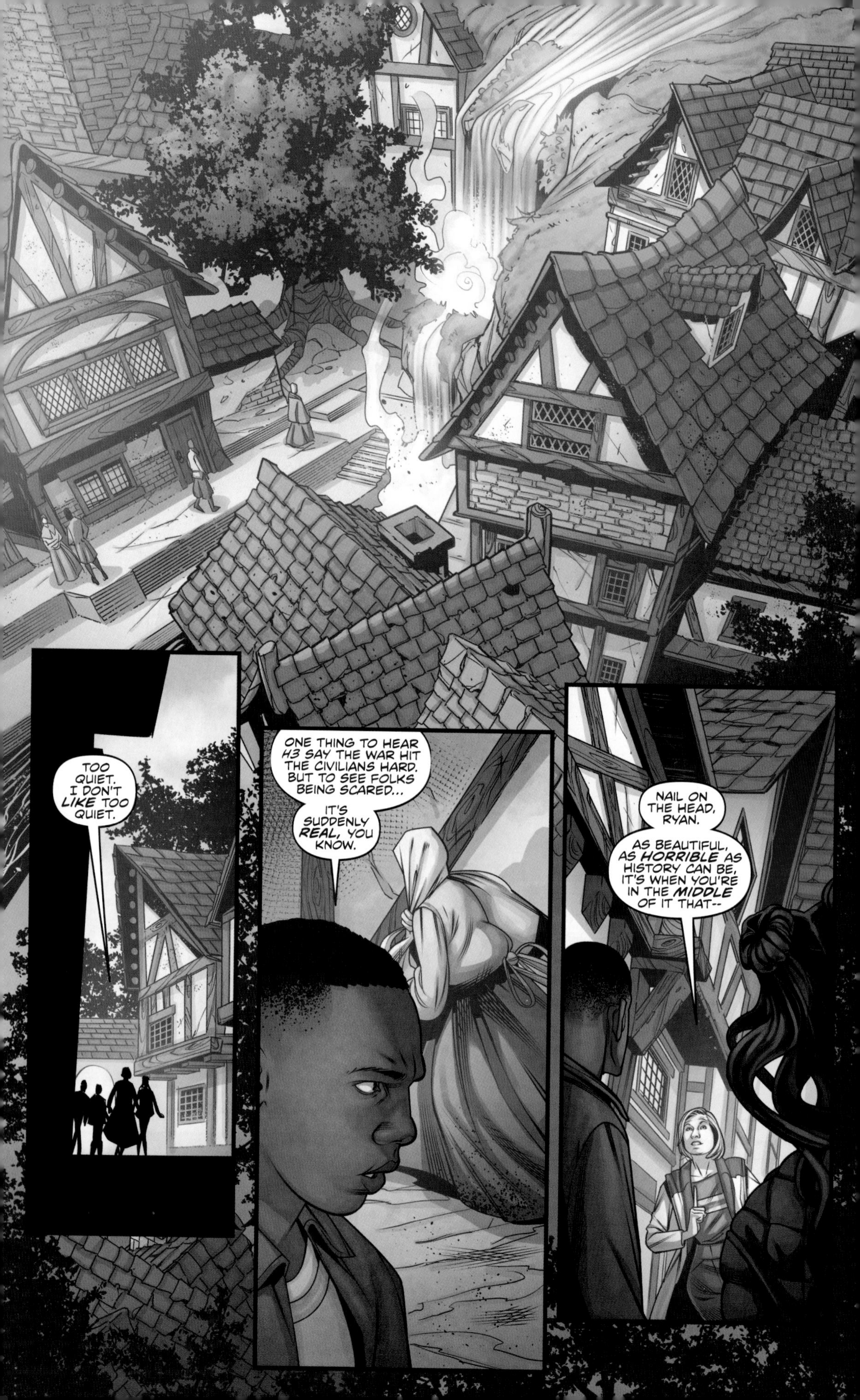
TOO QUIET. I DON'T LIKE TOO QUIET.
ONE THING TO HEAR H3 SAY THE WAR HIT THE CIVILIANS HARD. BUT TO SEE FOLKS BEING SCARED...
IT'S SUDDENLY REAL, YOU KNOW.
NAIL ON THE HEAD, RYAN.
AS BEAUTIFUL, AS HORRIBLE AS HISTORY CAN BE, IT'S WHEN YOU'RE IN THE MIDDLE OF IT THAT--

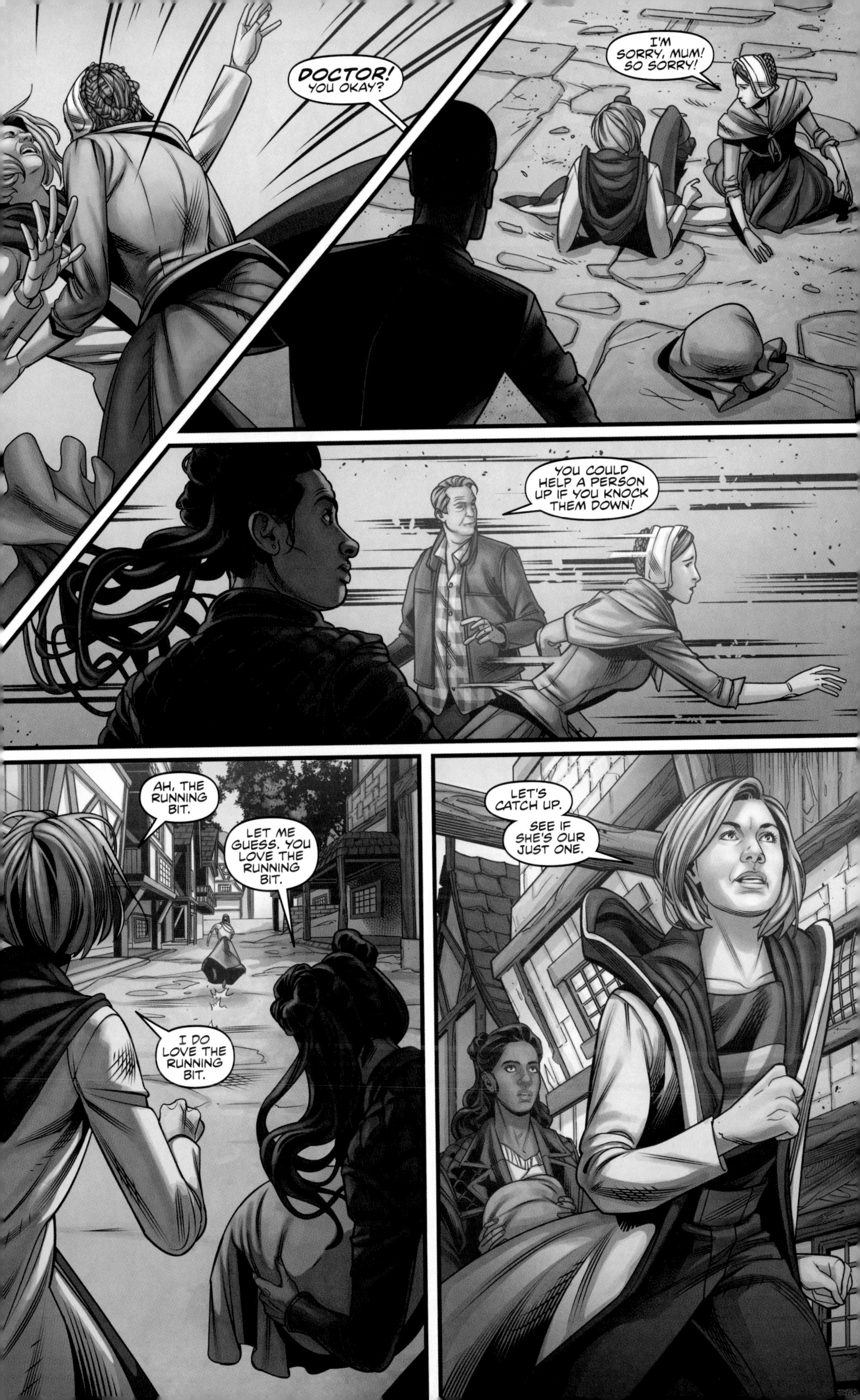
DOCTOR! YOU OKAY?
I'M SORRY, MUM! SO SORRY!
YOU COULD HELP A PERSON UP IF YOU KNOCK THEM DOWN!
AH, THE RUNNING BIT.
LET ME GUESS. YOU LOVE THE RUNNING BIT.
I DO LOVE THE RUNNING BIT.
LET'S CATCH UP.
SEE IF SHE'S OUR JUST ONE.

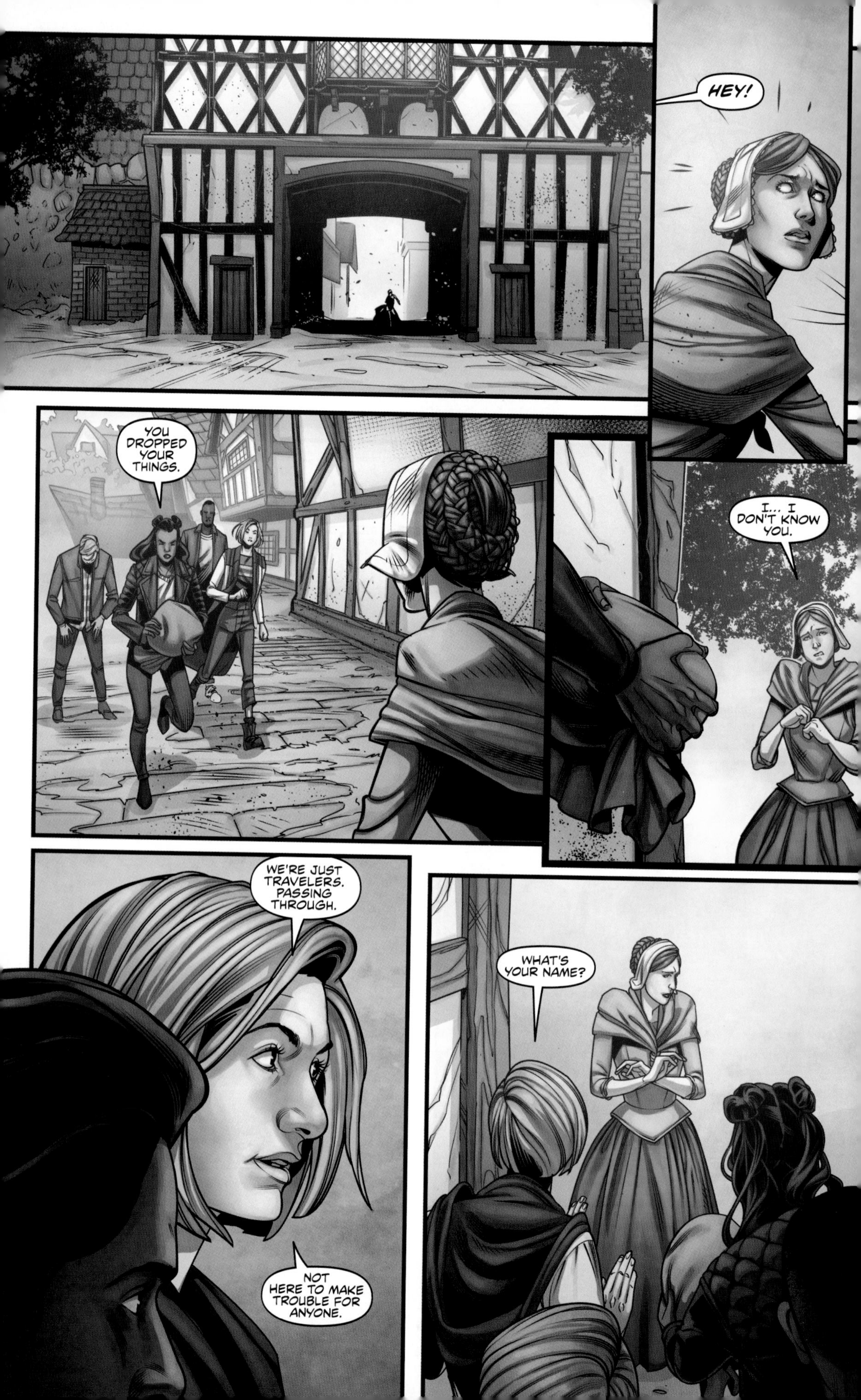
HEY!
YOU DROPPED YOUR THINGS.
I... I DON'T KNOW YOU.
WE'RE JUST TRAVELERS. PASSING THROUGH.
NOT HERE TO MAKE TROUBLE FOR ANYONE.
WHAT'S YOUR NAME?

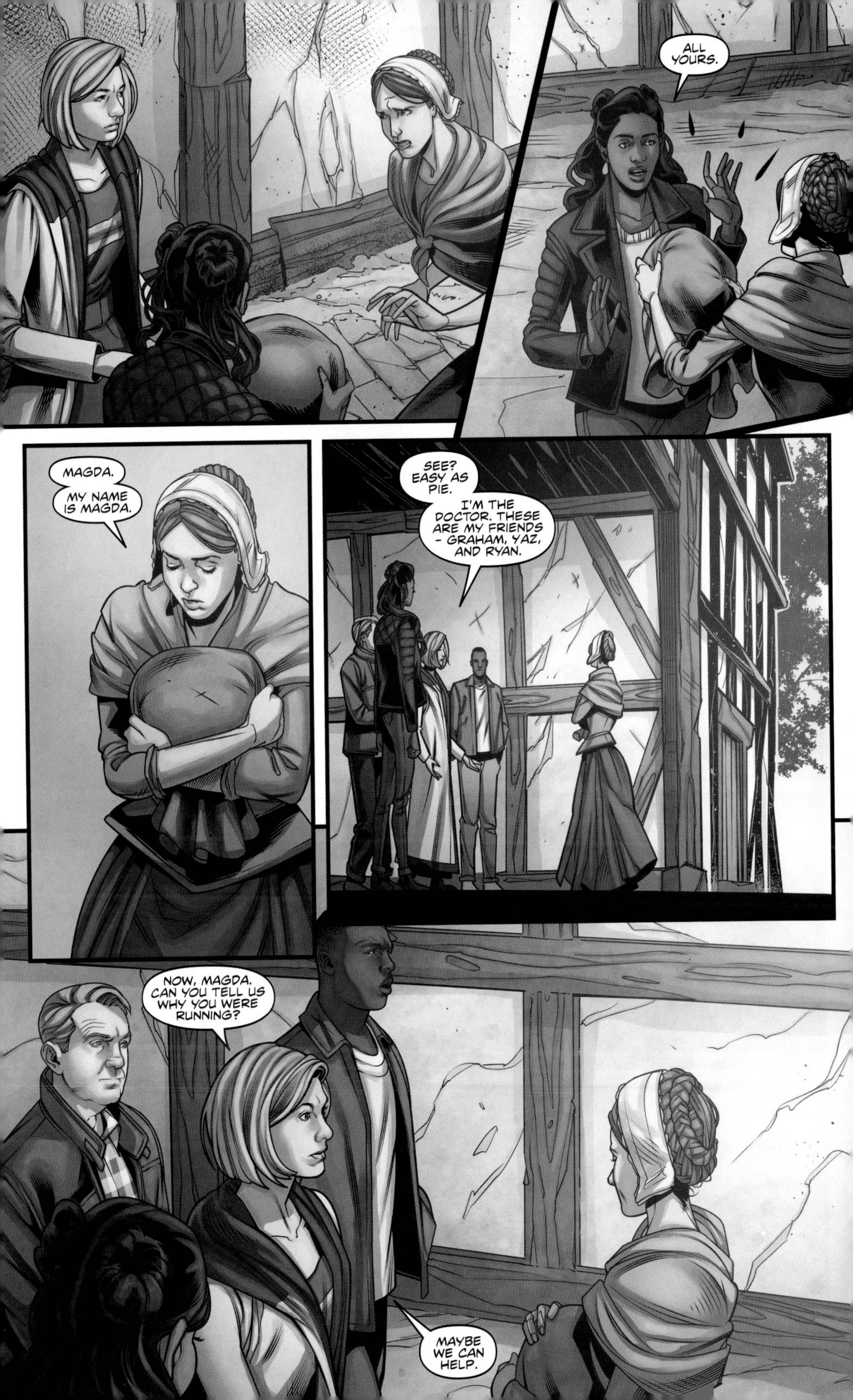
ALL YOURS.
MAGDA.
MY NAME IS MAGDA.
SEE? EASY AS PIE.
I'M THE DOCTOR. THESE ARE MY FRIENDS - GRAHAM, YAZ, AND RYAN.
NOW, MAGDA. CAN YOU TELL US WHY YOU WERE RUNNING?
MAYBE WE CAN HELP.

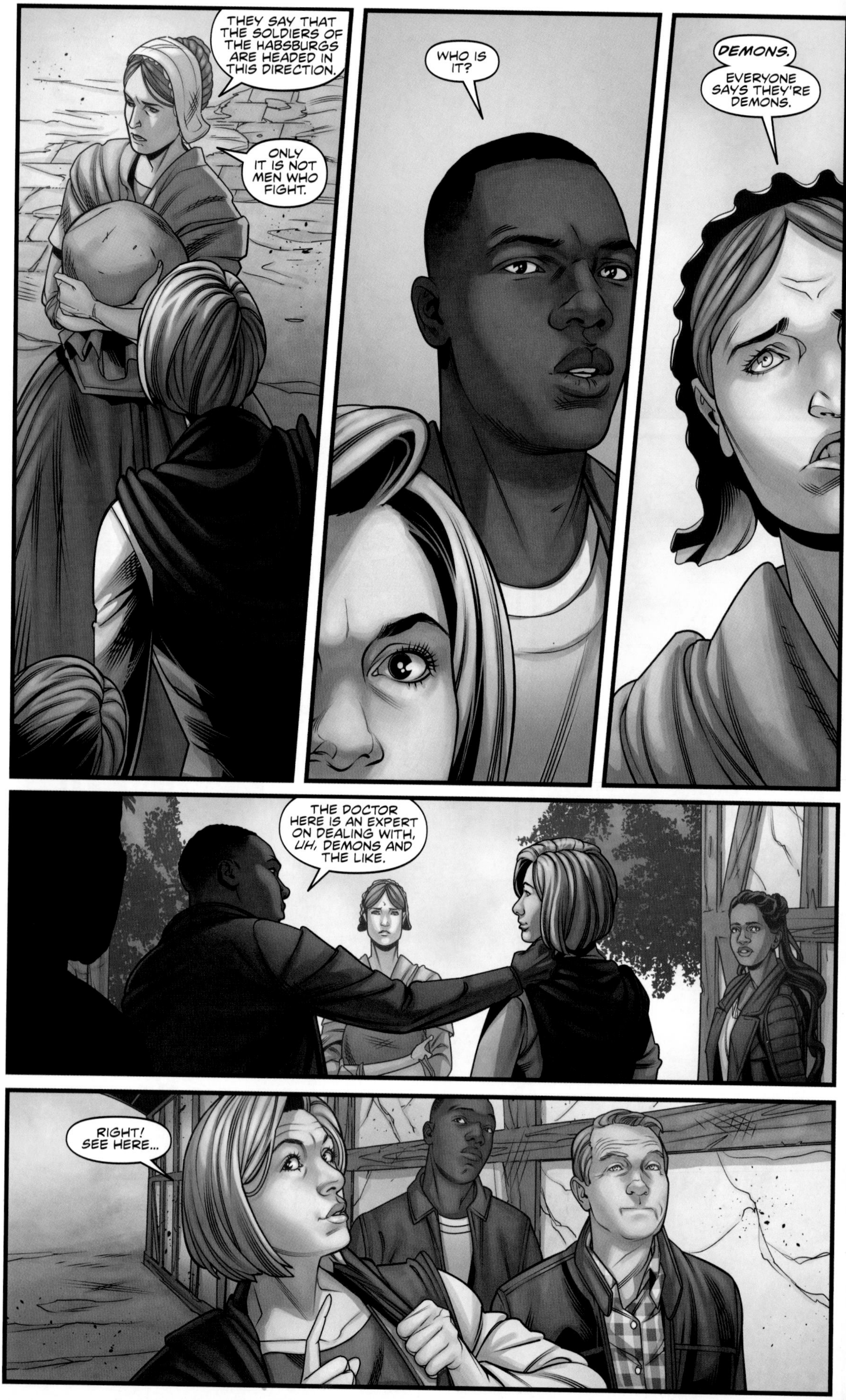
THEY SAY THAT THE SOLDIERS OF THE HABSBURGS ARE HEADED IN THIS DIRECTION.
ONLY IT IS NOT MEN WHO FIGHT.
WHO IS IT?
DEMONS.
EVERYONE SAYS THEY'RE DEMONS.
THE DOCTOR HERE IS AN EXPERT ON DEALING WITH, UH, DEMONS AND THE LIKE.
RIGHT! SEE HERE...

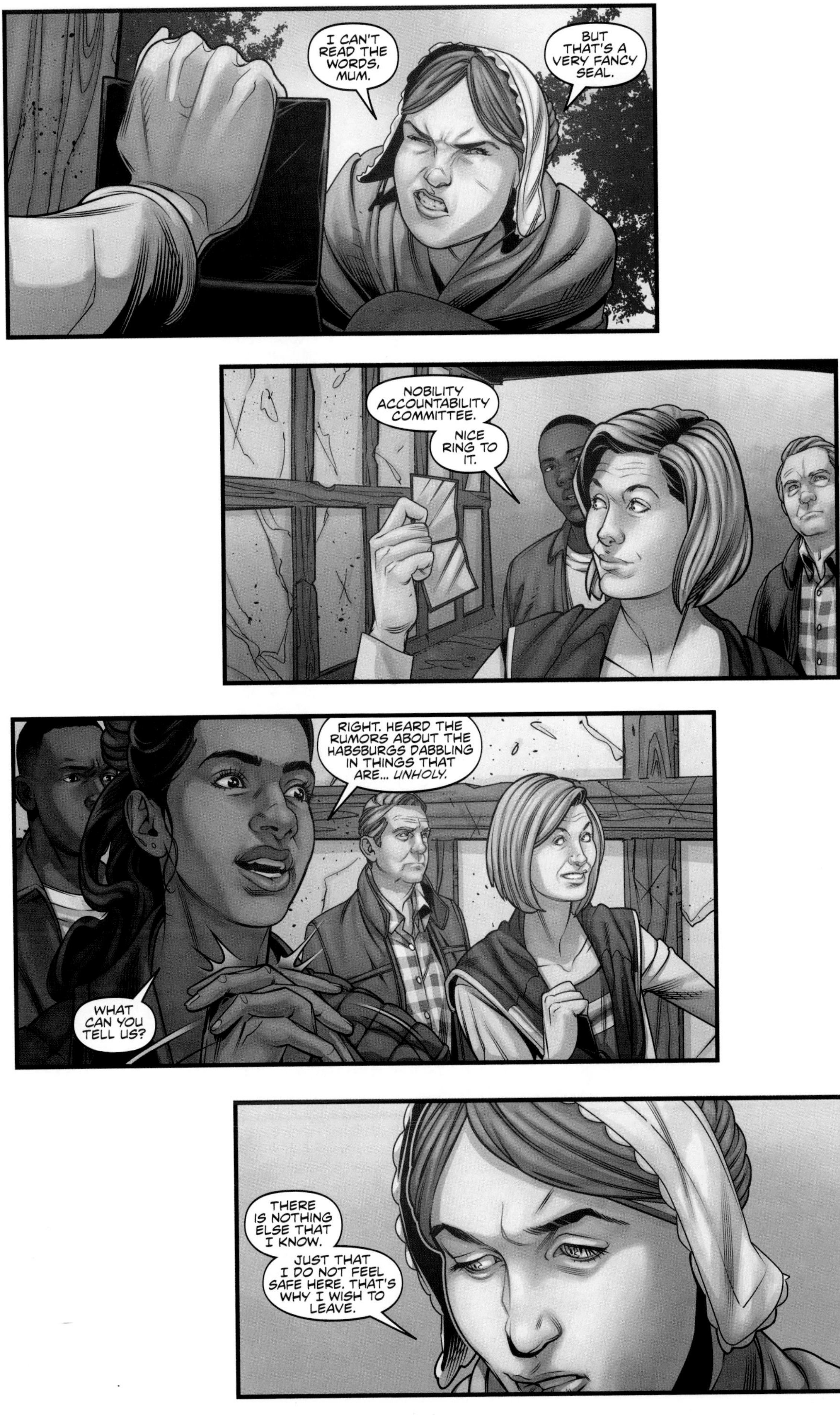
I CAN'T READ THE WORDS, MUM.
BUT THAT'S A VERY FANCY SEAL.
NOBILITY ACCOUNTABILITY COMMITTEE.
NICE RING TO IT.
RIGHT. HEARD THE RUMORS ABOUT THE HABSBURGS DABBLING IN THINGS THAT ARE... *UNHOLY*.
WHAT CAN YOU TELL US?
THERE IS NOTHING ELSE THAT I KNOW.
JUST THAT I DO NOT FEEL SAFE HERE. THAT'S WHY I WISH TO LEAVE.

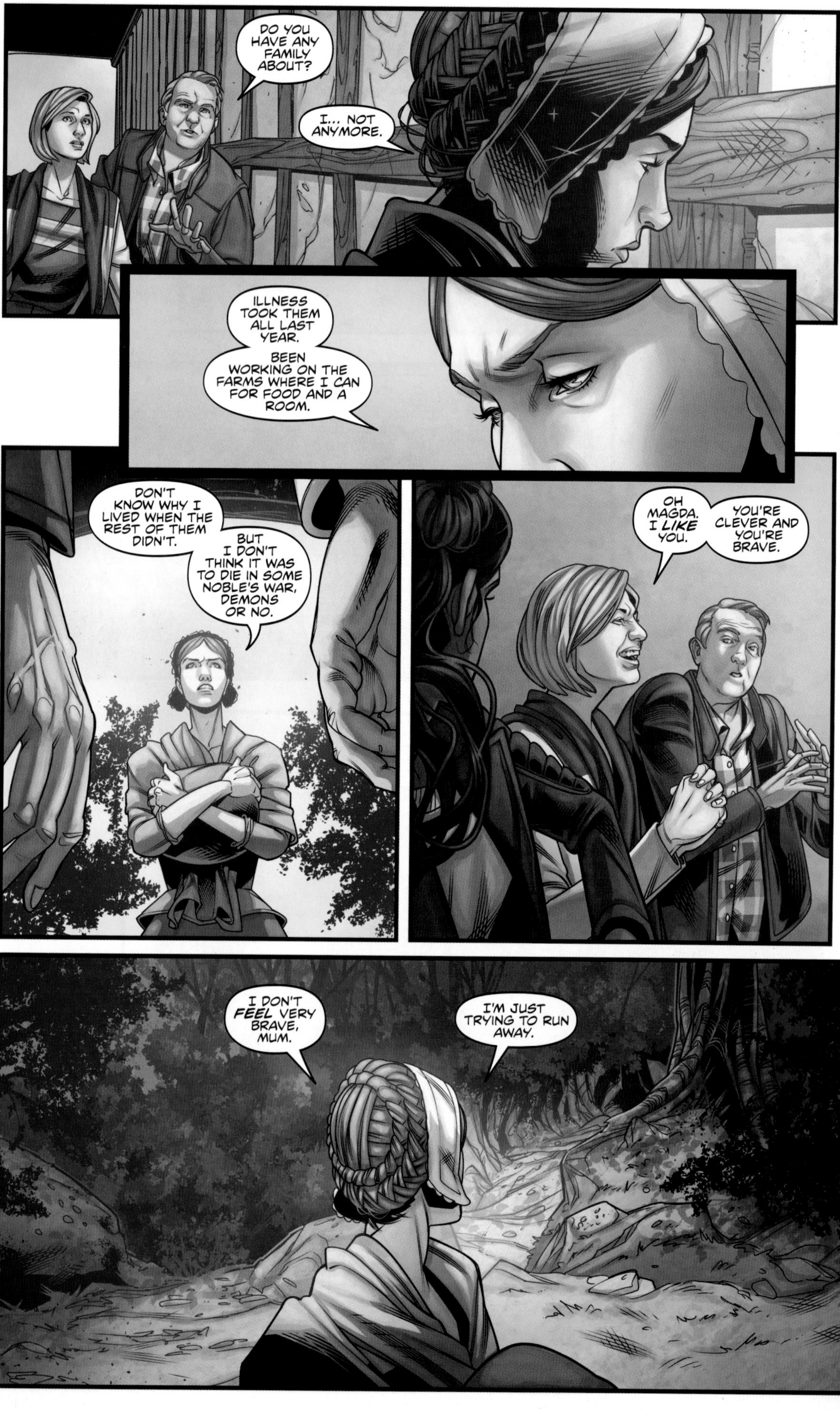
DO YOU HAVE ANY FAMILY ABOUT?
I... NOT ANYMORE.
ILLNESS TOOK THEM ALL LAST YEAR.
BEEN WORKING ON THE FARMS WHERE I CAN FOR FOOD AND A ROOM.
DON'T KNOW WHY I LIVED WHEN THE REST OF THEM DIDN'T.
BUT I DON'T THINK IT WAS TO DIE IN SOME NOBLE'S WAR, DEMONS OR NO.
OH MAGDA. I LIKE YOU.
YOU'RE CLEVER AND YOU'RE BRAVE.
I DON'T FEEL VERY BRAVE, MUM.
I'M JUST TRYING TO RUN AWAY.

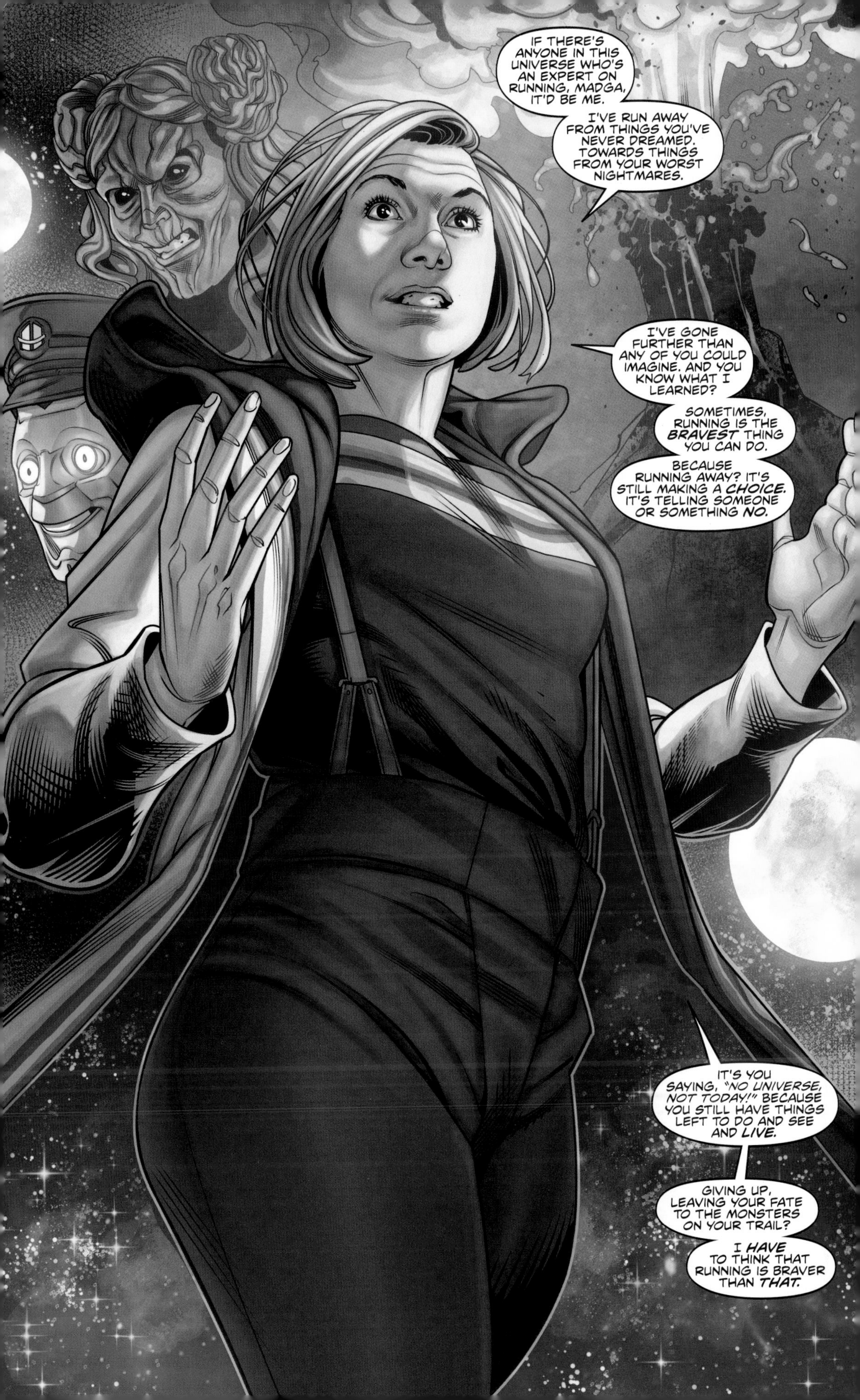
IF THERE'S ANYONE IN THIS UNIVERSE WHO'S AN EXPERT ON RUNNING, MADGA, IT'D BE ME.
I'VE RUN AWAY FROM THINGS YOU'VE NEVER DREAMED. TOWARDS THINGS FROM YOUR WORST NIGHTMARES.
I'VE GONE FURTHER THAN ANY OF YOU COULD IMAGINE. AND YOU KNOW WHAT I LEARNED?
SOMETIMES, RUNNING IS THE ***BRAVEST*** THING YOU CAN DO.
BECAUSE RUNNING AWAY? IT'S STILL MAKING A ***CHOICE***. IT'S TELLING SOMEONE OR SOMETHING ***NO***.
IT'S YOU SAYING, *"NO UNIVERSE, NOT TODAY!"* BECAUSE YOU STILL HAVE THINGS LEFT TO DO AND SEE AND ***LIVE***.
GIVING UP, LEAVING YOUR FATE TO THE MONSTERS ON YOUR TRAIL?
I ***HAVE*** TO THINK THAT RUNNING IS BRAVER THAN ***THAT***.

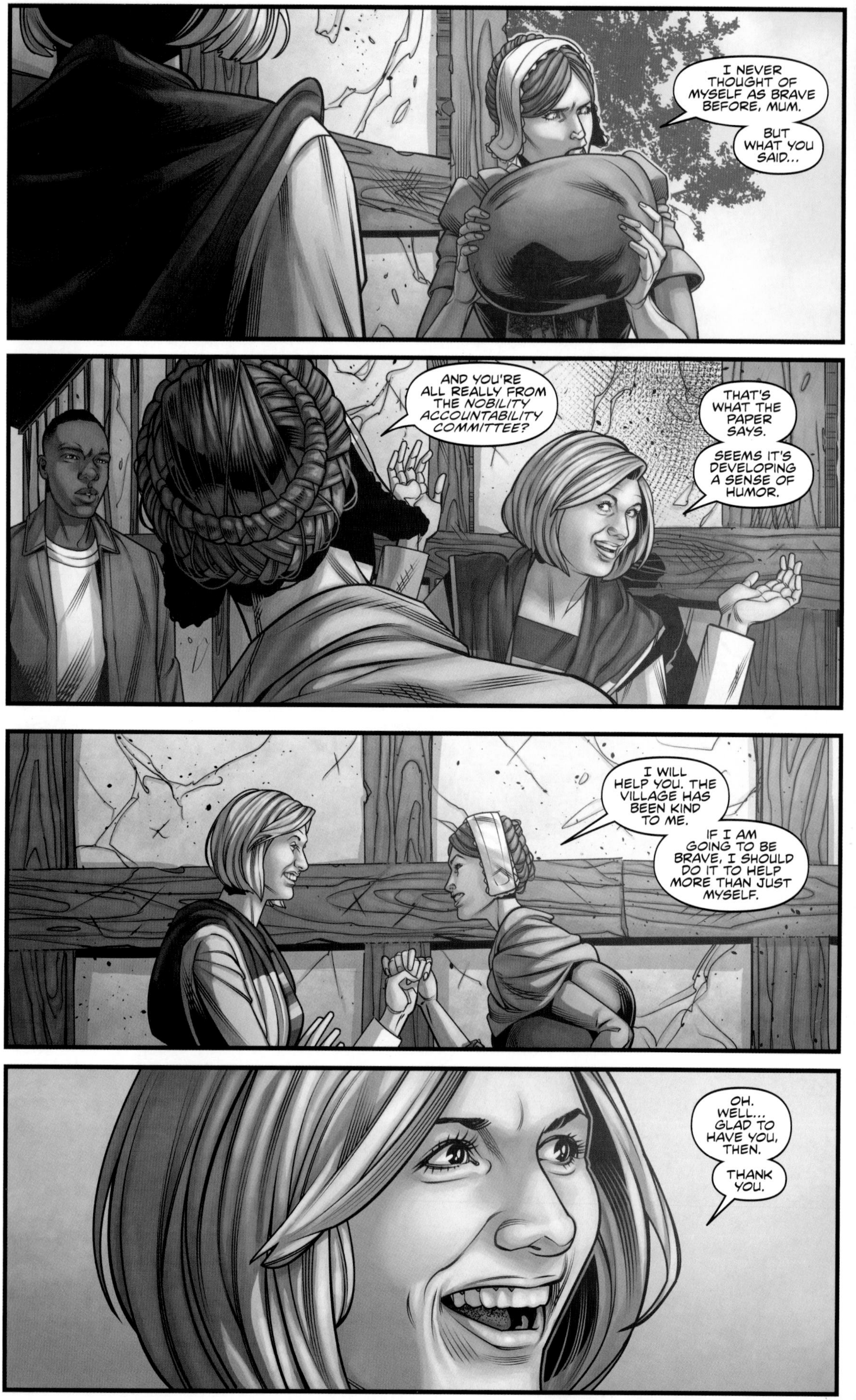
I NEVER THOUGHT OF MYSELF AS BRAVE BEFORE, MUM.
BUT WHAT YOU SAID...
AND YOU'RE ALL REALLY FROM THE *NOBILITY ACCOUNTABILITY COMMITTEE*?
THAT'S WHAT THE PAPER SAYS.
SEEMS IT'S DEVELOPING A SENSE OF HUMOR.
I WILL HELP YOU. THE VILLAGE HAS BEEN KIND TO ME.
IF I AM GOING TO BE BRAVE, I SHOULD DO IT TO HELP MORE THAN JUST MYSELF.
OH. WELL... GLAD TO HAVE YOU, THEN.
THANK YOU.

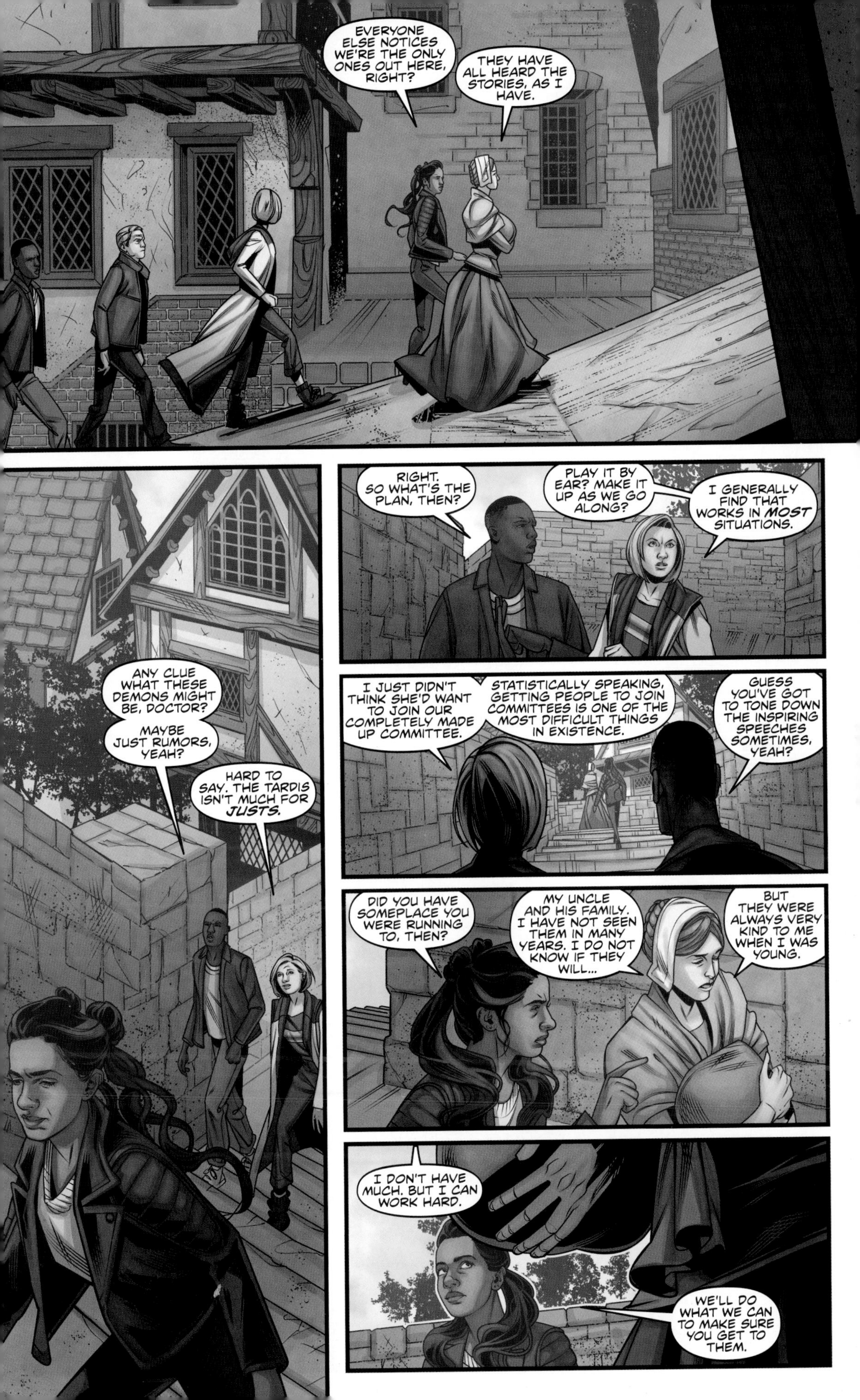
EVERYONE ELSE NOTICES WE'RE THE ONLY ONES OUT HERE, RIGHT?
THEY HAVE ALL HEARD THE STORIES, AS I HAVE.
ANY CLUE WHAT THESE DEMONS MIGHT BE, DOCTOR?
MAYBE JUST RUMORS, YEAH?
HARD TO SAY. THE TARDIS ISN'T MUCH FOR JUSTS.
RIGHT. SO WHAT'S THE PLAN, THEN?
PLAY IT BY EAR? MAKE IT UP AS WE GO ALONG?
I GENERALLY FIND THAT WORKS IN MOST SITUATIONS.
I JUST DIDN'T THINK SHE'D WANT TO JOIN OUR COMPLETELY MADE UP COMMITTEE.
STATISTICALLY SPEAKING, GETTING PEOPLE TO JOIN COMMITTEES IS ONE OF THE MOST DIFFICULT THINGS IN EXISTENCE.
GUESS YOU'VE GOT TO TONE DOWN THE INSPIRING SPEECHES SOMETIMES, YEAH?
DID YOU HAVE SOMEPLACE YOU WERE RUNNING TO, THEN?
MY UNCLE AND HIS FAMILY. I HAVE NOT SEEN THEM IN MANY YEARS. I DO NOT KNOW IF THEY WILL...
BUT THEY WERE ALWAYS VERY KIND TO ME WHEN I WAS YOUNG.
I DON'T HAVE MUCH. BUT I CAN WORK HARD.
WE'LL DO WHAT WE CAN TO MAKE SURE YOU GET TO THEM.

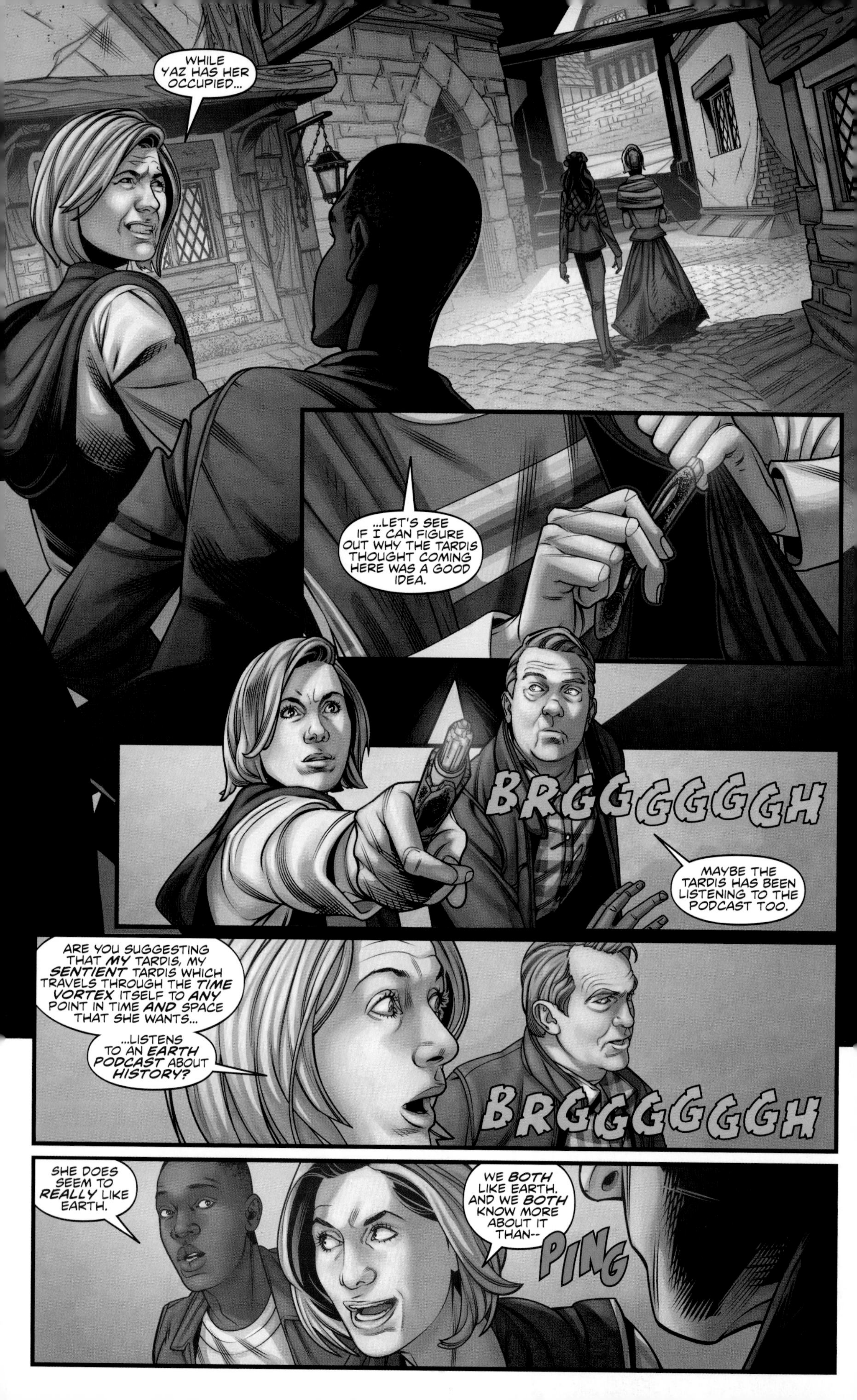
WHILE YAZ HAS HER OCCUPIED...
...LET'S SEE IF I CAN FIGURE OUT WHY THE TARDIS THOUGHT COMING HERE WAS A GOOD IDEA.
BRGGGGGGH
MAYBE THE TARDIS HAS BEEN LISTENING TO THE PODCAST TOO.
ARE YOU SUGGESTING THAT MY TARDIS, MY SENTIENT TARDIS WHICH TRAVELS THROUGH THE TIME VORTEX ITSELF TO ANY POINT IN TIME AND SPACE THAT SHE WANTS...
...LISTENS TO AN EARTH PODCAST ABOUT HISTORY?
BRGGGGGGH
SHE DOES SEEM TO REALLY LIKE EARTH.
WE BOTH LIKE EARTH. AND WE BOTH KNOW MORE ABOUT IT THAN--
PING

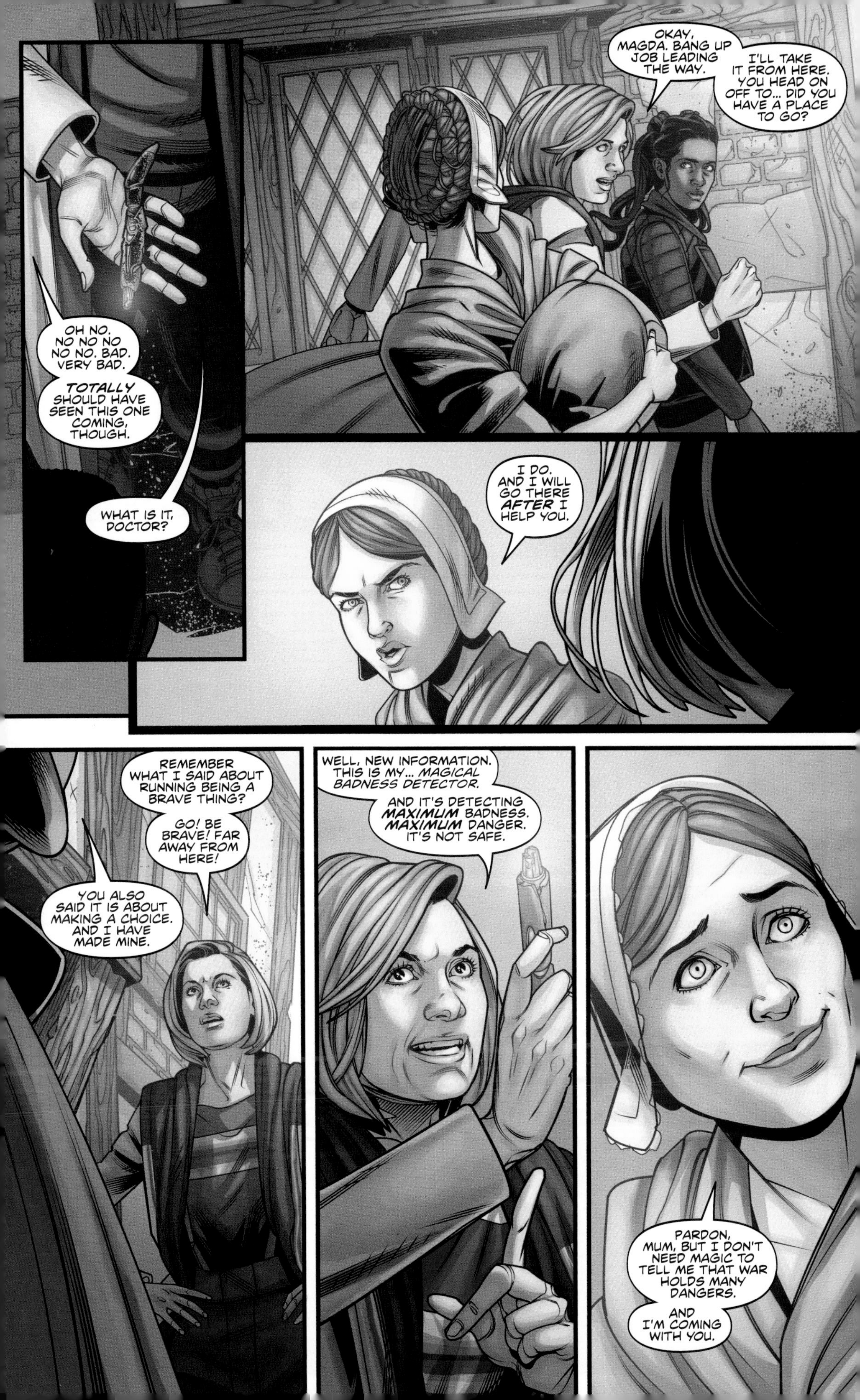
OH NO. NO NO NO NO NO. BAD. VERY BAD.
TOTALLY SHOULD HAVE SEEN THIS ONE COMING, THOUGH.
OKAY, MAGDA. BANG UP JOB LEADING THE WAY.
I'LL TAKE IT FROM HERE. YOU HEAD ON OFF TO... DID YOU HAVE A PLACE TO GO?
WHAT IS IT, DOCTOR?
I DO. AND I WILL GO THERE AFTER I HELP YOU.
REMEMBER WHAT I SAID ABOUT RUNNING BEING A BRAVE THING?
GO! BE BRAVE! FAR AWAY FROM HERE!
YOU ALSO SAID IT IS ABOUT MAKING A CHOICE. AND I HAVE MADE MINE.
WELL, NEW INFORMATION. THIS IS MY... MAGICAL BADNESS DETECTOR.
AND IT'S DETECTING MAXIMUM BADNESS. MAXIMUM DANGER. IT'S NOT SAFE.
PARDON, MUM, BUT I DON'T NEED MAGIC TO TELL ME THAT WAR HOLDS MANY DANGERS.
AND I'M COMING WITH YOU.

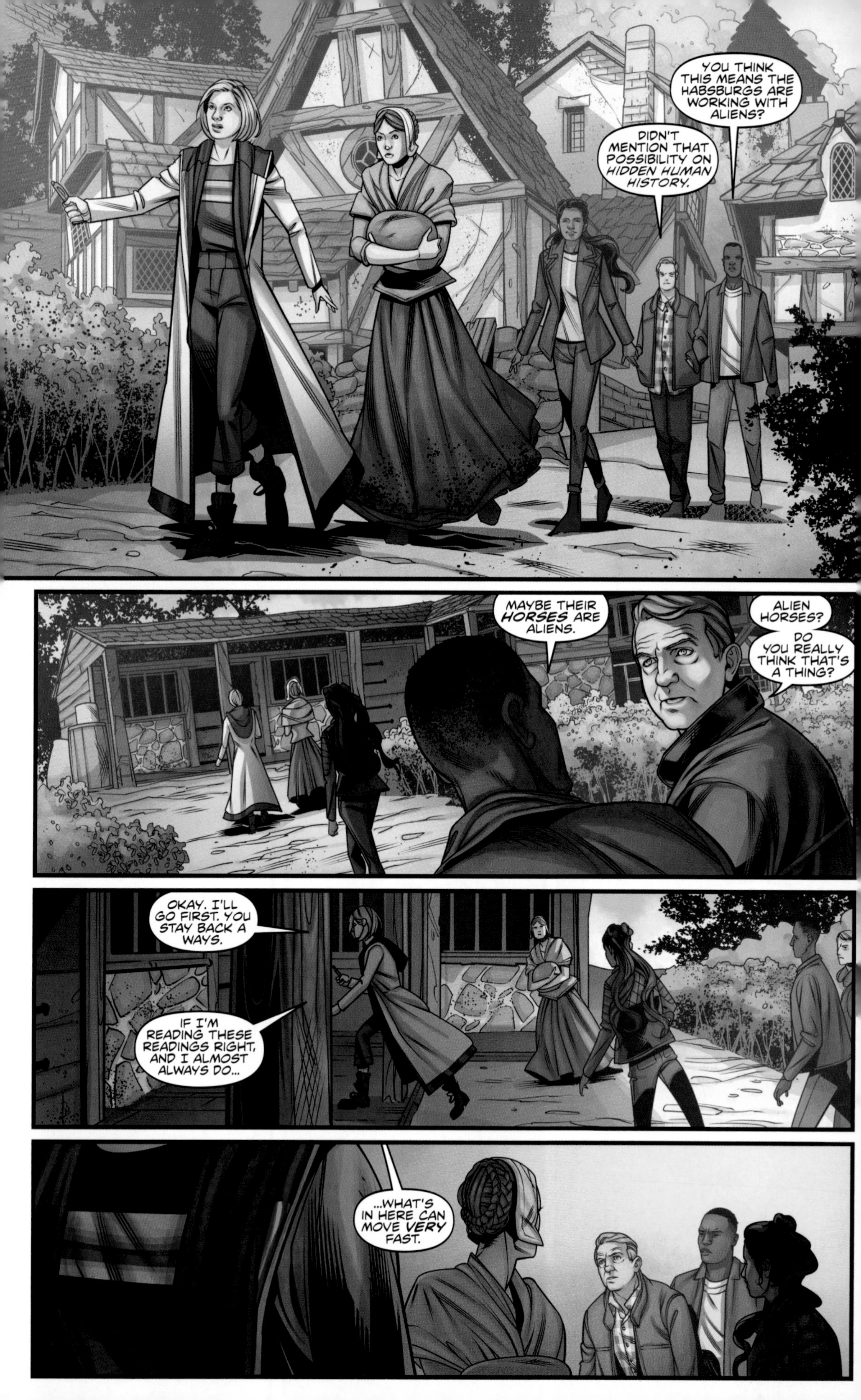
YOU THINK THIS MEANS THE HABSBURGS ARE WORKING WITH ALIENS?
DIDN'T MENTION THAT POSSIBILITY ON *HIDDEN HUMAN HISTORY.*
MAYBE THEIR ***HORSES*** ARE ALIENS.
ALIEN HORSES?
DO YOU REALLY THINK THAT'S A THING?
OKAY. I'LL GO FIRST. YOU STAY BACK A WAYS.
IF I'M READING THESE READINGS RIGHT, AND I ALMOST ALWAYS DO...
...WHAT'S IN HERE CAN MOVE ***VERY*** FAST.

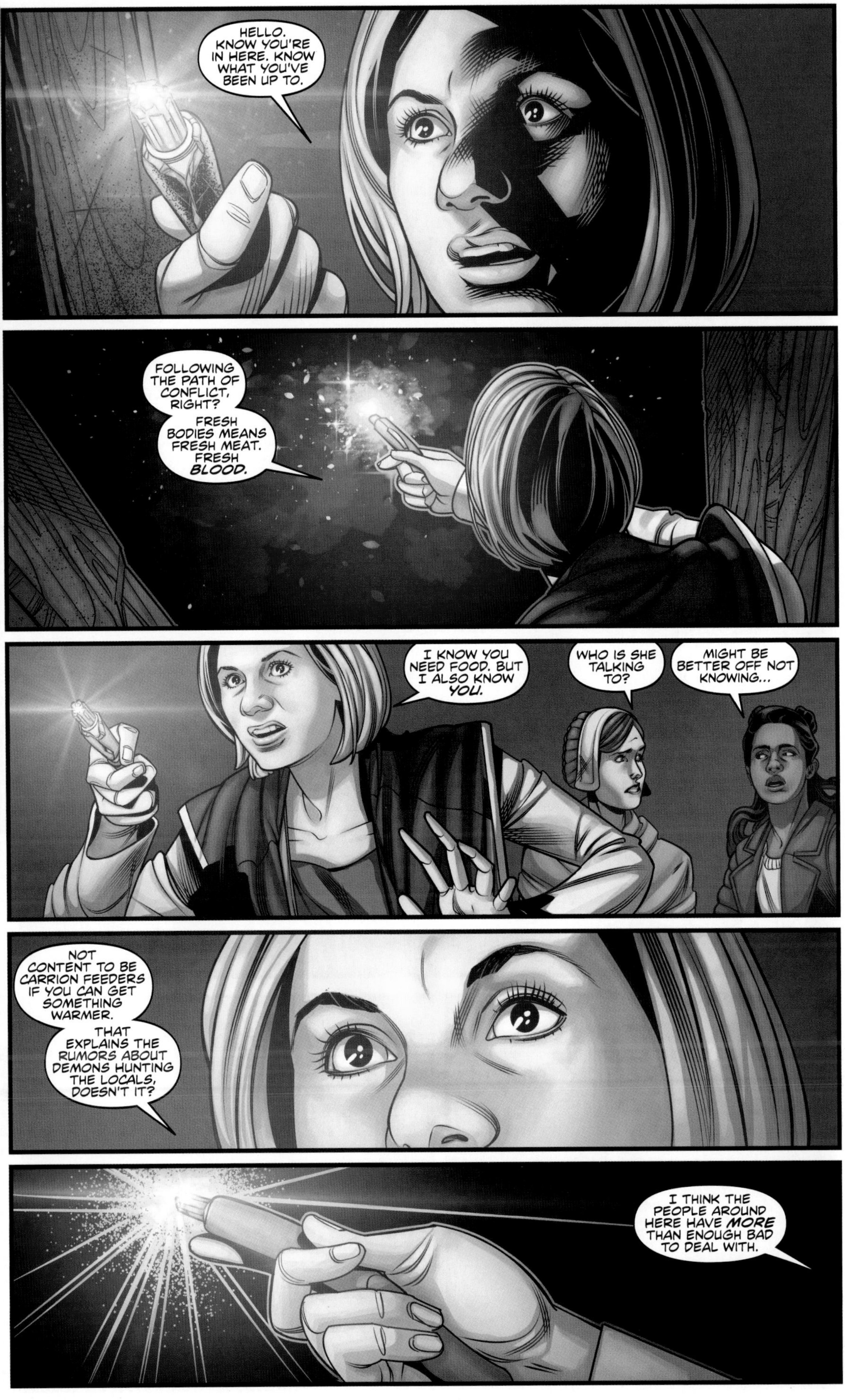
HELLO. KNOW YOU'RE IN HERE. KNOW WHAT YOU'VE BEEN UP TO.
FOLLOWING THE PATH OF CONFLICT, RIGHT?
FRESH BODIES MEANS FRESH MEAT. FRESH *BLOOD.*
I KNOW YOU NEED FOOD. BUT I ALSO KNOW *YOU.*
WHO IS SHE TALKING TO?
MIGHT BE BETTER OFF NOT KNOWING...
NOT CONTENT TO BE CARRION FEEDERS IF YOU CAN GET SOMETHING WARMER.
THAT EXPLAINS THE RUMORS ABOUT DEMONS HUNTING THE LOCALS, DOESN'T IT?
I THINK THE PEOPLE AROUND HERE HAVE *MORE* THAN ENOUGH BAD TO DEAL WITH.

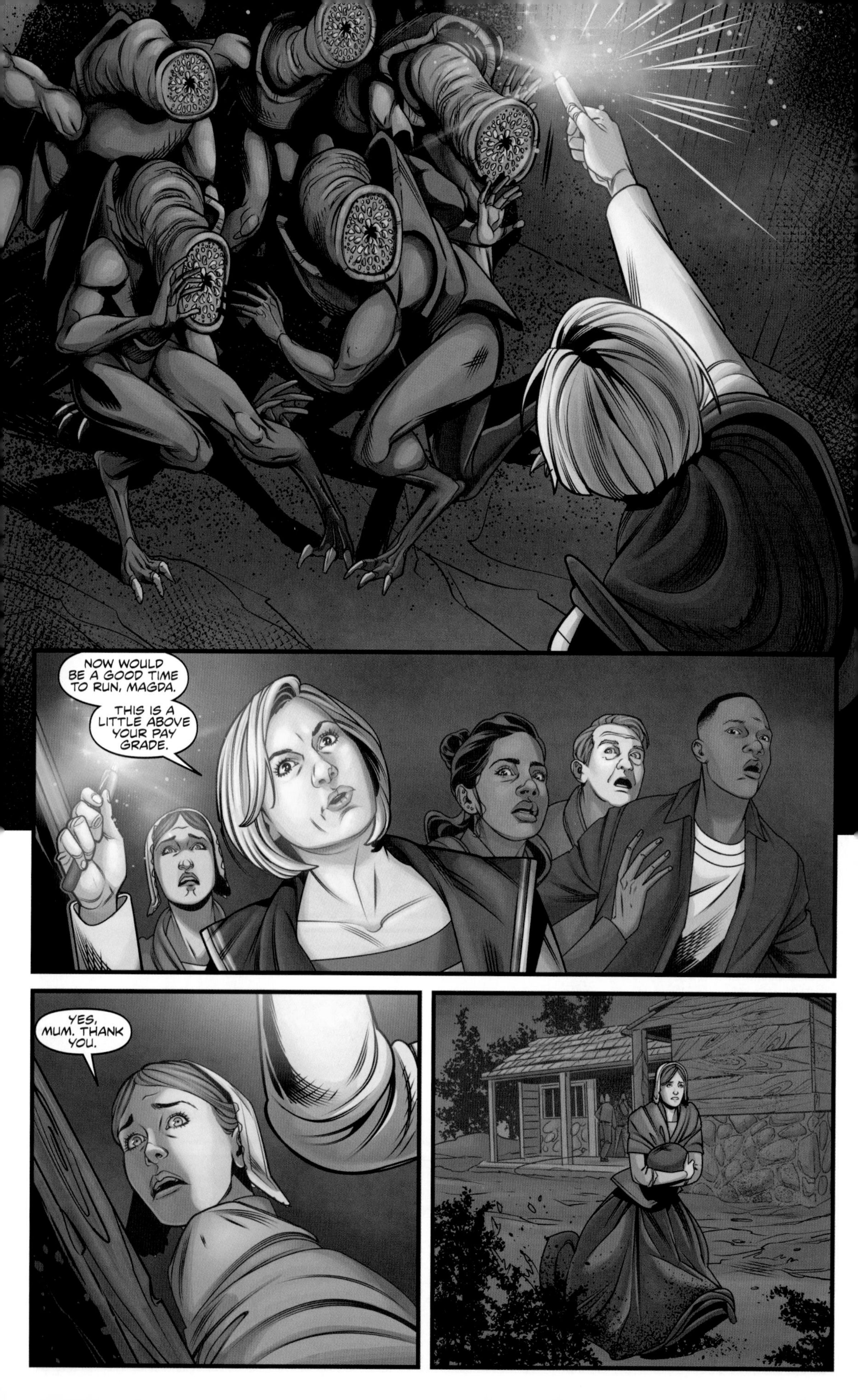
NOW WOULD BE A GOOD TIME TO RUN, MAGDA.
THIS IS A LITTLE ABOVE YOUR PAY GRADE.
YES, MUM. THANK YOU.

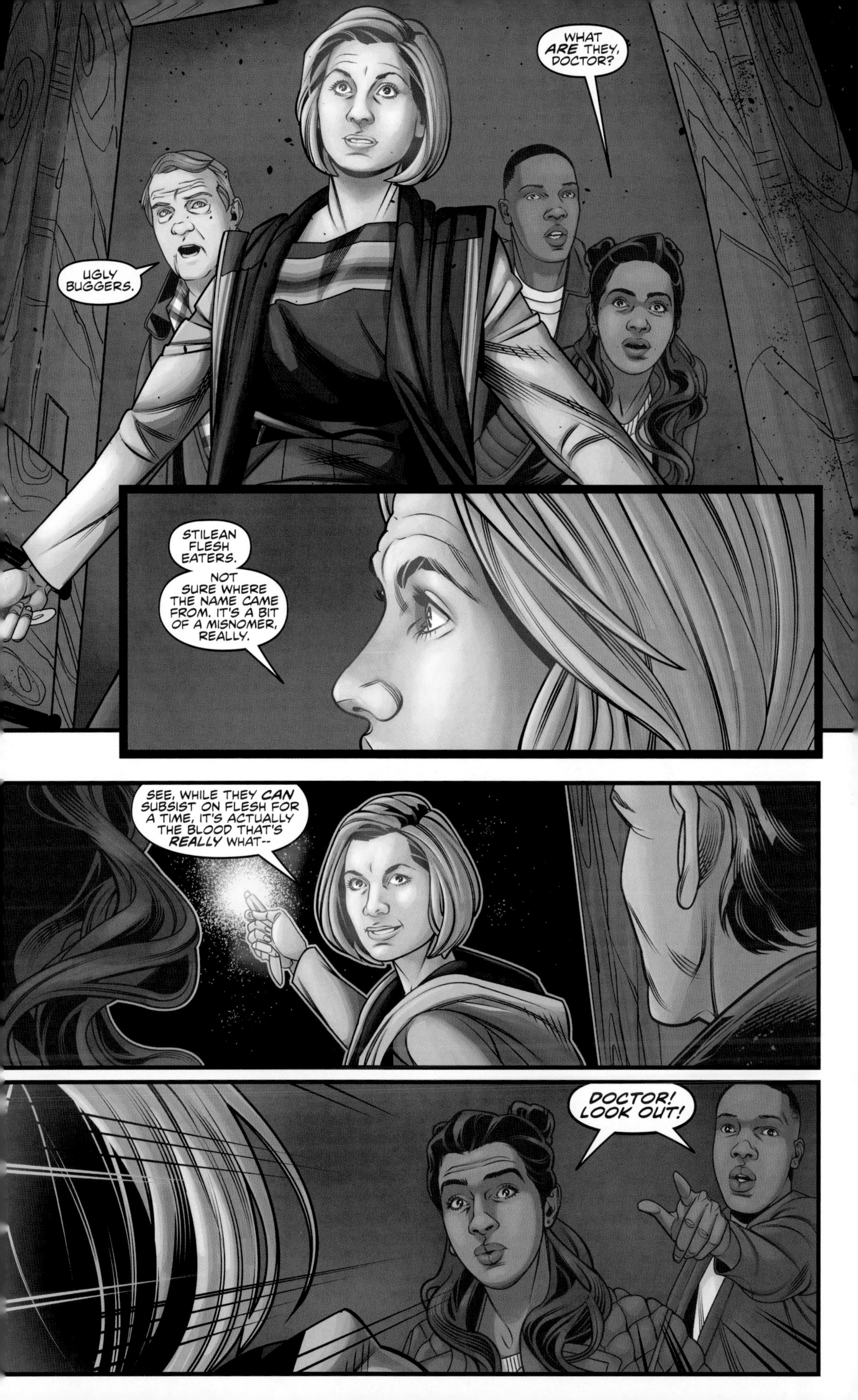
WHAT ARE THEY, DOCTOR?
UGLY BUGGERS.
STILEAN FLESH EATERS.
NOT SURE WHERE THE NAME CAME FROM. IT'S A BIT OF A MISNOMER, REALLY.
SEE, WHILE THEY CAN SUBSIST ON FLESH FOR A TIME, IT'S ACTUALLY THE BLOOD THAT'S REALLY WHAT--
DOCTOR! LOOK OUT!

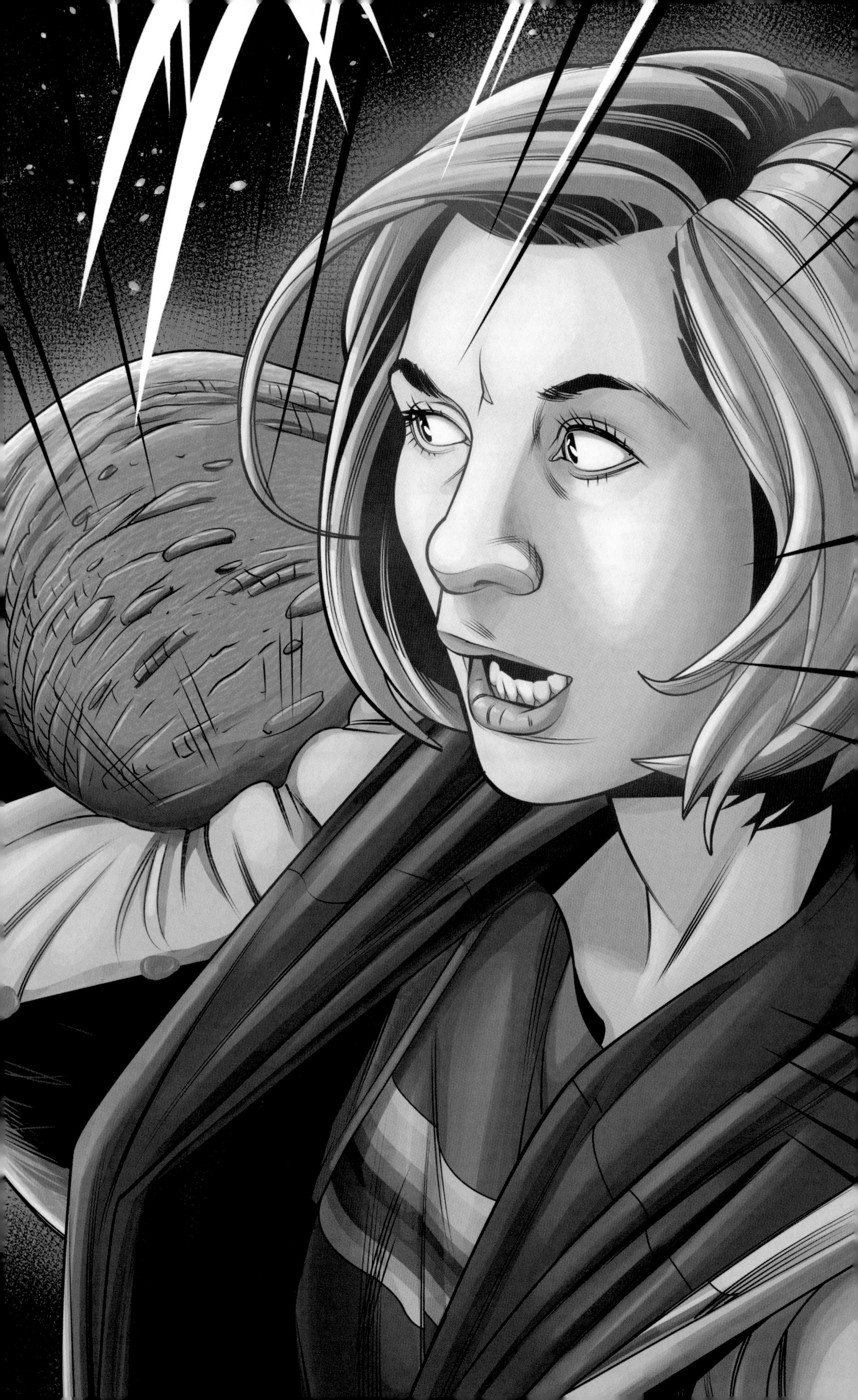

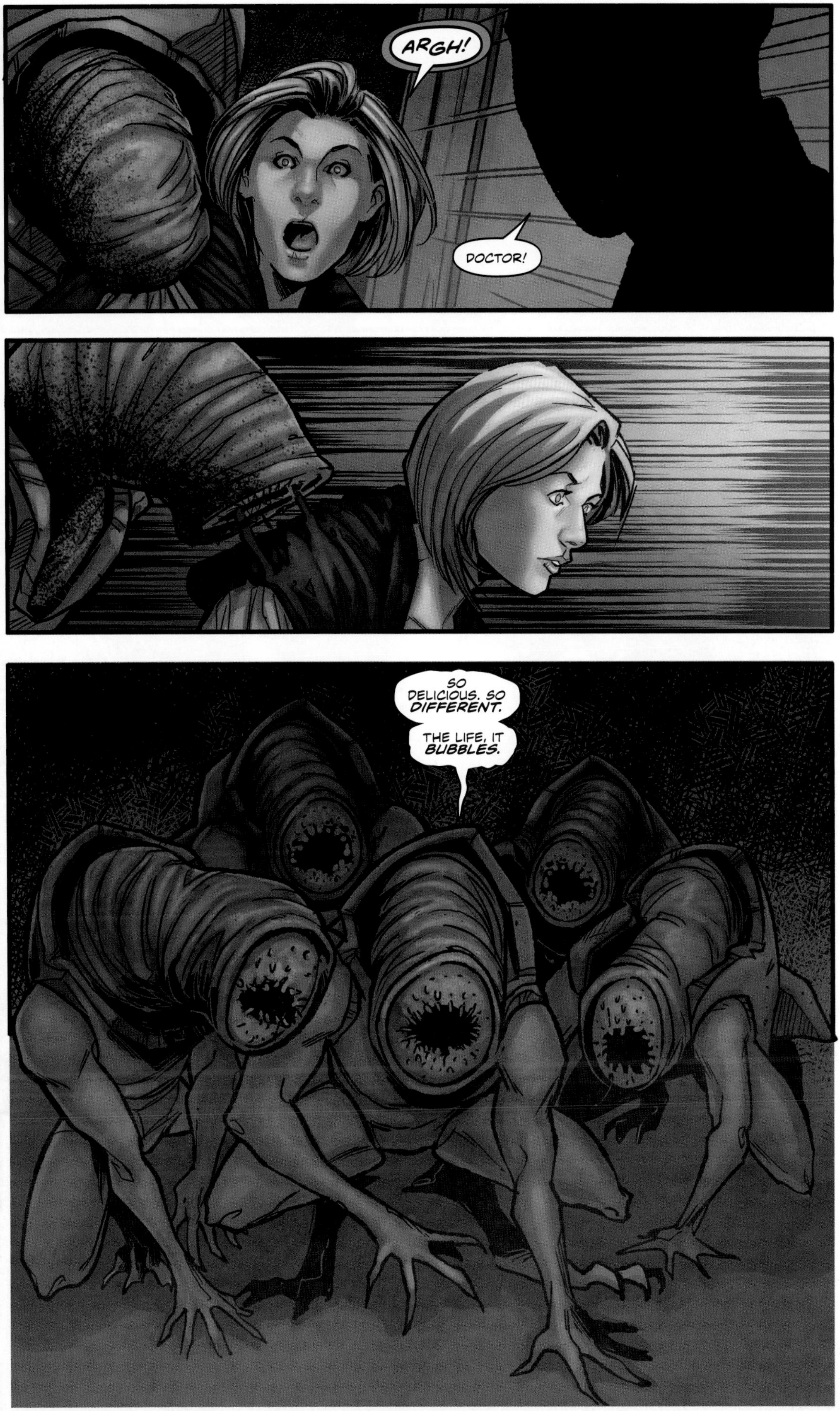
ARGH!
DOCTOR!
SO DELICIOUS. SO DIFFERENT.
THE LIFE, IT BUBBLES.

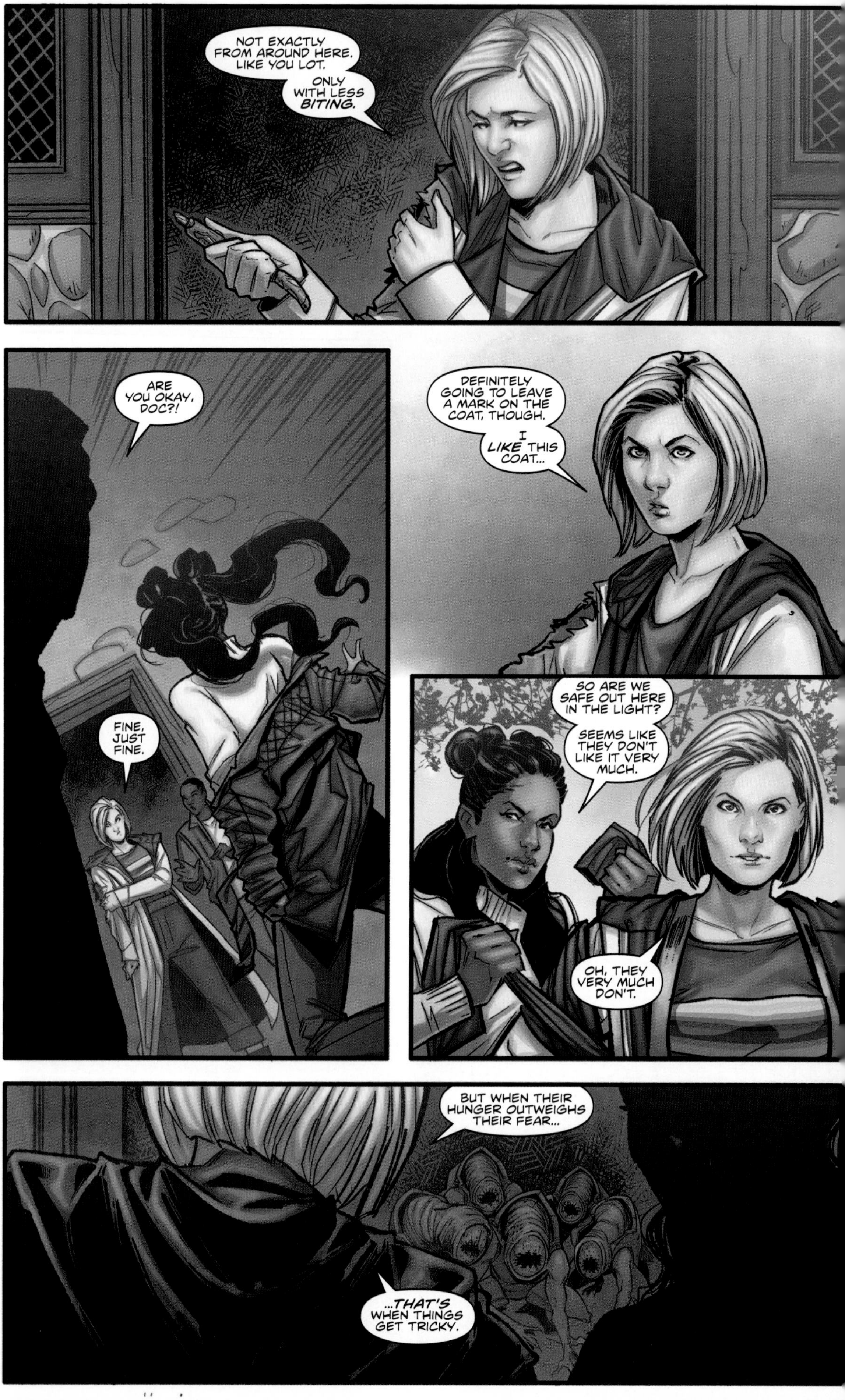
NOT EXACTLY FROM AROUND HERE. LIKE YOU LOT.
ONLY WITH LESS *BITING*.
ARE YOU OKAY, DOC?!
FINE, JUST FINE.
DEFINITELY GOING TO LEAVE A MARK ON THE COAT, THOUGH.
I *LIKE* THIS COAT...
SO ARE WE SAFE OUT HERE IN THE LIGHT?
SEEMS LIKE THEY DON'T LIKE IT VERY MUCH.
OH, THEY VERY MUCH DON'T.
BUT WHEN THEIR HUNGER OUTWEIGHS THEIR FEAR...
...*THAT'S* WHEN THINGS GET TRICKY.

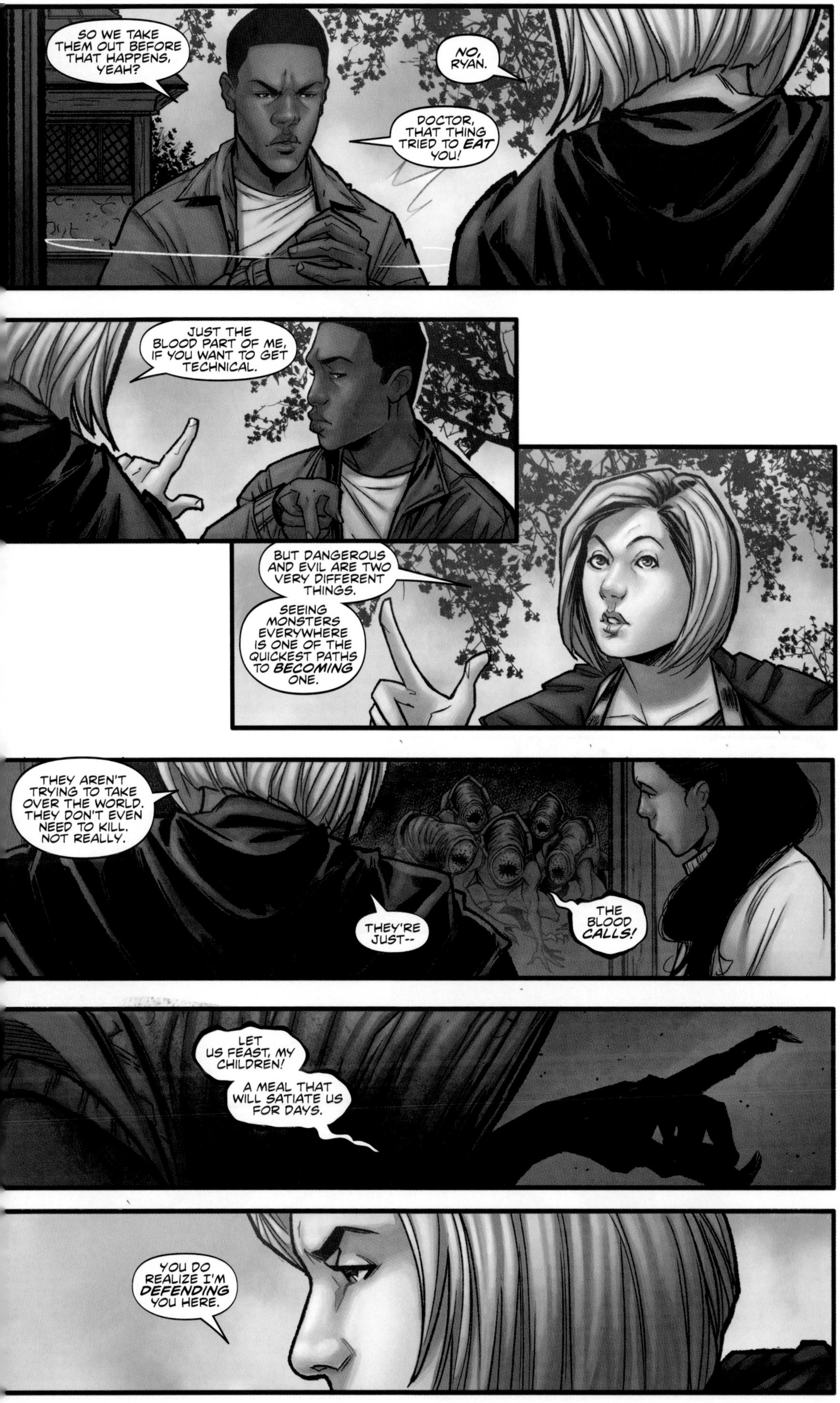

SO WE TAKE THEM OUT BEFORE THAT HAPPENS, YEAH?
NO, RYAN.
DOCTOR, THAT THING TRIED TO EAT YOU!
JUST THE BLOOD PART OF ME, IF YOU WANT TO GET TECHNICAL.
BUT DANGEROUS AND EVIL ARE TWO VERY DIFFERENT THINGS.
SEEING MONSTERS EVERYWHERE IS ONE OF THE QUICKEST PATHS TO BECOMING ONE.
THEY AREN'T TRYING TO TAKE OVER THE WORLD. THEY DON'T EVEN NEED TO KILL. NOT REALLY.
THEY'RE JUST--
THE BLOOD CALLS!
LET US FEAST, MY CHILDREN!
A MEAL THAT WILL SATIATE US FOR DAYS.
YOU DO REALIZE I'M DEFENDING YOU HERE.

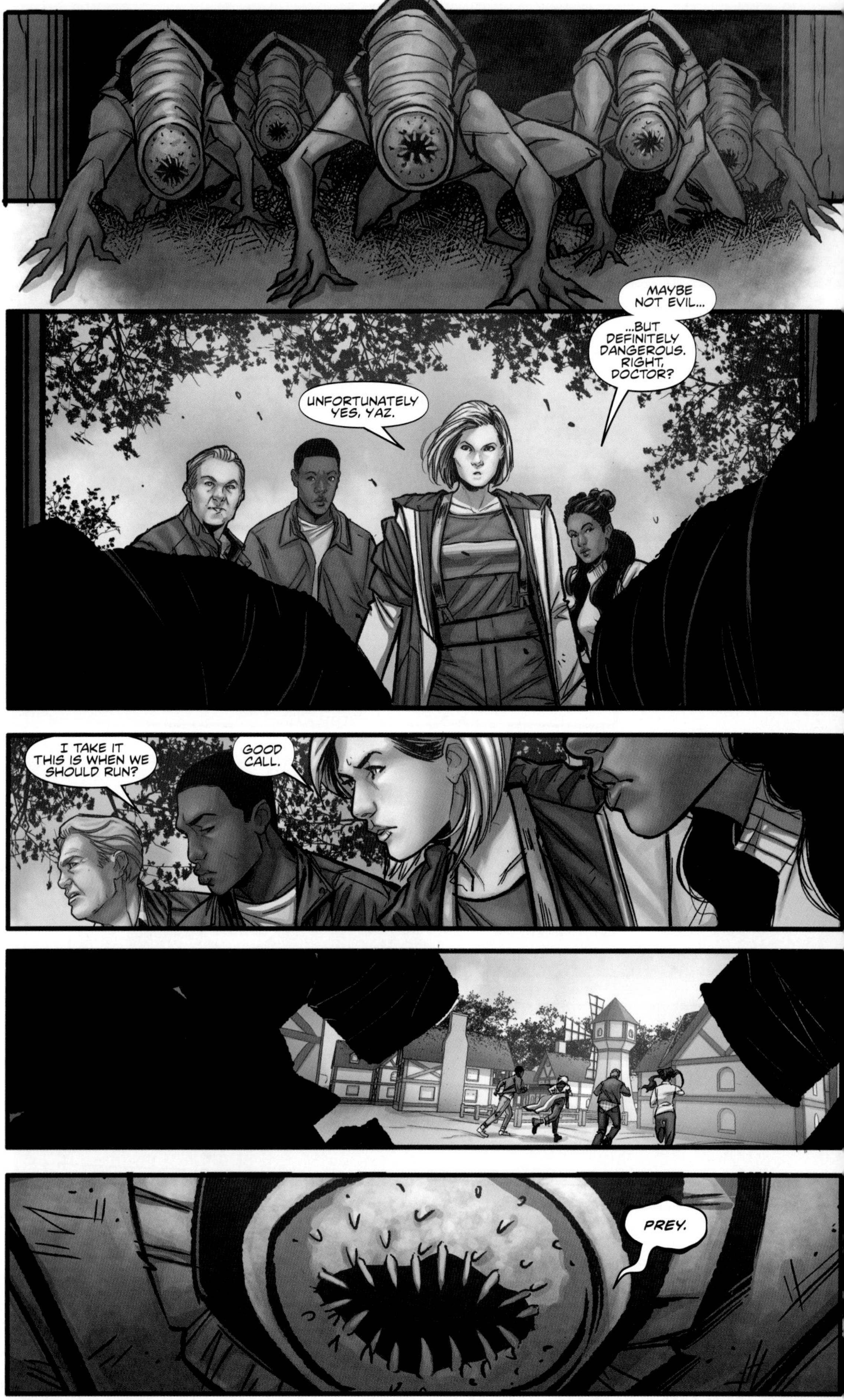

MAYBE NOT EVIL...
...BUT DEFINITELY DANGEROUS. RIGHT, DOCTOR?
UNFORTUNATELY YES, YAZ.
I TAKE IT THIS IS WHEN WE SHOULD RUN?
GOOD CALL.
PREY.

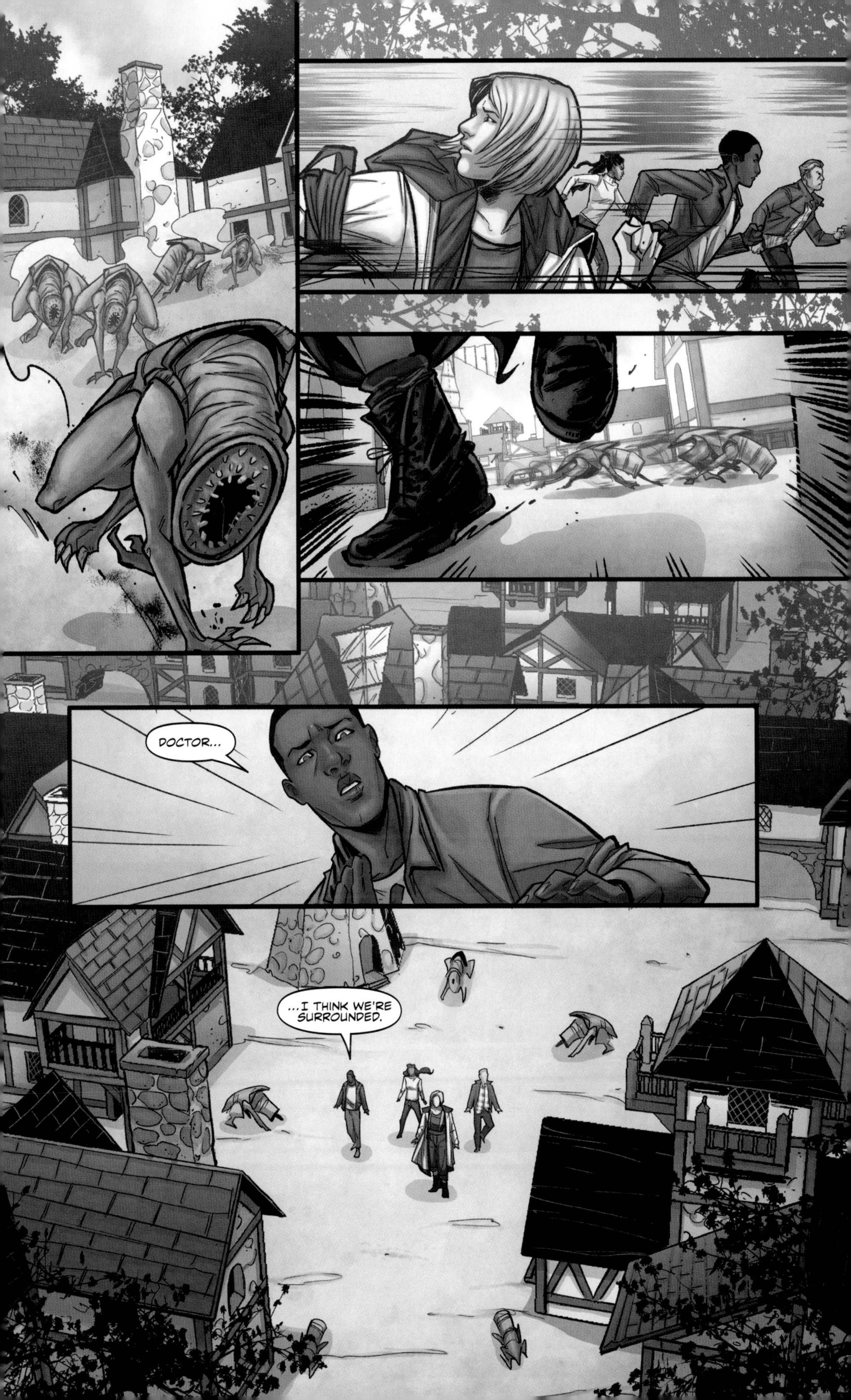
DOCTOR...
...I THINK WE'RE SURROUNDED.

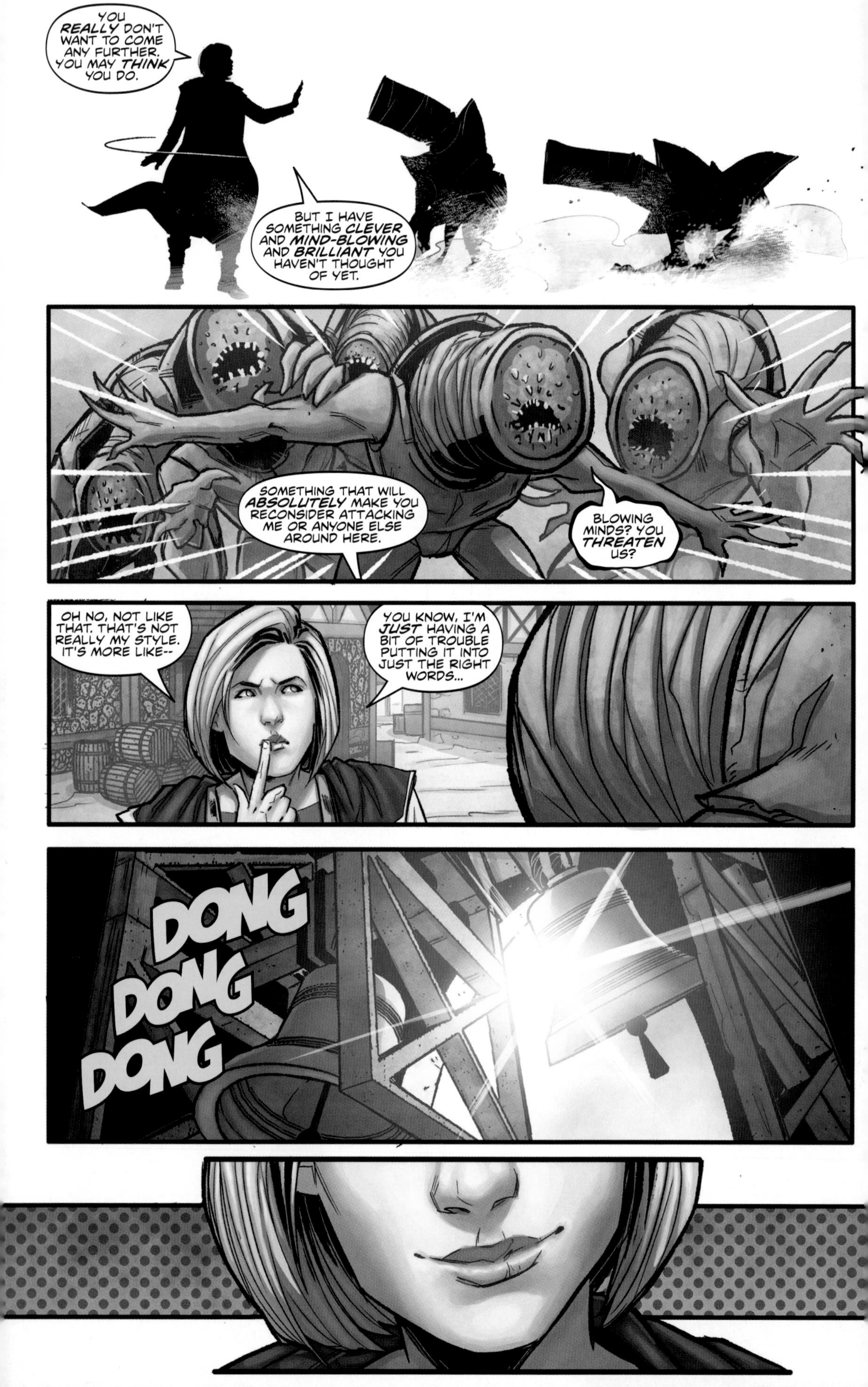
YOU REALLY DON'T WANT TO COME ANY FURTHER. YOU MAY THINK YOU DO.
BUT I HAVE SOMETHING CLEVER AND MIND-BLOWING AND BRILLIANT YOU HAVEN'T THOUGHT OF YET.
SOMETHING THAT WILL ABSOLUTELY MAKE YOU RECONSIDER ATTACKING ME OR ANYONE ELSE AROUND HERE.
BLOWING MINDS? YOU THREATEN US?
OH NO, NOT LIKE THAT. THAT'S NOT REALLY MY STYLE. IT'S MORE LIKE--
YOU KNOW, I'M JUST HAVING A BIT OF TROUBLE PUTTING IT INTO JUST THE RIGHT WORDS...
DONG
DONG
DONG

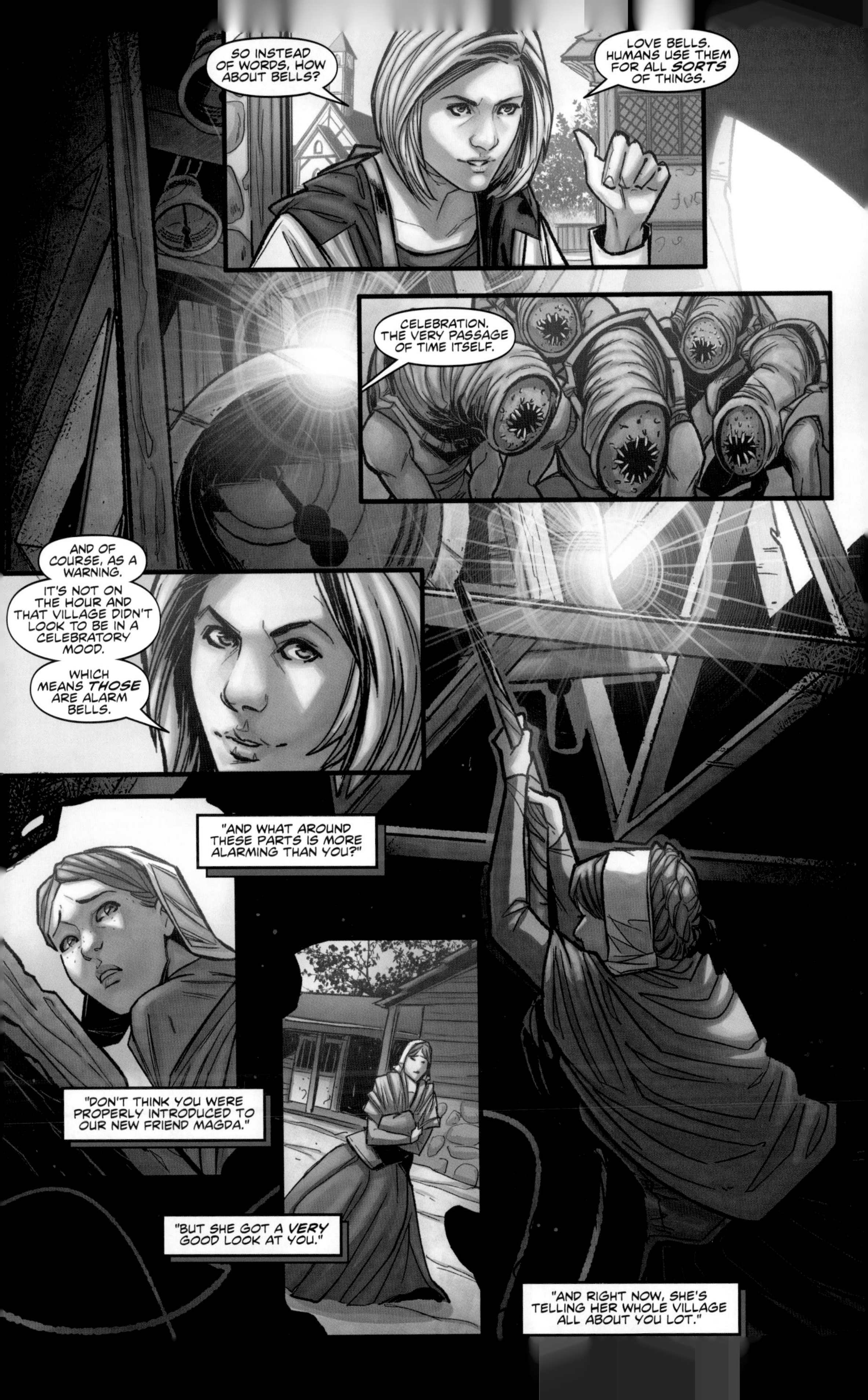
SO INSTEAD OF WORDS, HOW ABOUT BELLS?
LOVE BELLS. HUMANS USE THEM FOR ALL *SORTS* OF THINGS.
CELEBRATION. THE VERY PASSAGE OF TIME ITSELF.
AND OF COURSE, AS A WARNING.
IT'S NOT ON THE HOUR AND THAT VILLAGE DIDN'T LOOK TO BE IN A CELEBRATORY MOOD.
WHICH MEANS *THOSE* ARE ALARM BELLS.
"AND WHAT AROUND THESE PARTS IS MORE ALARMING THAN YOU?"
"DON'T THINK YOU WERE PROPERLY INTRODUCED TO OUR NEW FRIEND MAGDA."
"BUT SHE GOT A *VERY* GOOD LOOK AT YOU."
"AND RIGHT NOW, SHE'S TELLING HER WHOLE VILLAGE ALL ABOUT YOU LOT."

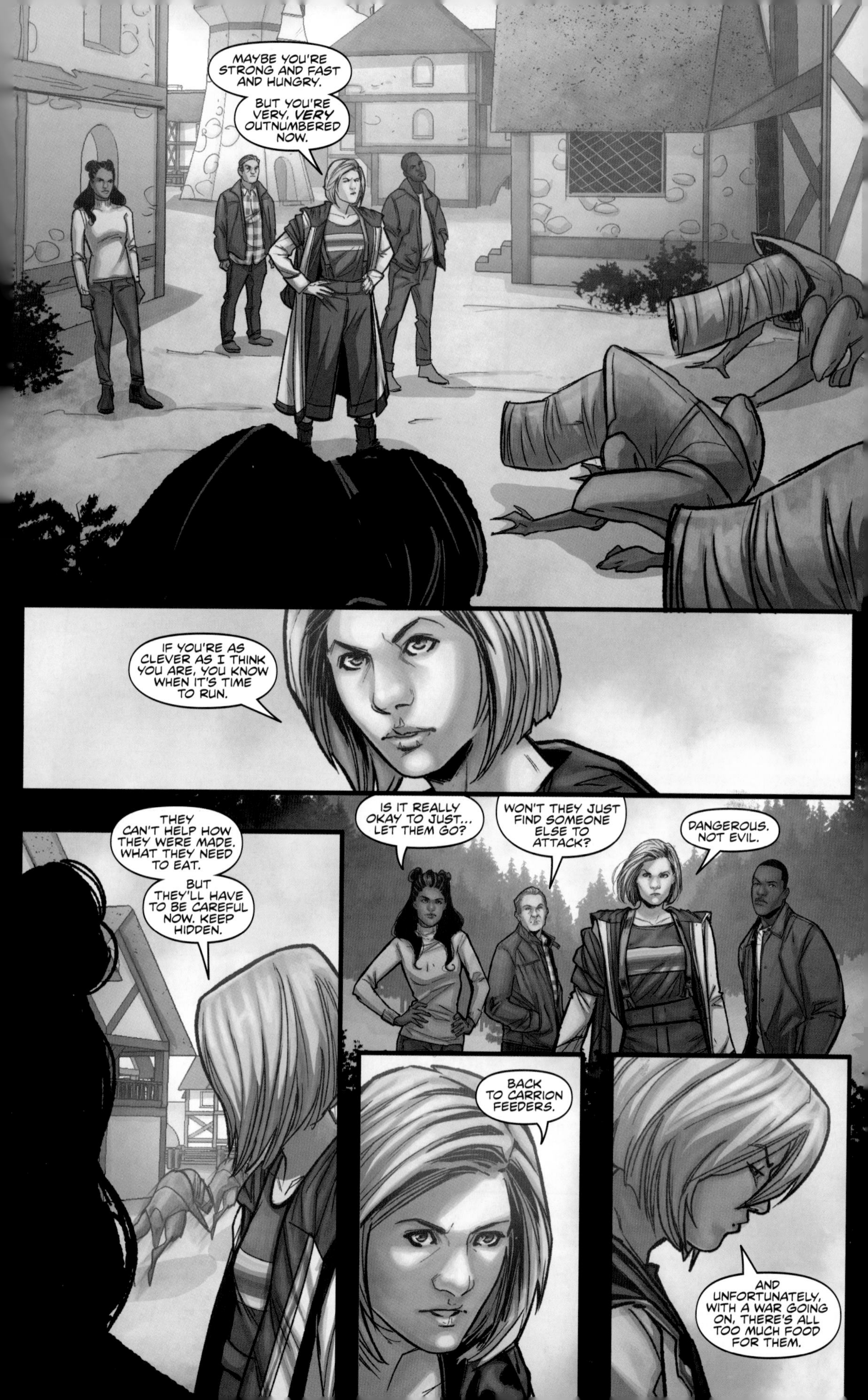

MAYBE YOU'RE STRONG AND FAST AND HUNGRY.
BUT YOU'RE VERY, ***VERY*** OUTNUMBERED NOW.
IF YOU'RE AS CLEVER AS I THINK YOU ARE, YOU KNOW WHEN IT'S TIME TO RUN.
THEY CAN'T HELP HOW THEY WERE MADE. WHAT THEY NEED TO EAT.
BUT THEY'LL HAVE TO BE CAREFUL NOW. KEEP HIDDEN.
IS IT REALLY OKAY TO JUST... LET THEM GO?
WON'T THEY JUST FIND SOMEONE ELSE TO ATTACK?
DANGEROUS. NOT EVIL.
BACK TO CARRION FEEDERS.
AND UNFORTUNATELY, WITH A WAR GOING ON, THERE'S ALL TOO MUCH FOOD FOR THEM.

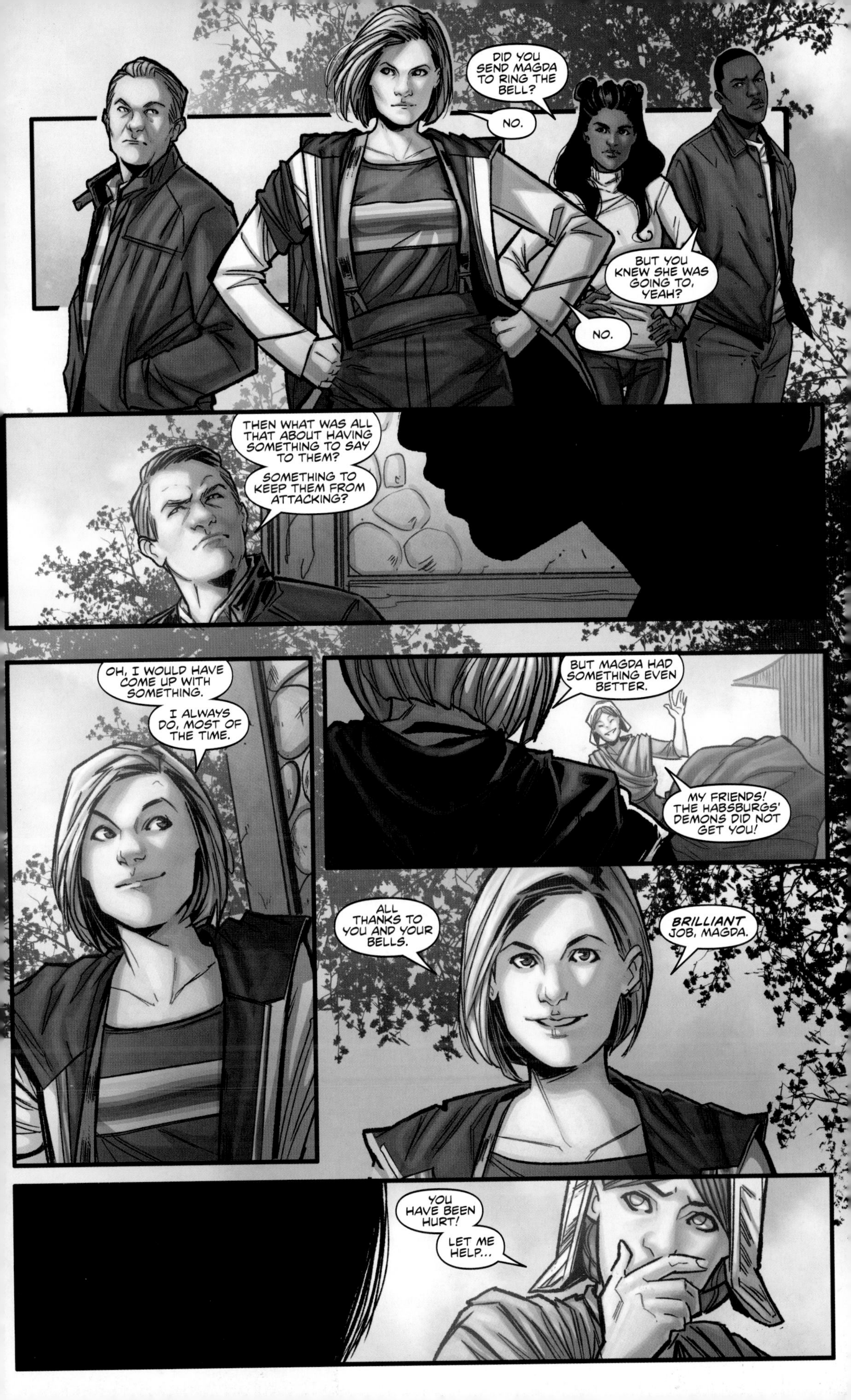
DID YOU SEND MAGDA TO RING THE BELL?
NO.
BUT YOU KNEW SHE WAS GOING TO, YEAH?
NO.
THEN WHAT WAS ALL THAT ABOUT HAVING SOMETHING TO SAY TO THEM?
SOMETHING TO KEEP THEM FROM ATTACKING?
OH, I WOULD HAVE COME UP WITH SOMETHING.
I ALWAYS DO, MOST OF THE TIME.
BUT MAGDA HAD SOMETHING EVEN BETTER.
MY FRIENDS! THE HABSBURGS' DEMONS DID NOT GET YOU!
ALL THANKS TO YOU AND YOUR BELLS.
BRILLIANT JOB, MAGDA.
YOU HAVE BEEN HURT!
LET ME HELP...

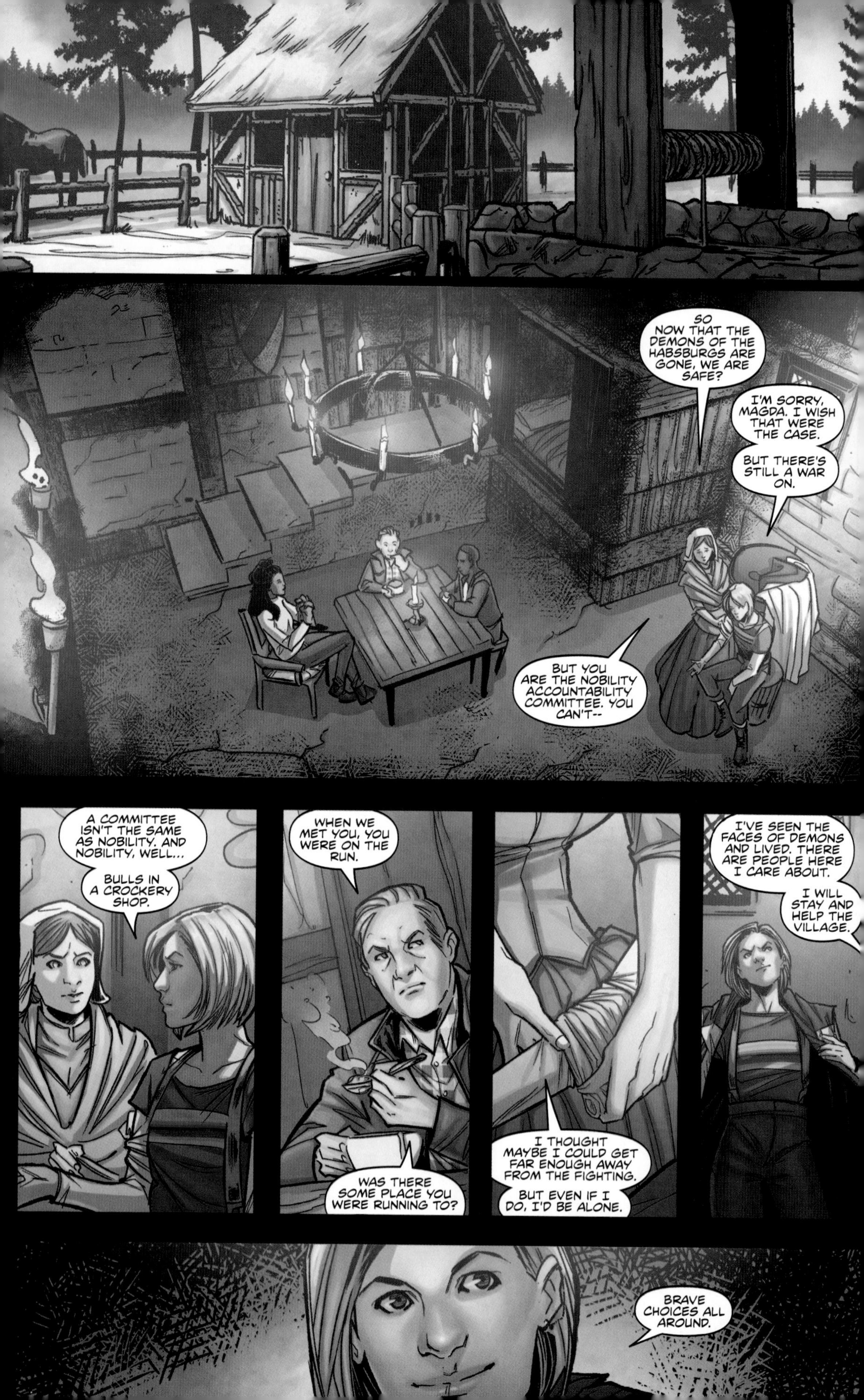
SO NOW THAT THE DEMONS OF THE HABSBURGS ARE GONE, WE ARE SAFE?
I'M SORRY, MAGDA. I WISH THAT WERE THE CASE.
BUT THERE'S STILL A WAR ON.
BUT YOU ARE THE NOBILITY ACCOUNTABILITY COMMITTEE. YOU CAN'T--
A COMMITTEE ISN'T THE SAME AS NOBILITY. AND NOBILITY, WELL...
BULLS IN A CROCKERY SHOP.
WHEN WE MET YOU, YOU WERE ON THE RUN.
WAS THERE SOME PLACE YOU WERE RUNNING TO?
I THOUGHT MAYBE I COULD GET FAR ENOUGH AWAY FROM THE FIGHTING.
BUT EVEN IF I DO, I'D BE ALONE.
I'VE SEEN THE FACES OF DEMONS AND LIVED. THERE ARE PEOPLE HERE I CARE ABOUT.
I WILL STAY AND HELP THE VILLAGE.
BRAVE CHOICES ALL AROUND.

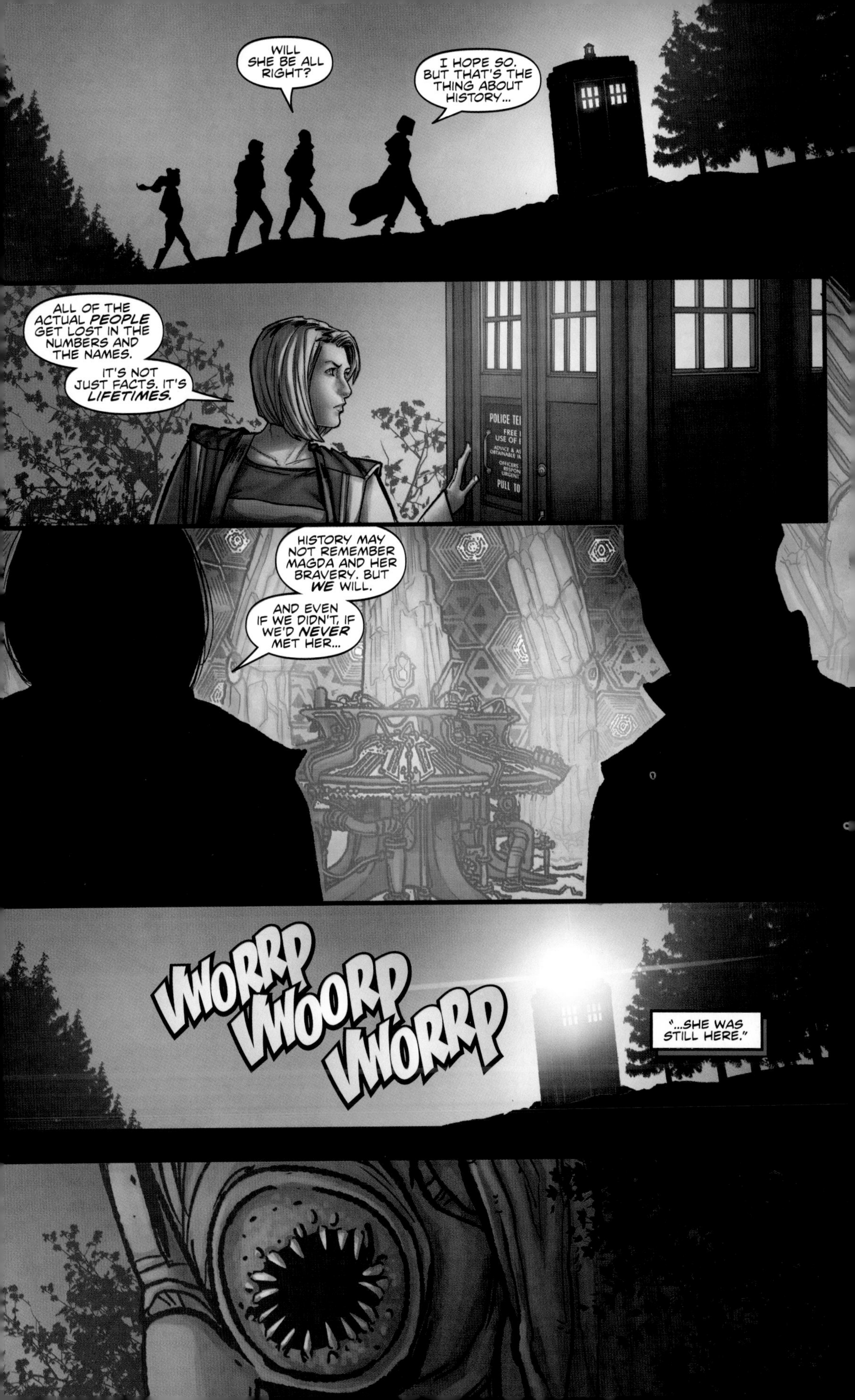
WILL SHE BE ALL RIGHT?
I HOPE SO. BUT THAT'S THE THING ABOUT HISTORY...
ALL OF THE ACTUAL PEOPLE GET LOST IN THE NUMBERS AND THE NAMES.
IT'S NOT JUST FACTS. IT'S LIFETIMES.
POLICE TE
FREE USE OF
PULL TO
HISTORY MAY NOT REMEMBER MAGDA AND HER BRAVERY. BUT WE WILL.
AND EVEN IF WE DIDN'T, IF WE'D NEVER MET HER...
VWORRP VWOORP VWORRP
"...SHE WAS STILL HERE."

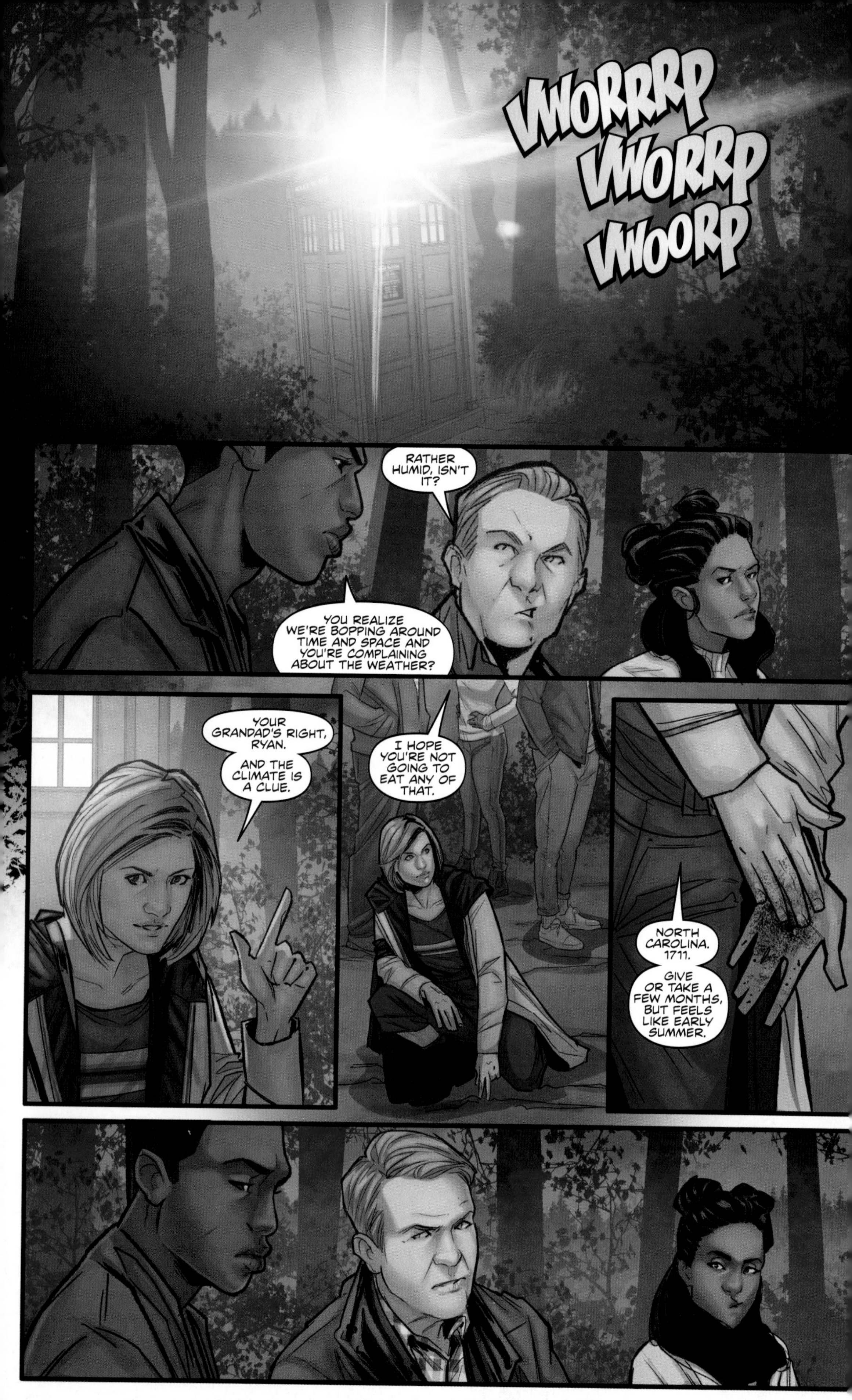
VWORRRP
VWORRP
VWOORP
RATHER HUMID, ISN'T IT?
YOU REALIZE WE'RE BOPPING AROUND TIME AND SPACE AND YOU'RE COMPLAINING ABOUT THE WEATHER?
YOUR GRANDAD'S RIGHT, RYAN.
AND THE CLIMATE IS A CLUE.
I HOPE YOU'RE NOT GOING TO EAT ANY OF THAT.
NORTH CAROLINA. 1711.
GIVE OR TAKE A FEW MONTHS, BUT FEELS LIKE EARLY SUMMER.

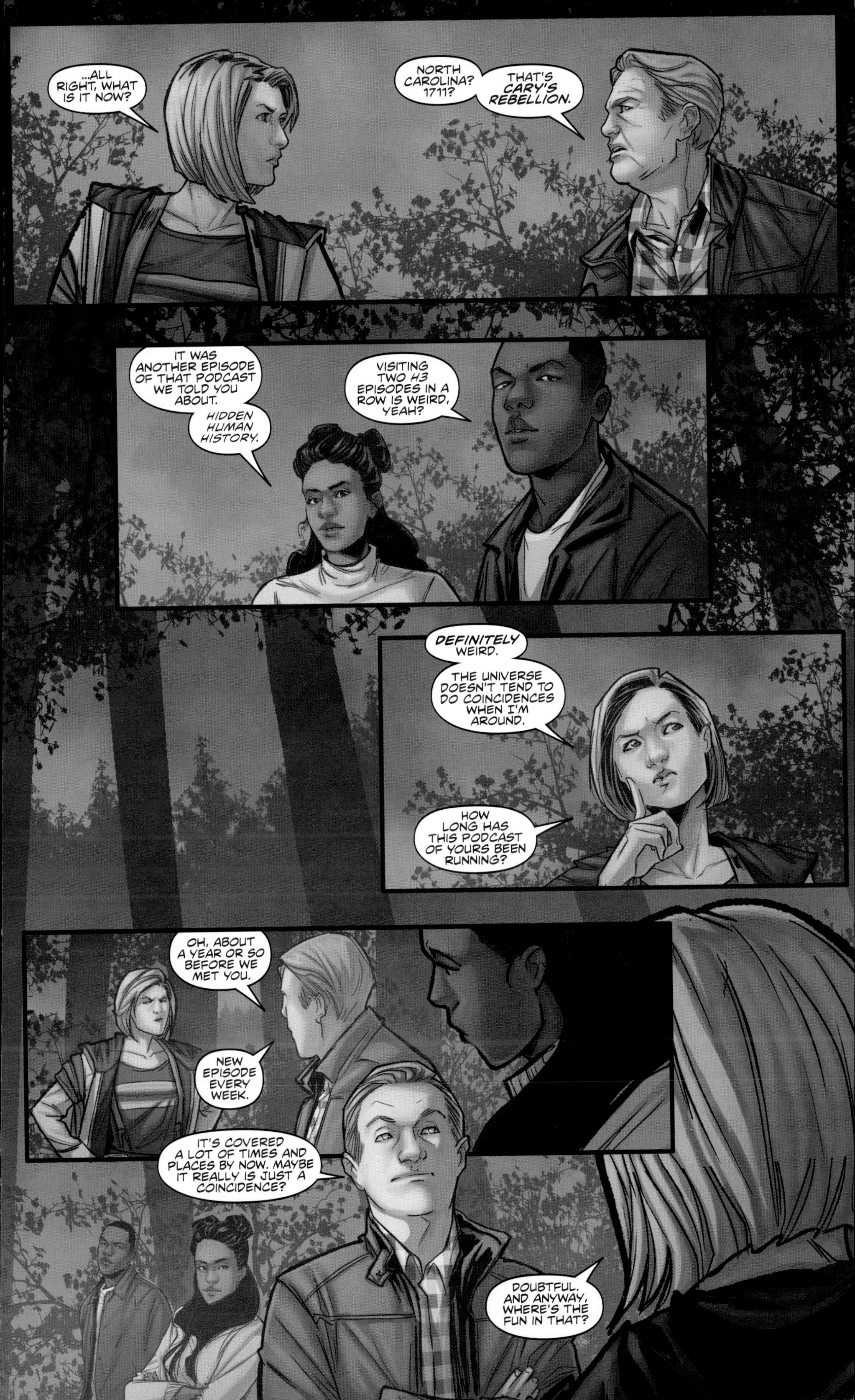
...ALL RIGHT, WHAT IS IT NOW?
NORTH CAROLINA? 1711?
THAT'S *CARY'S REBELLION.*
IT WAS ANOTHER EPISODE OF THAT PODCAST WE TOLD YOU ABOUT.
HIDDEN HUMAN HISTORY.
VISITING TWO *H3* EPISODES IN A ROW IS WEIRD, YEAH?
DEFINITELY WEIRD.
THE UNIVERSE DOESN'T TEND TO DO COINCIDENCES WHEN I'M AROUND.
HOW LONG HAS THIS PODCAST OF YOURS BEEN RUNNING?
OH, ABOUT A YEAR OR SO BEFORE WE MET YOU.
NEW EPISODE EVERY WEEK.
IT'S COVERED A LOT OF TIMES AND PLACES BY NOW. MAYBE IT REALLY IS JUST A COINCIDENCE?
DOUBTFUL. AND ANYWAY, WHERE'S THE FUN IN THAT?

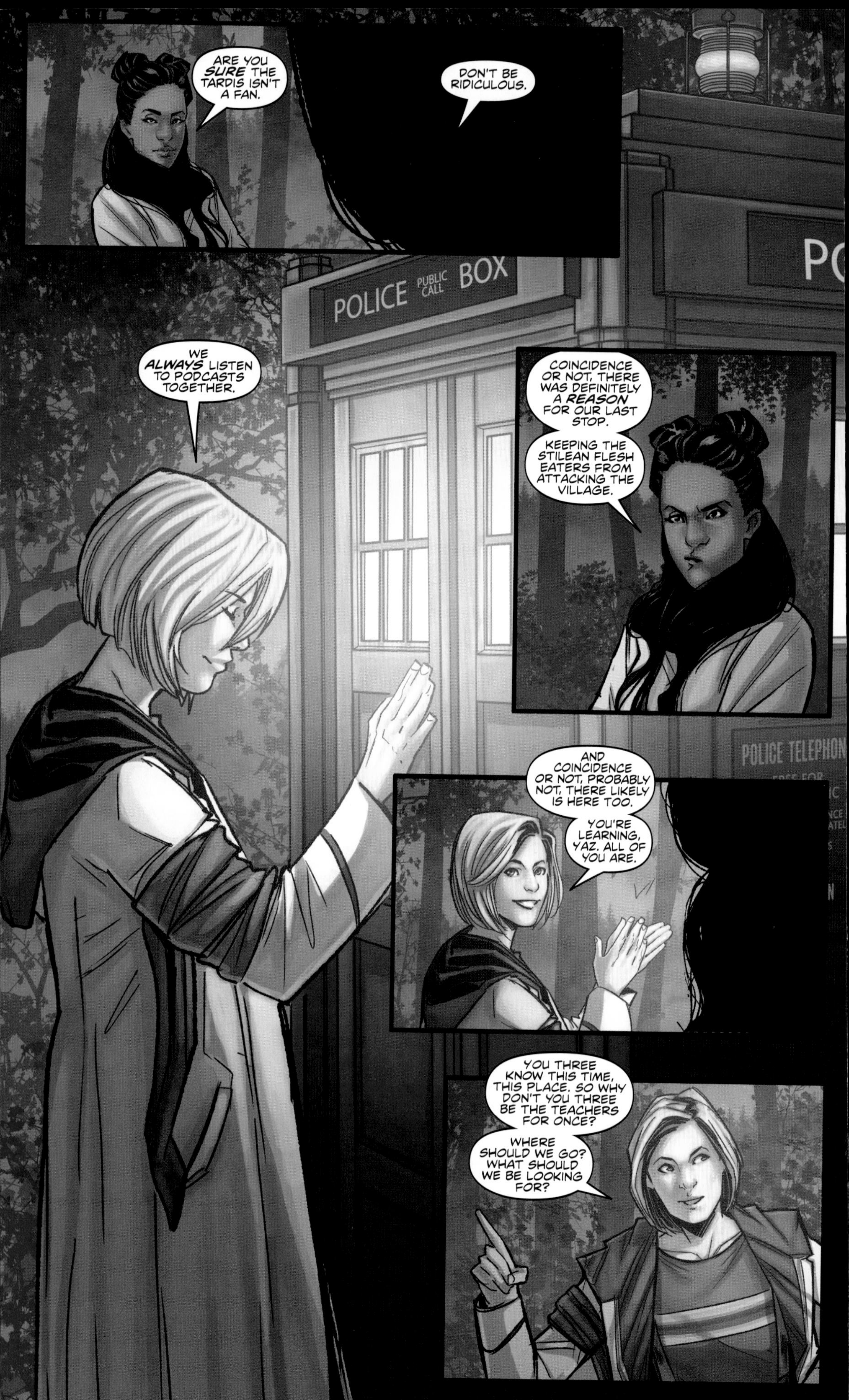
ARE YOU SURE THE TARDIS ISN'T A FAN.
DON'T BE RIDICULOUS.
POLICE PUBLIC CALL BOX
WE ALWAYS LISTEN TO PODCASTS TOGETHER.
COINCIDENCE OR NOT, THERE WAS DEFINITELY A REASON FOR OUR LAST STOP.
KEEPING THE STILEAN FLESH EATERS FROM ATTACKING THE VILLAGE.
POLICE TELEPHON
AND COINCIDENCE OR NOT, PROBABLY NOT, THERE LIKELY IS HERE TOO.
YOU'RE LEARNING, YAZ. ALL OF YOU ARE.
YOU THREE KNOW THIS TIME, THIS PLACE. SO WHY DON'T YOU THREE BE THE TEACHERS FOR ONCE?
WHERE SHOULD WE GO? WHAT SHOULD WE BE LOOKING FOR?

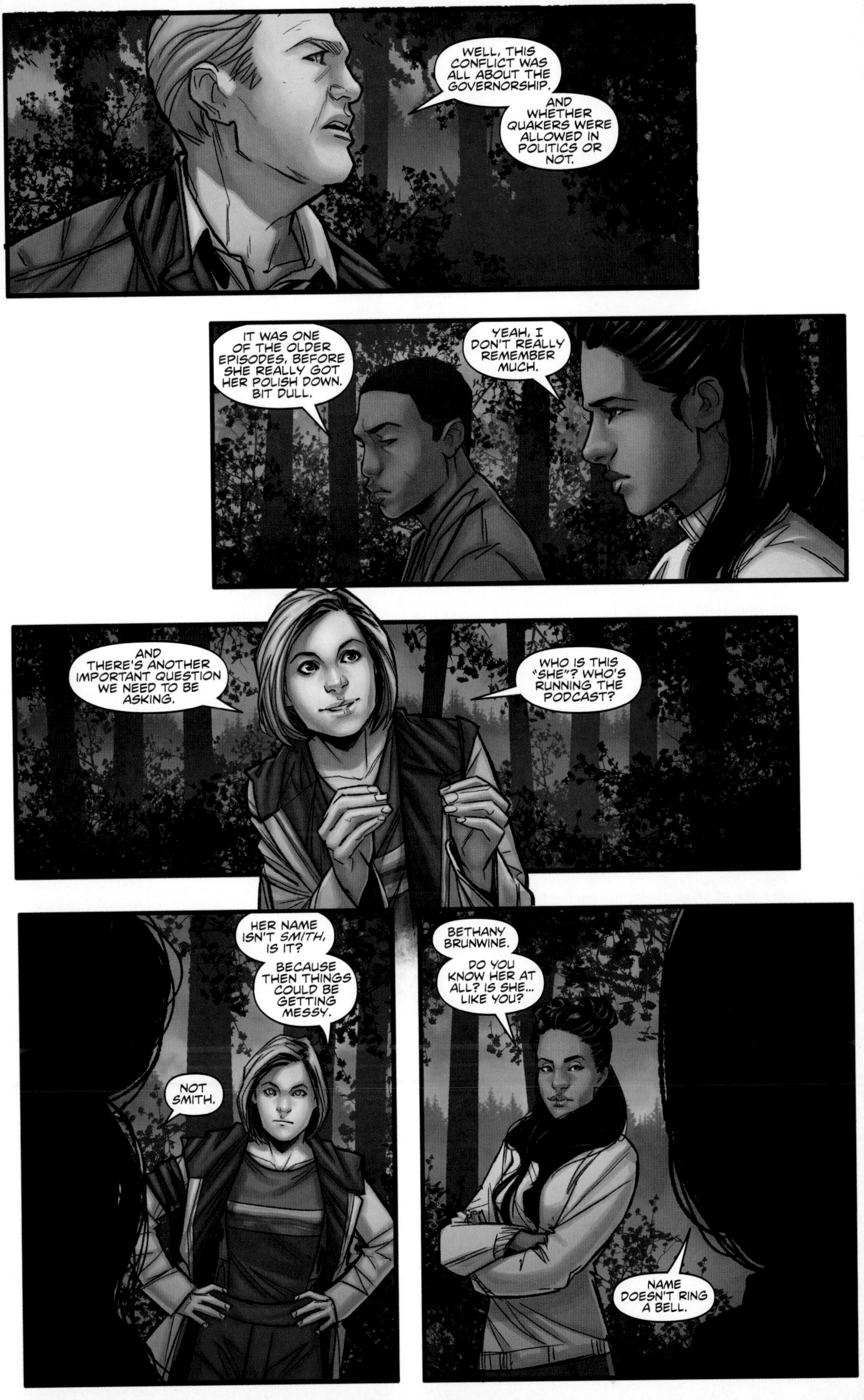
WELL, THIS CONFLICT WAS ALL ABOUT THE GOVERNORSHIP.
AND WHETHER QUAKERS WERE ALLOWED IN POLITICS OR NOT.
IT WAS ONE OF THE OLDER EPISODES, BEFORE SHE REALLY GOT HER POLISH DOWN. BIT DULL.
YEAH, I DON'T REALLY REMEMBER MUCH.
AND THERE'S ANOTHER IMPORTANT QUESTION WE NEED TO BE ASKING.
WHO IS THIS "SHE"? WHO'S RUNNING THE PODCAST?
HER NAME ISN'T SMITH, IS IT?
BECAUSE THEN THINGS COULD BE GETTING MESSY.
NOT SMITH.
BETHANY BRUNWINE.
DO YOU KNOW HER AT ALL? IS SHE... LIKE YOU?
NAME DOESN'T RING A BELL.

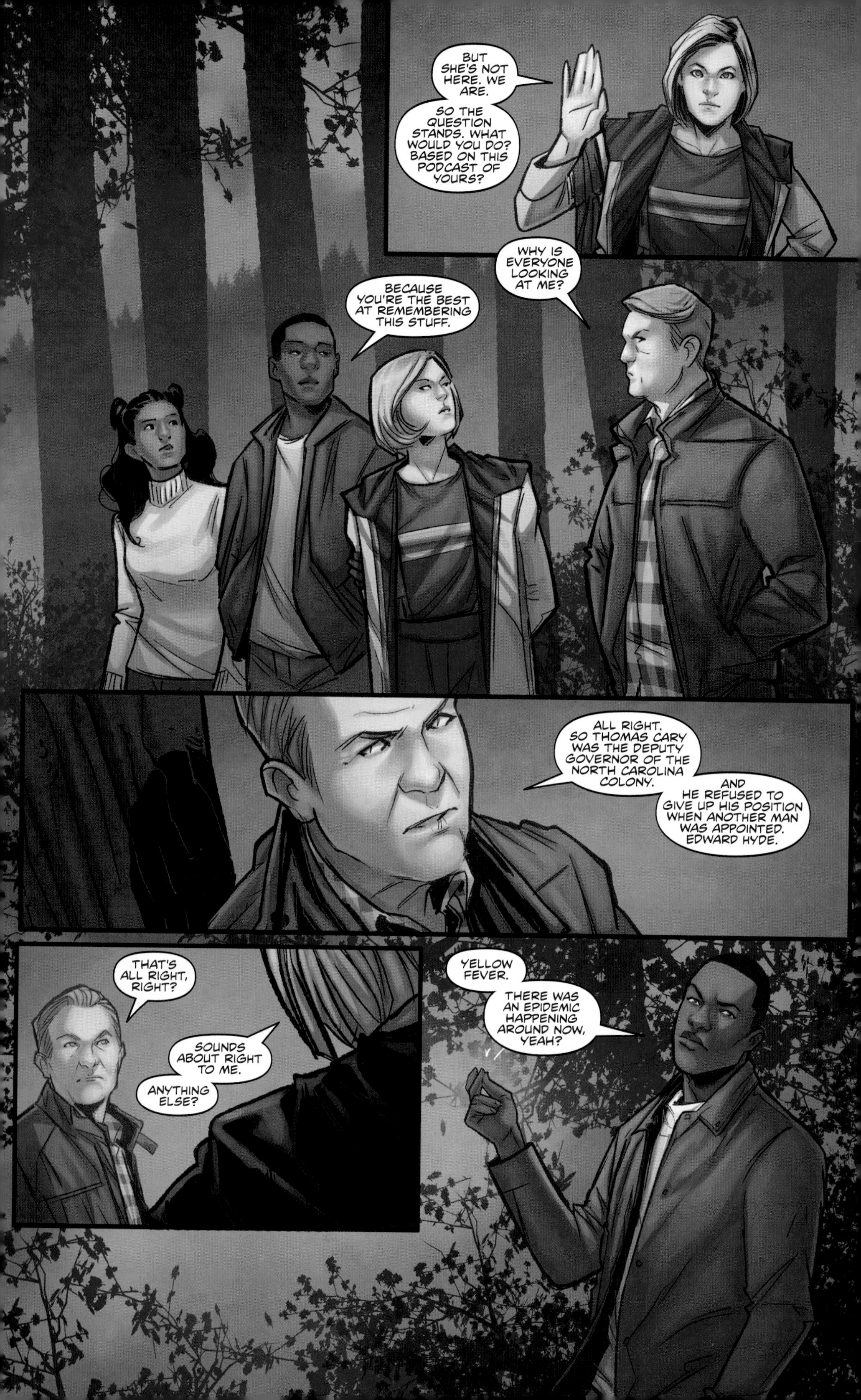
BUT SHE'S NOT HERE. WE ARE.
SO THE QUESTION STANDS. WHAT WOULD YOU DO? BASED ON THIS PODCAST OF YOURS?
WHY IS EVERYONE LOOKING AT ME?
BECAUSE YOU'RE THE BEST AT REMEMBERING THIS STUFF.
ALL RIGHT. SO THOMAS CARY WAS THE DEPUTY GOVERNOR OF THE NORTH CAROLINA COLONY.
AND HE REFUSED TO GIVE UP HIS POSITION WHEN ANOTHER MAN WAS APPOINTED. EDWARD HYDE.
THAT'S ALL RIGHT, RIGHT?
SOUNDS ABOUT RIGHT TO ME.
ANYTHING ELSE?
YELLOW FEVER.
THERE WAS AN EPIDEMIC HAPPENING AROUND NOW, YEAH?

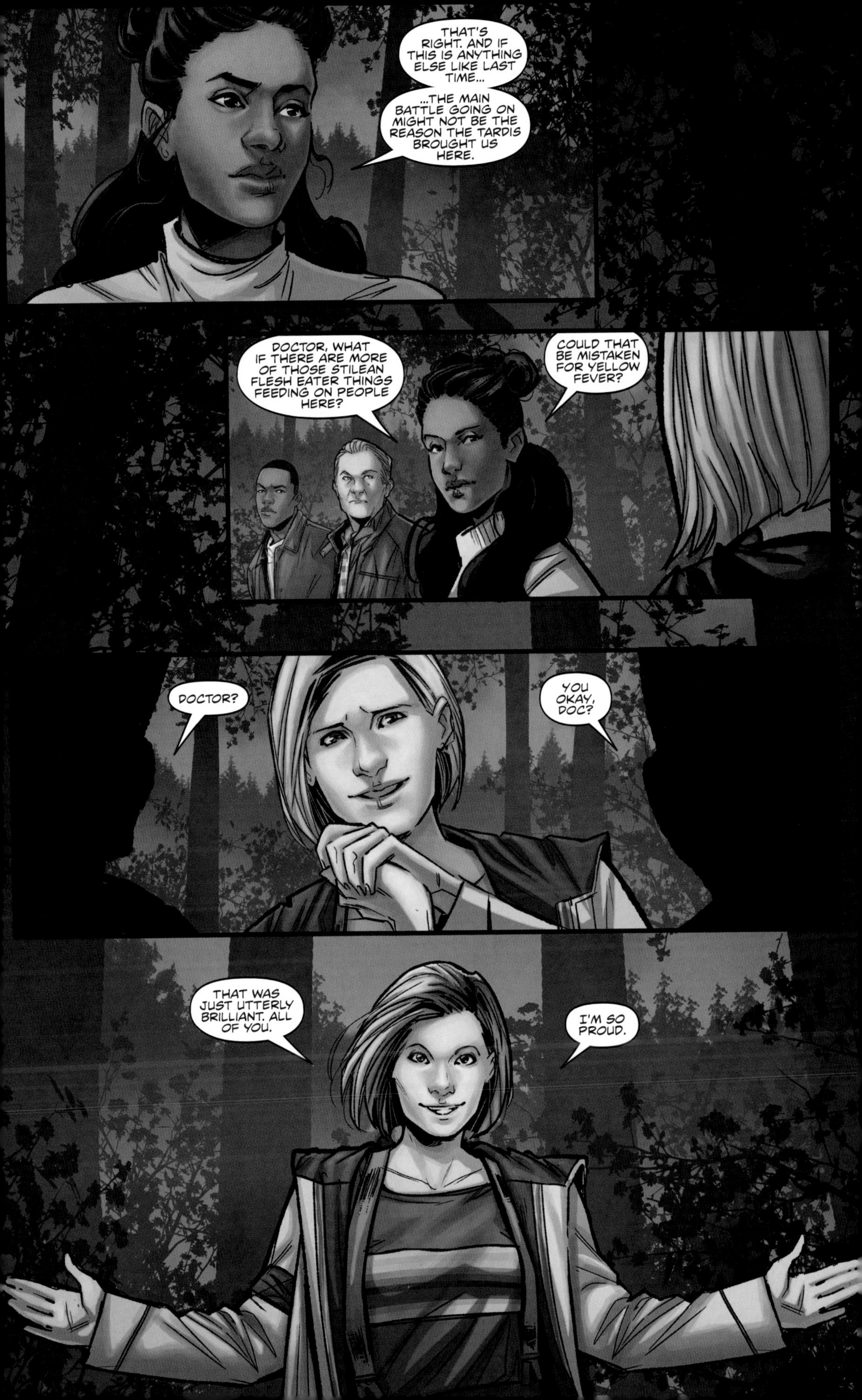
THAT'S RIGHT. AND IF THIS IS ANYTHING ELSE LIKE LAST TIME...
...THE MAIN BATTLE GOING ON MIGHT NOT BE THE REASON THE TARDIS BROUGHT US HERE.
DOCTOR, WHAT IF THERE ARE MORE OF THOSE STILEAN FLESH EATER THINGS FEEDING ON PEOPLE HERE?
COULD THAT BE MISTAKEN FOR YELLOW FEVER?
DOCTOR?
YOU OKAY, DOC?
THAT WAS JUST UTTERLY BRILLIANT. ALL OF YOU.
I'M SO PROUD.

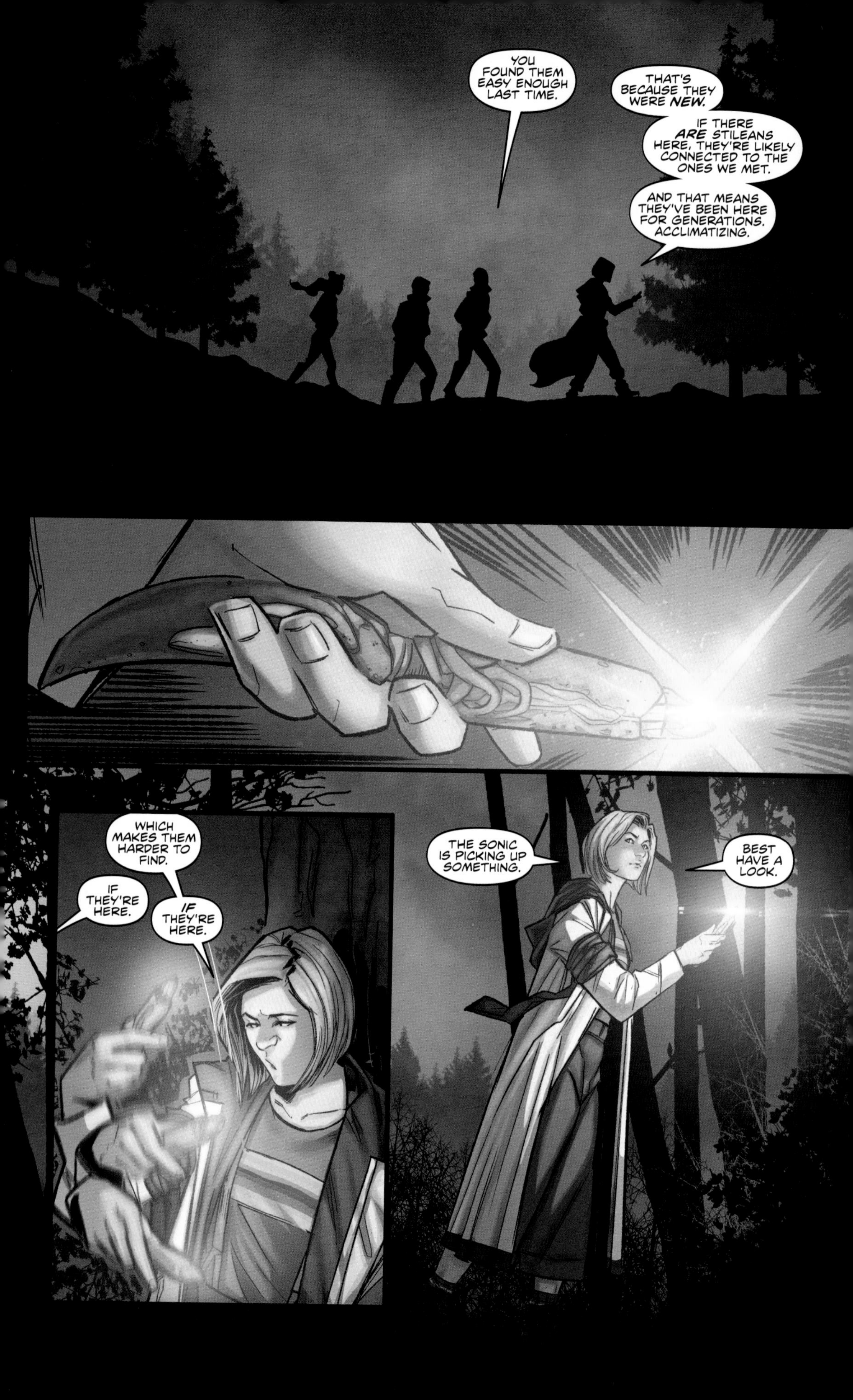
YOU FOUND THEM EASY ENOUGH LAST TIME.
THAT'S BECAUSE THEY WERE *NEW.*
IF THERE *ARE* STILEANS HERE, THEY'RE LIKELY CONNECTED TO THE ONES WE MET.
AND THAT MEANS THEY'VE BEEN HERE FOR GENERATIONS. ACCLIMATIZING.
WHICH MAKES THEM HARDER TO FIND.
IF THEY'RE HERE.
IF THEY'RE HERE.
THE SONIC IS PICKING UP SOMETHING.
BEST HAVE A LOOK.

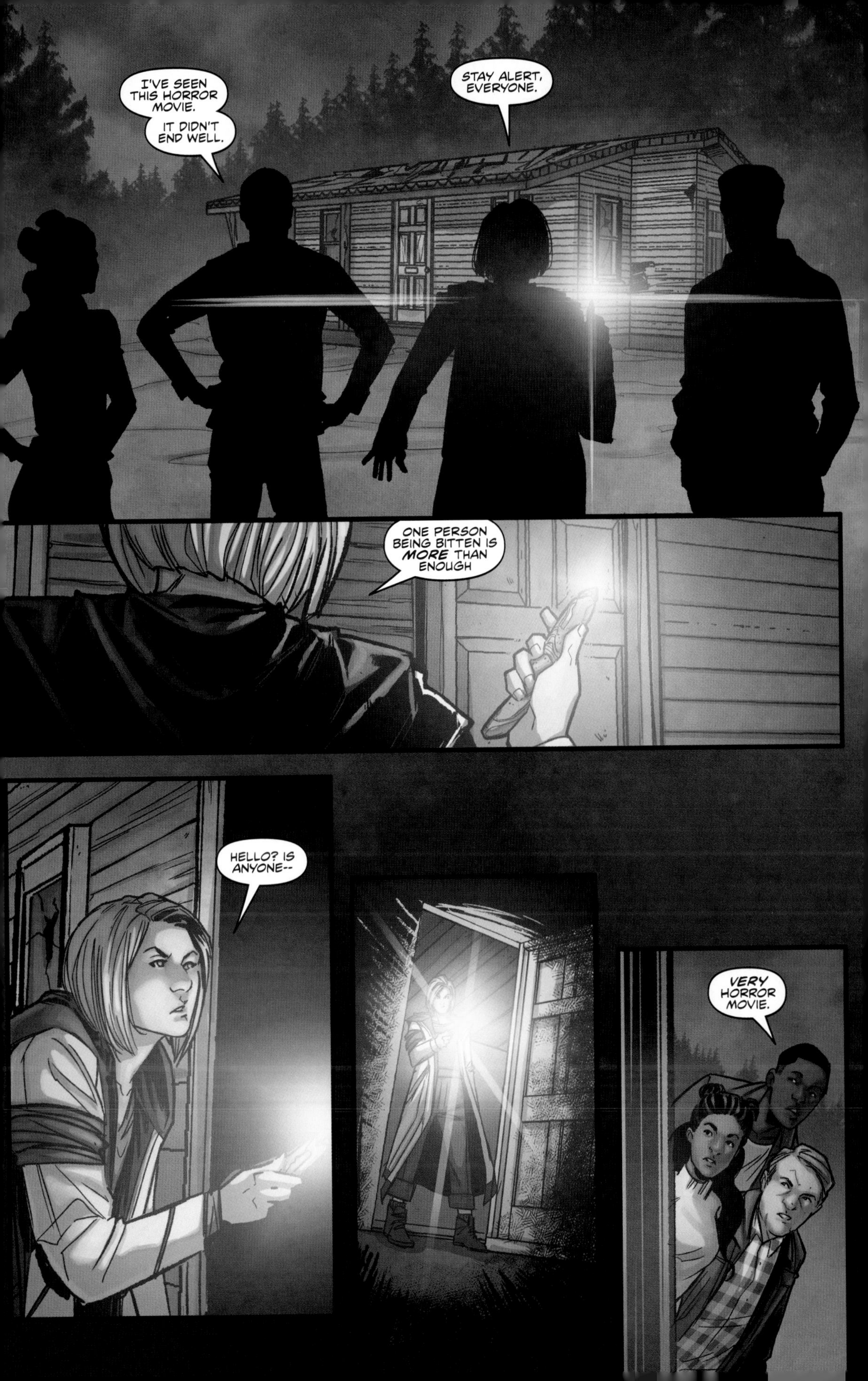
I'VE SEEN THIS HORROR MOVIE.
IT DIDN'T END WELL.
STAY ALERT, EVERYONE.
ONE PERSON BEING BITTEN IS *MORE* THAN ENOUGH
HELLO? IS ANYONE--
VERY HORROR MOVIE.

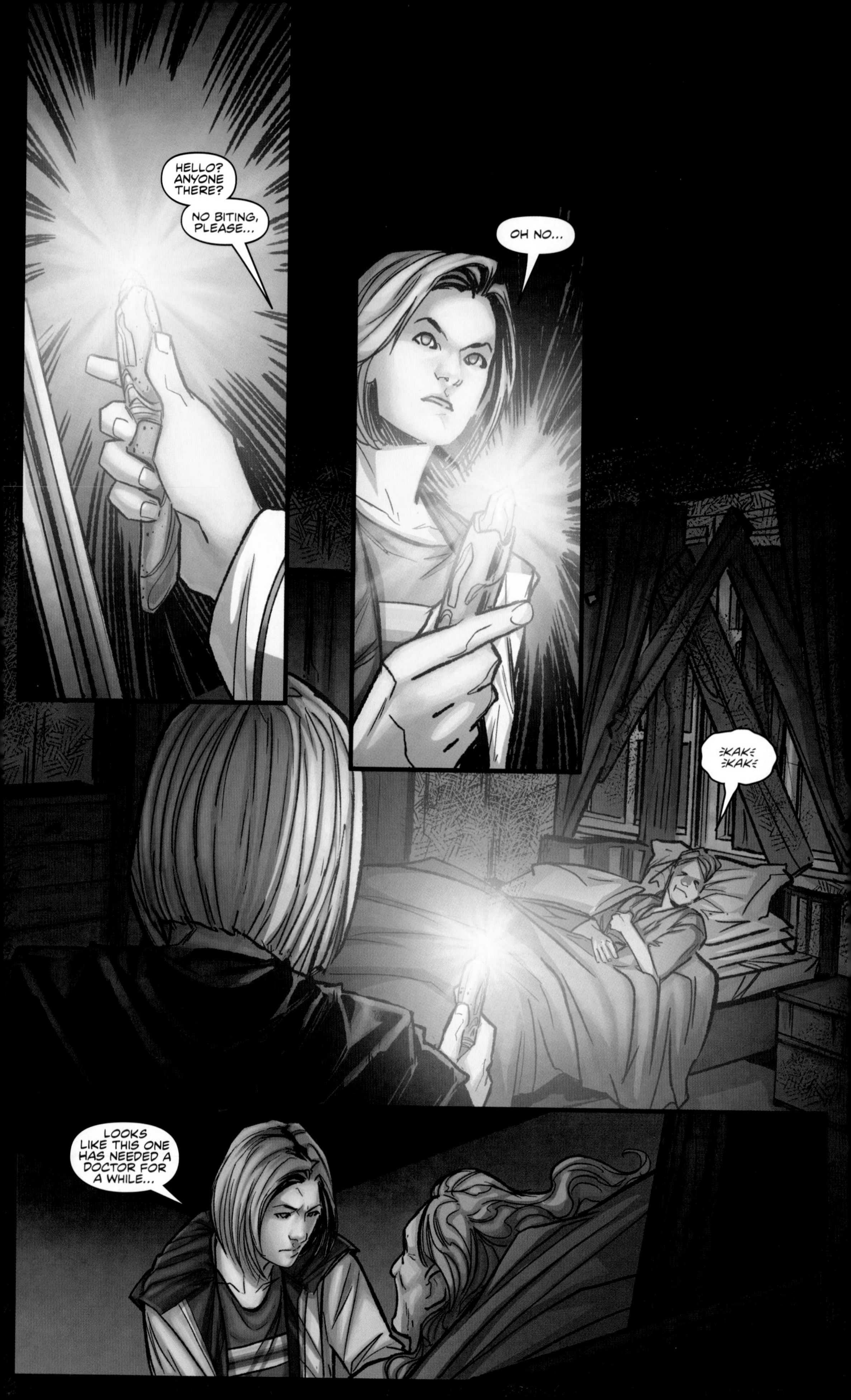
HELLO? ANYONE THERE?
NO BITING, PLEASE...
OH NO...
KAK KAK
LOOKS LIKE THIS ONE HAS NEEDED A DOCTOR FOR A WHILE...

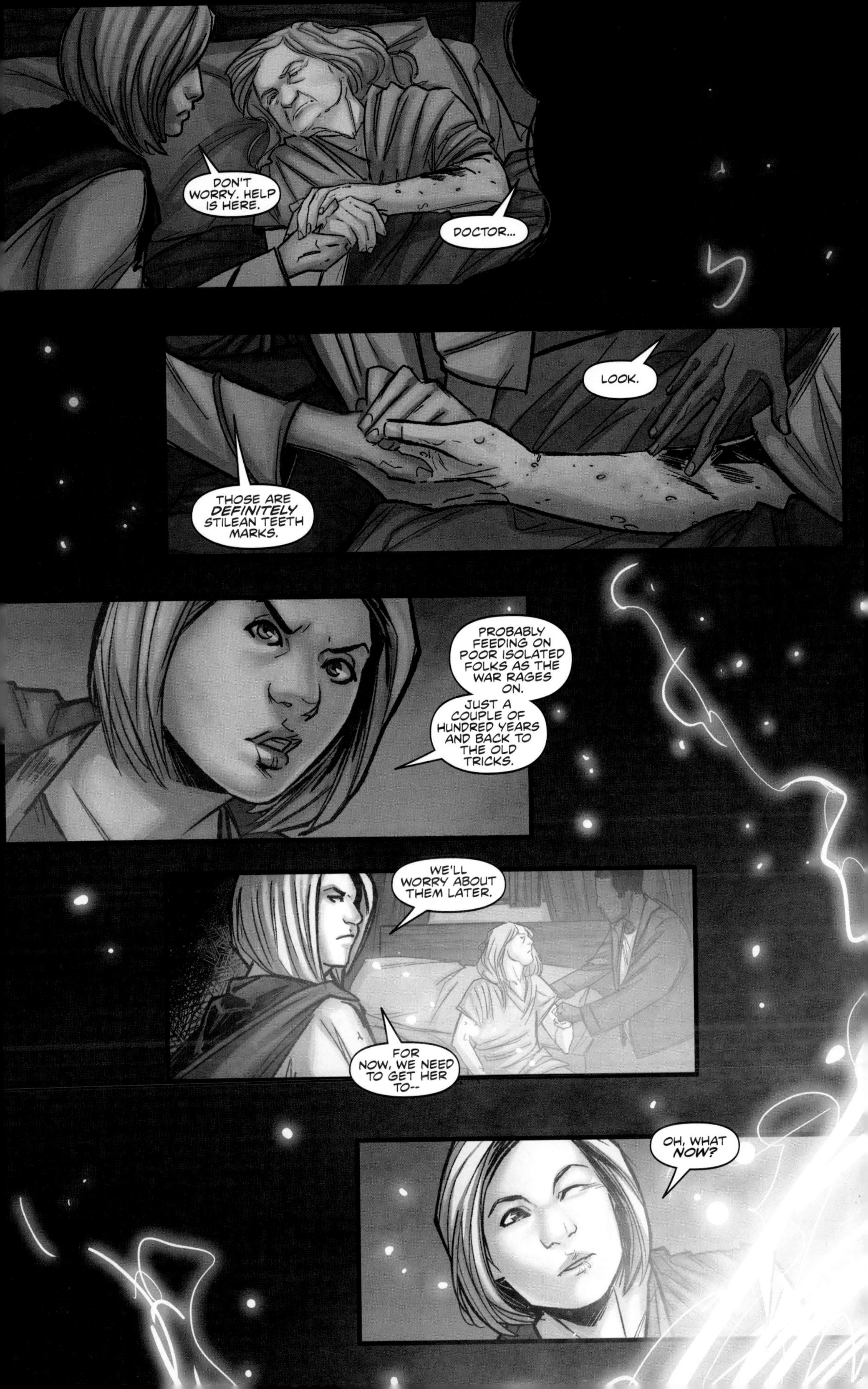
DON'T WORRY. HELP IS HERE.
DOCTOR...
LOOK.
THOSE ARE *DEFINITELY* STILEAN TEETH MARKS.
PROBABLY FEEDING ON POOR ISOLATED FOLKS AS THE WAR RAGES ON.
JUST A COUPLE OF HUNDRED YEARS AND BACK TO THE OLD TRICKS.
WE'LL WORRY ABOUT THEM LATER.
FOR NOW, WE NEED TO GET HER TO--
OH, WHAT *NOW?*

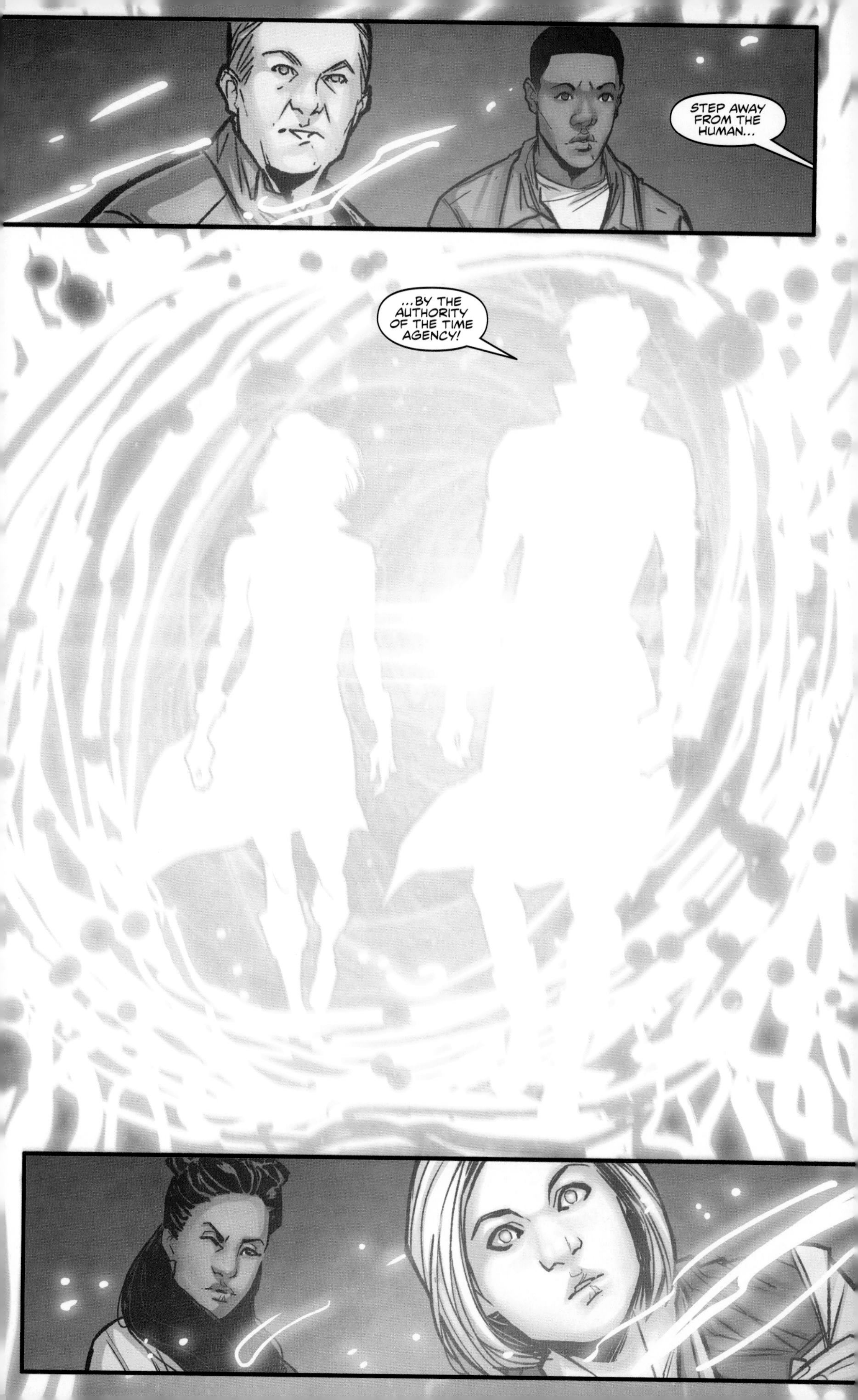
STEP AWAY FROM THE HUMAN...
...BY THE AUTHORITY OF THE TIME AGENCY!

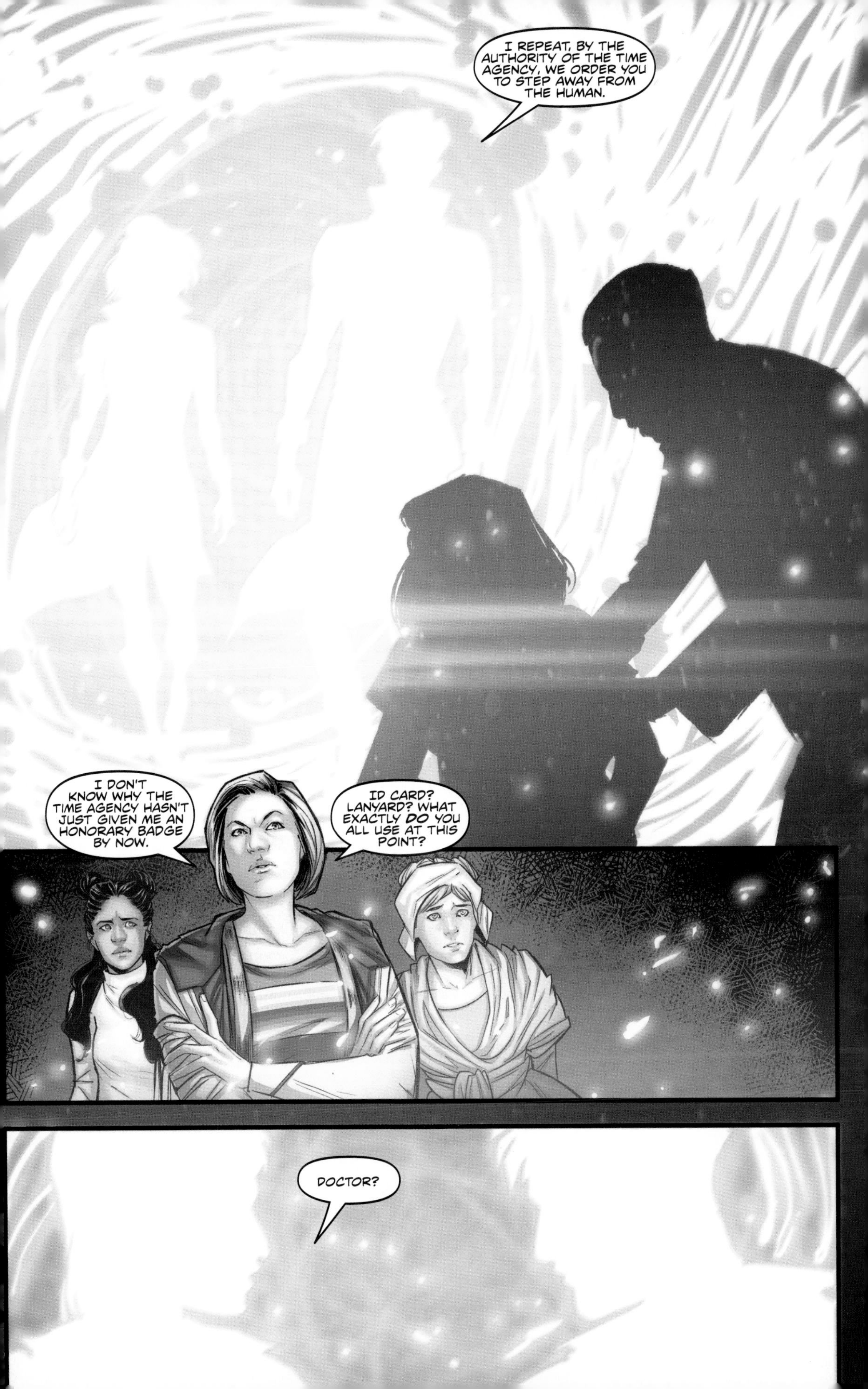
I REPEAT, BY THE AUTHORITY OF THE TIME AGENCY, WE ORDER YOU TO STEP AWAY FROM THE HUMAN.
I DON'T KNOW WHY THE TIME AGENCY HASN'T JUST GIVEN ME AN HONORARY BADGE BY NOW.
ID CARD? LANYARD? WHAT EXACTLY **DO** YOU ALL USE AT THIS POINT?
DOCTOR?

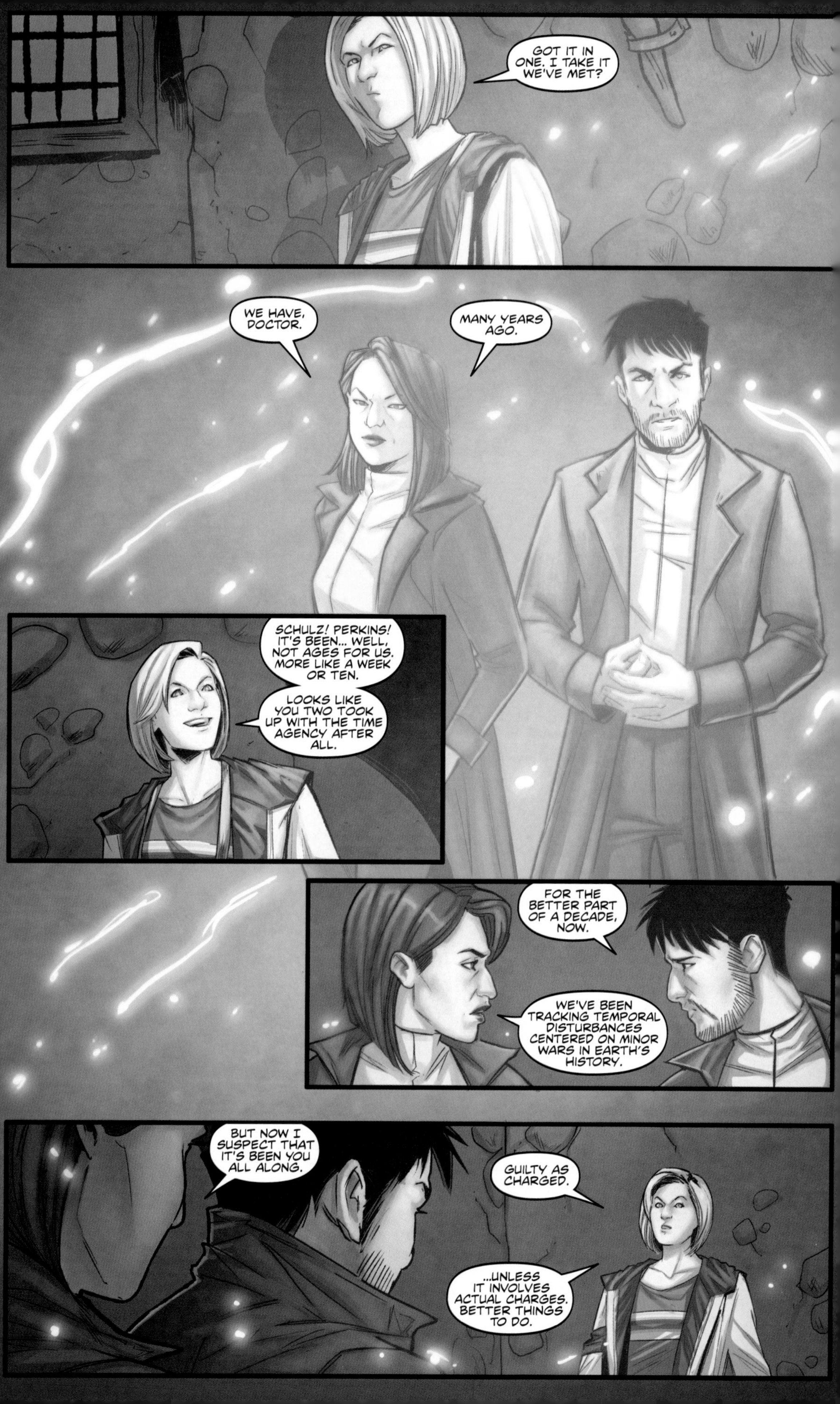
GOT IT IN ONE. I TAKE IT WE'VE MET?
WE HAVE, DOCTOR.
MANY YEARS AGO.
SCHULZ! PERKINS! IT'S BEEN... WELL, NOT AGES FOR US. MORE LIKE A WEEK OR TEN.
LOOKS LIKE YOU TWO TOOK UP WITH THE TIME AGENCY AFTER ALL.
FOR THE BETTER PART OF A DECADE, NOW.
WE'VE BEEN TRACKING TEMPORAL DISTURBANCES CENTERED ON MINOR WARS IN EARTH'S HISTORY.
BUT NOW I SUSPECT THAT IT'S BEEN YOU ALL ALONG.
GUILTY AS CHARGED.
...UNLESS IT INVOLVES ACTUAL CHARGES. BETTER THINGS TO DO.

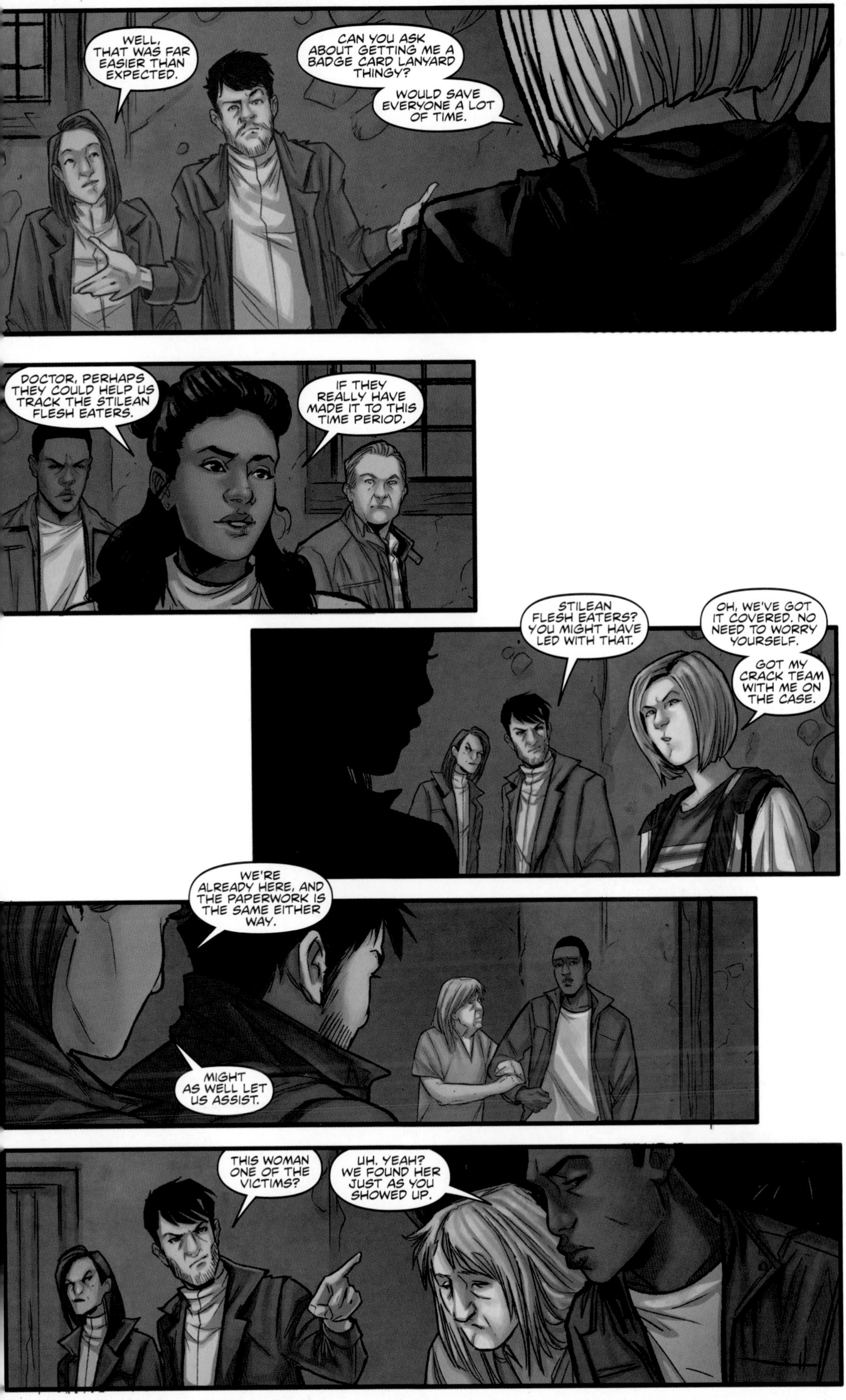
WELL, THAT WAS FAR EASIER THAN EXPECTED.
CAN YOU ASK ABOUT GETTING ME A BADGE CARD LANYARD THINGY?
WOULD SAVE EVERYONE A LOT OF TIME.
DOCTOR, PERHAPS THEY COULD HELP US TRACK THE STILEAN FLESH EATERS.
IF THEY REALLY HAVE MADE IT TO THIS TIME PERIOD.
STILEAN FLESH EATERS? YOU MIGHT HAVE LED WITH THAT.
OH, WE'VE GOT IT COVERED. NO NEED TO WORRY YOURSELF.
GOT MY CRACK TEAM WITH ME ON THE CASE.
WE'RE ALREADY HERE, AND THE PAPERWORK IS THE SAME EITHER WAY.
MIGHT AS WELL LET US ASSIST.
THIS WOMAN ONE OF THE VICTIMS?
UH. YEAH? WE FOUND HER JUST AS YOU SHOWED UP.

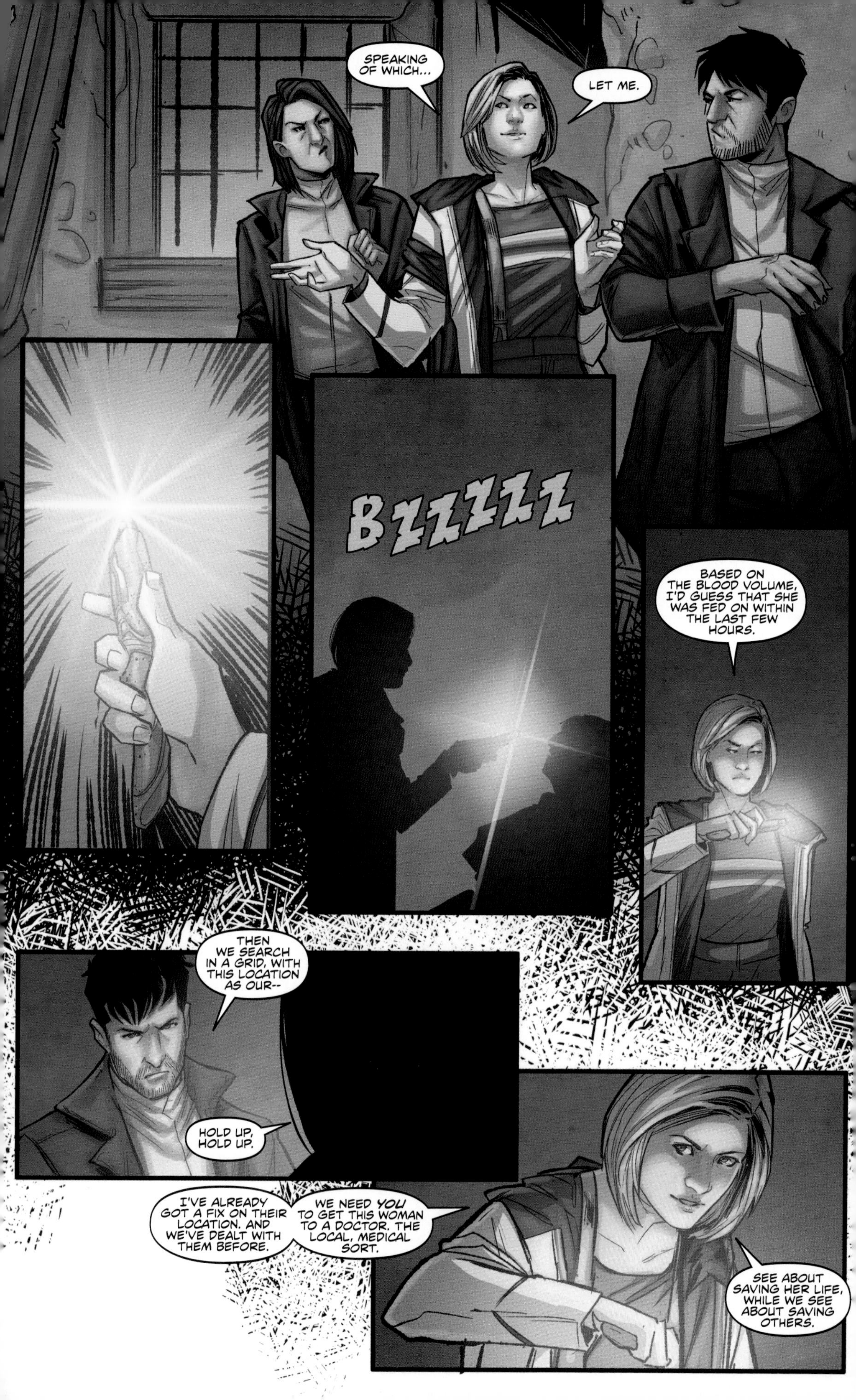
SPEAKING OF WHICH...
LET ME.
BZZZZZ
BASED ON THE BLOOD VOLUME, I'D GUESS THAT SHE WAS FED ON WITHIN THE LAST FEW HOURS.
THEN WE SEARCH IN A GRID, WITH THIS LOCATION AS OUR--
HOLD UP, HOLD UP.
I'VE ALREADY GOT A FIX ON THEIR LOCATION. AND WE'VE DEALT WITH THEM BEFORE.
WE NEED YOU TO GET THIS WOMAN TO A DOCTOR. THE LOCAL, MEDICAL SORT.
SEE ABOUT SAVING HER LIFE, WHILE WE SEE ABOUT SAVING OTHERS.

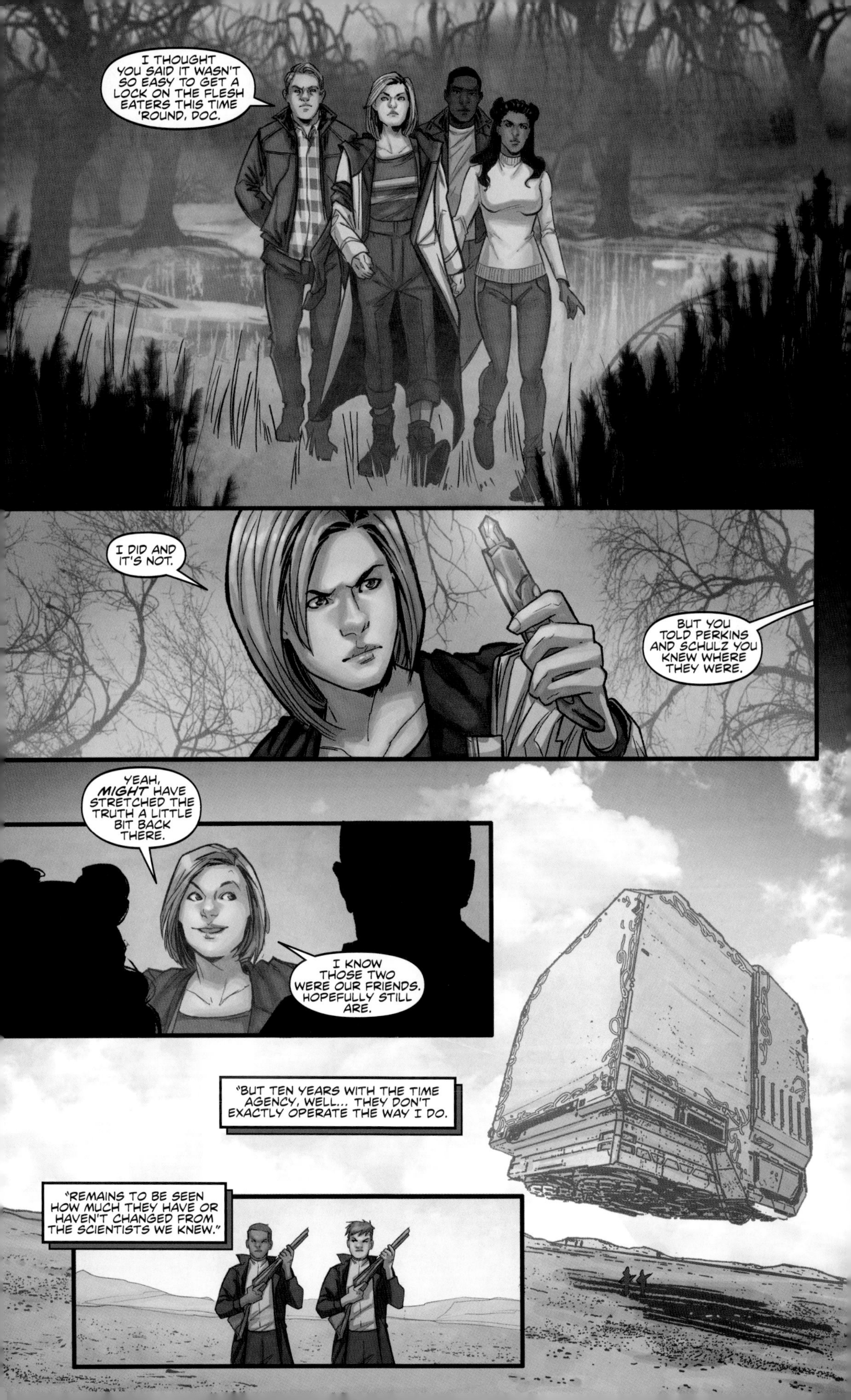
I THOUGHT YOU SAID IT WASN'T SO EASY TO GET A LOCK ON THE FLESH EATERS THIS TIME 'ROUND, DOC.
I DID AND IT'S NOT.
BUT YOU TOLD PERKINS AND SCHULZ YOU KNEW WHERE THEY WERE.
YEAH, *MIGHT* HAVE STRETCHED THE TRUTH A LITTLE BIT BACK THERE.
I KNOW THOSE TWO WERE OUR FRIENDS. HOPEFULLY STILL ARE.
"BUT TEN YEARS WITH THE TIME AGENCY, WELL... THEY DON'T EXACTLY OPERATE THE WAY I DO.
"REMAINS TO BE SEEN HOW MUCH THEY HAVE OR HAVEN'T CHANGED FROM THE SCIENTISTS WE KNEW."

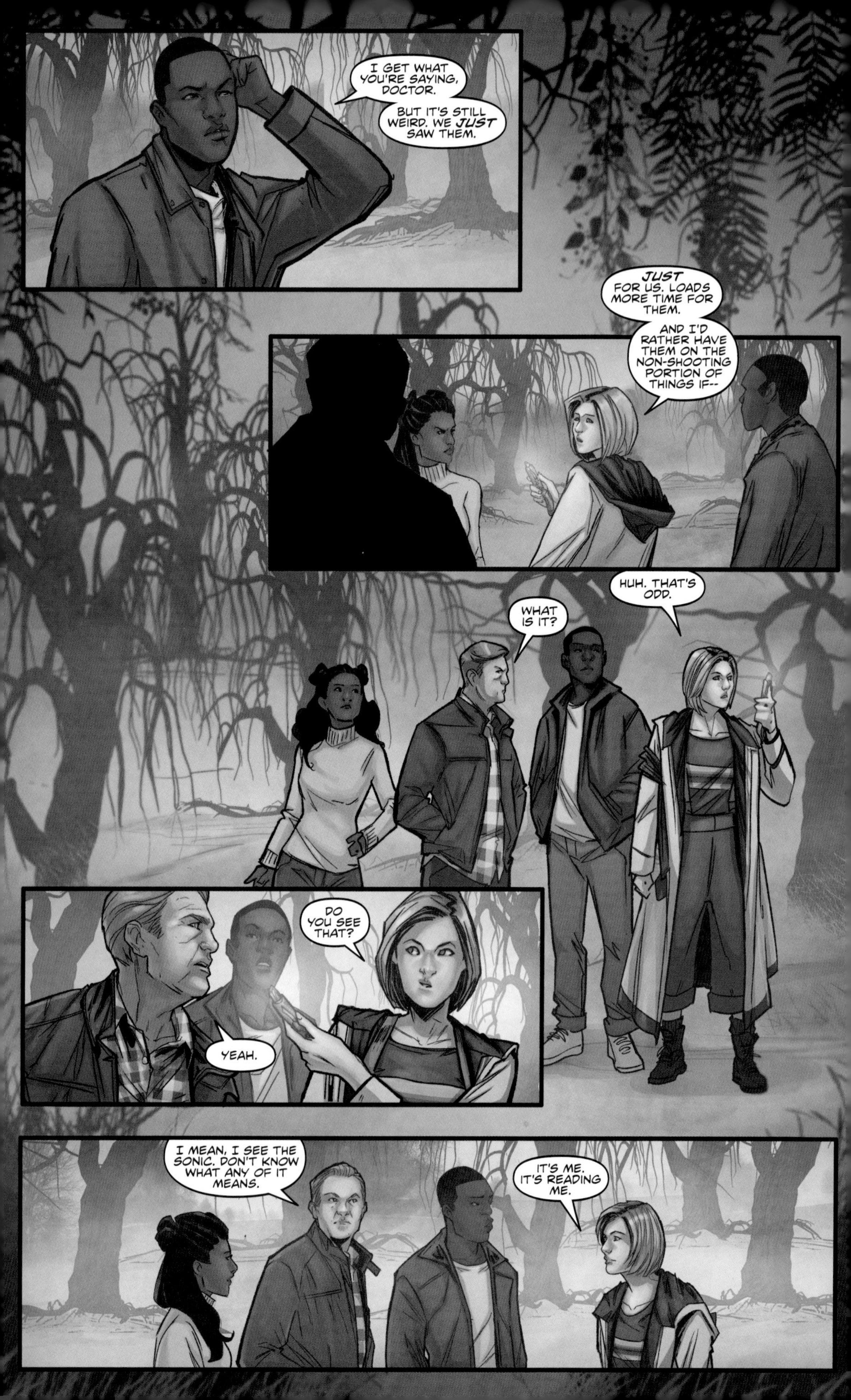
I GET WHAT YOU'RE SAYING, DOCTOR.
BUT IT'S STILL WEIRD. WE *JUST* SAW THEM.
JUST FOR US. LOADS MORE TIME FOR THEM.
AND I'D RATHER HAVE THEM ON THE NON-SHOOTING PORTION OF THINGS IF--
HUH. THAT'S ODD.
WHAT IS IT?
DO YOU SEE THAT?
YEAH.
I MEAN, I SEE THE SONIC. DON'T KNOW WHAT ANY OF IT MEANS.
IT'S ME. IT'S READING ME.

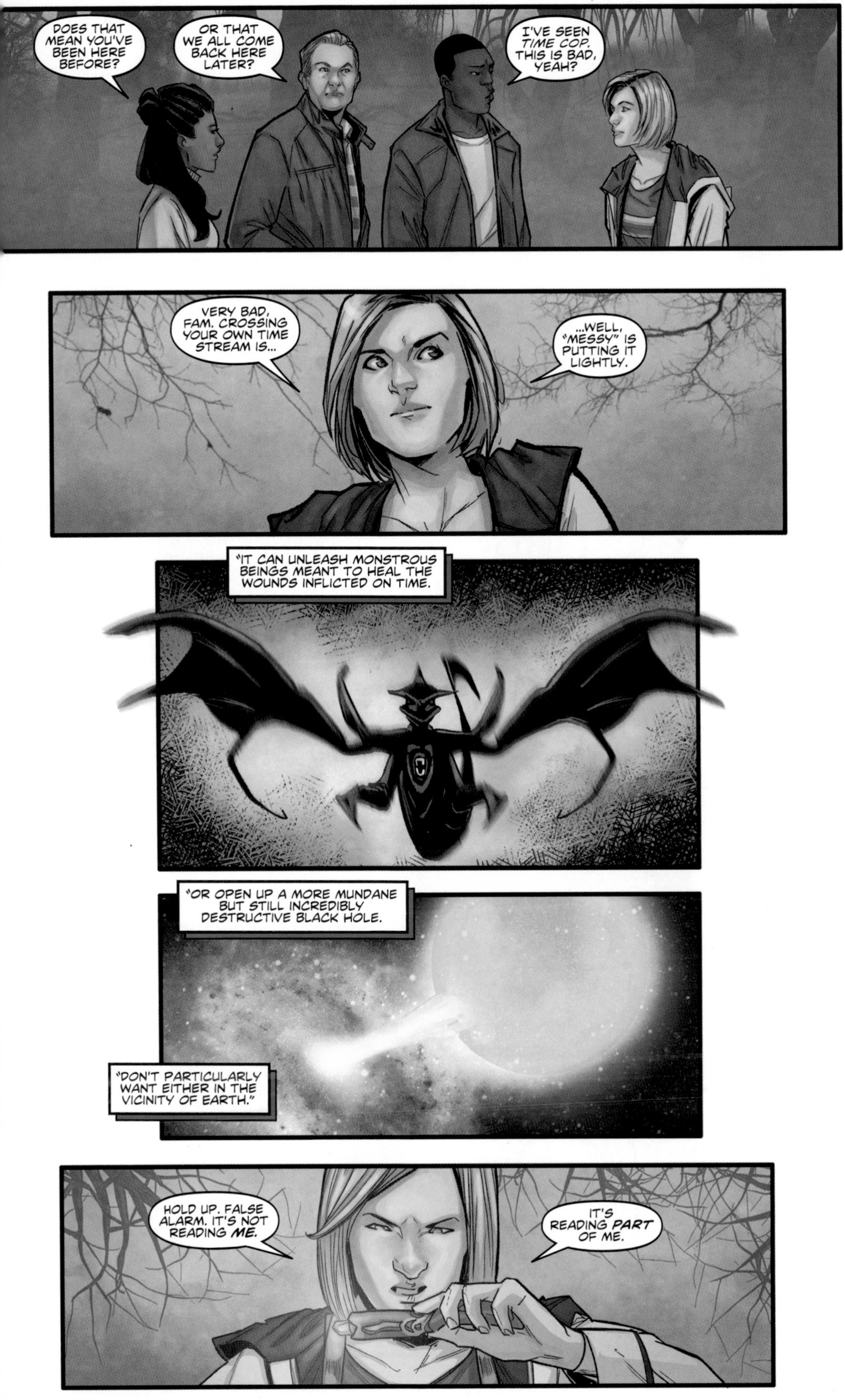
DOES THAT MEAN YOU'VE BEEN HERE BEFORE?
OR THAT WE ALL COME BACK HERE LATER?
I'VE SEEN *TIME COP.* THIS IS BAD, YEAH?
VERY BAD, FAM. CROSSING YOUR OWN TIME STREAM IS...
...WELL, "MESSY" IS PUTTING IT LIGHTLY.
"IT CAN UNLEASH MONSTROUS BEINGS MEANT TO HEAL THE WOUNDS INFLICTED ON TIME.
"OR OPEN UP A MORE MUNDANE BUT STILL INCREDIBLY DESTRUCTIVE BLACK HOLE.
"DON'T PARTICULARLY WANT EITHER IN THE VICINITY OF EARTH."
HOLD UP. FALSE ALARM. IT'S NOT READING **ME.**
IT'S READING ***PART*** OF ME.

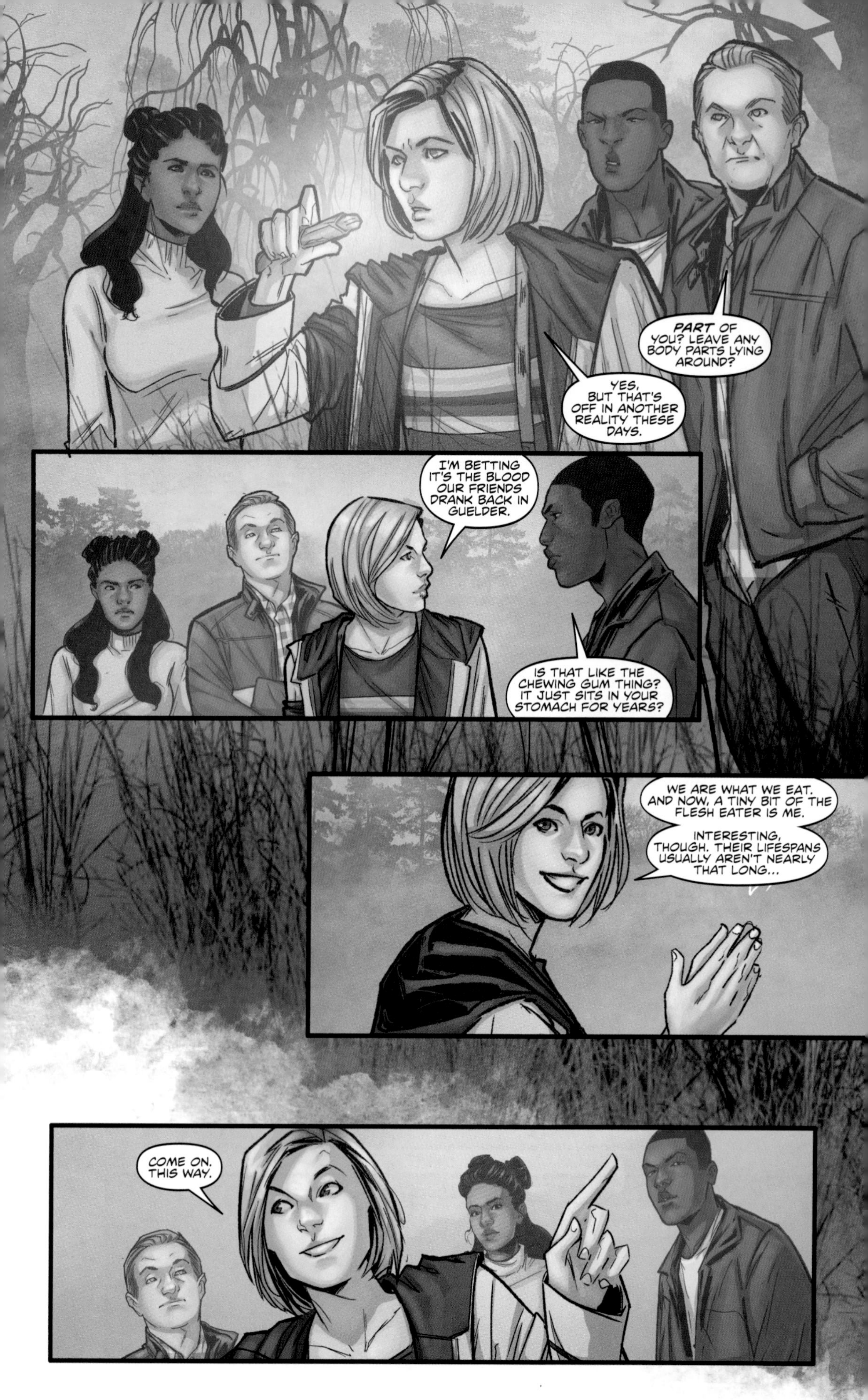
PART OF YOU? LEAVE ANY BODY PARTS LYING AROUND?
YES, BUT THAT'S OFF IN ANOTHER REALITY THESE DAYS.
I'M BETTING IT'S THE BLOOD OUR FRIENDS DRANK BACK IN GUELDER.
IS THAT LIKE THE CHEWING GUM THING? IT JUST SITS IN YOUR STOMACH FOR YEARS?
WE ARE WHAT WE EAT. AND NOW, A TINY BIT OF THE FLESH EATER IS ME.
INTERESTING, THOUGH. THEIR LIFESPANS USUALLY AREN'T NEARLY THAT LONG...
COME ON. THIS WAY.

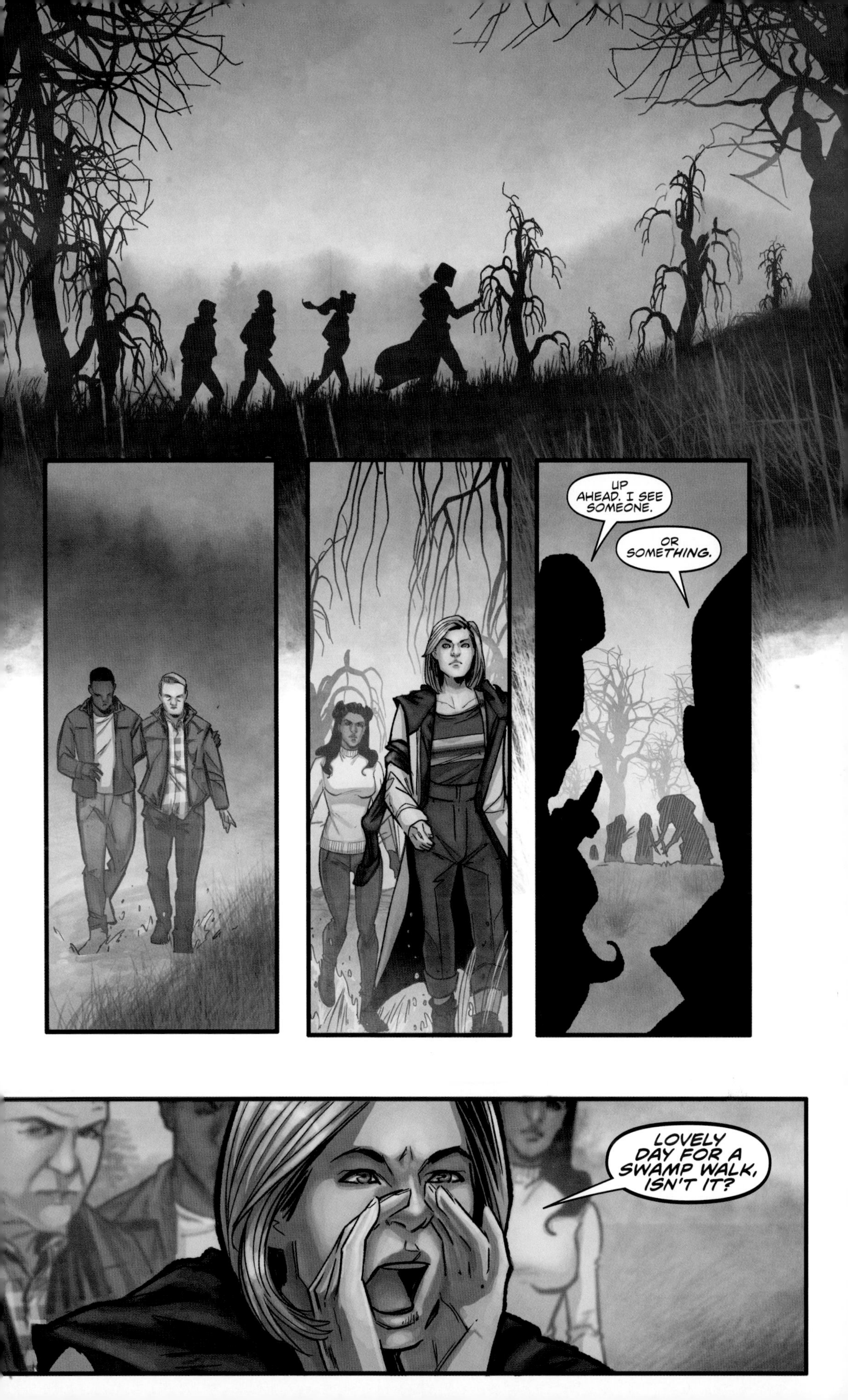
UP AHEAD. I SEE SOMEONE.
OR SOMETHING.
LOVELY DAY FOR A SWAMP WALK, ISN'T IT?

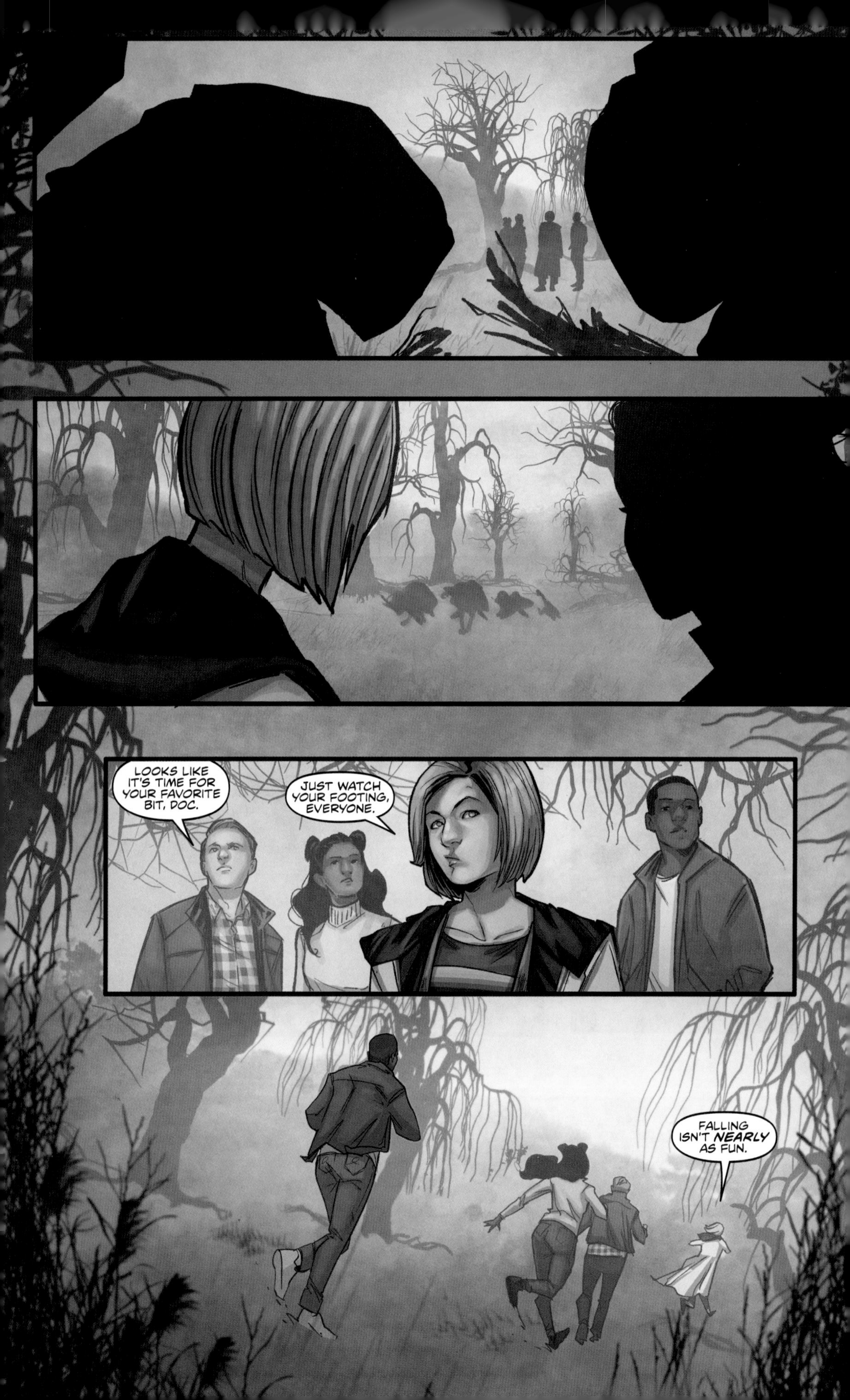
LOOKS LIKE IT'S TIME FOR YOUR FAVORITE BIT, DOC.
JUST WATCH YOUR FOOTING, EVERYONE.
FALLING ISN'T NEARLY AS FUN.

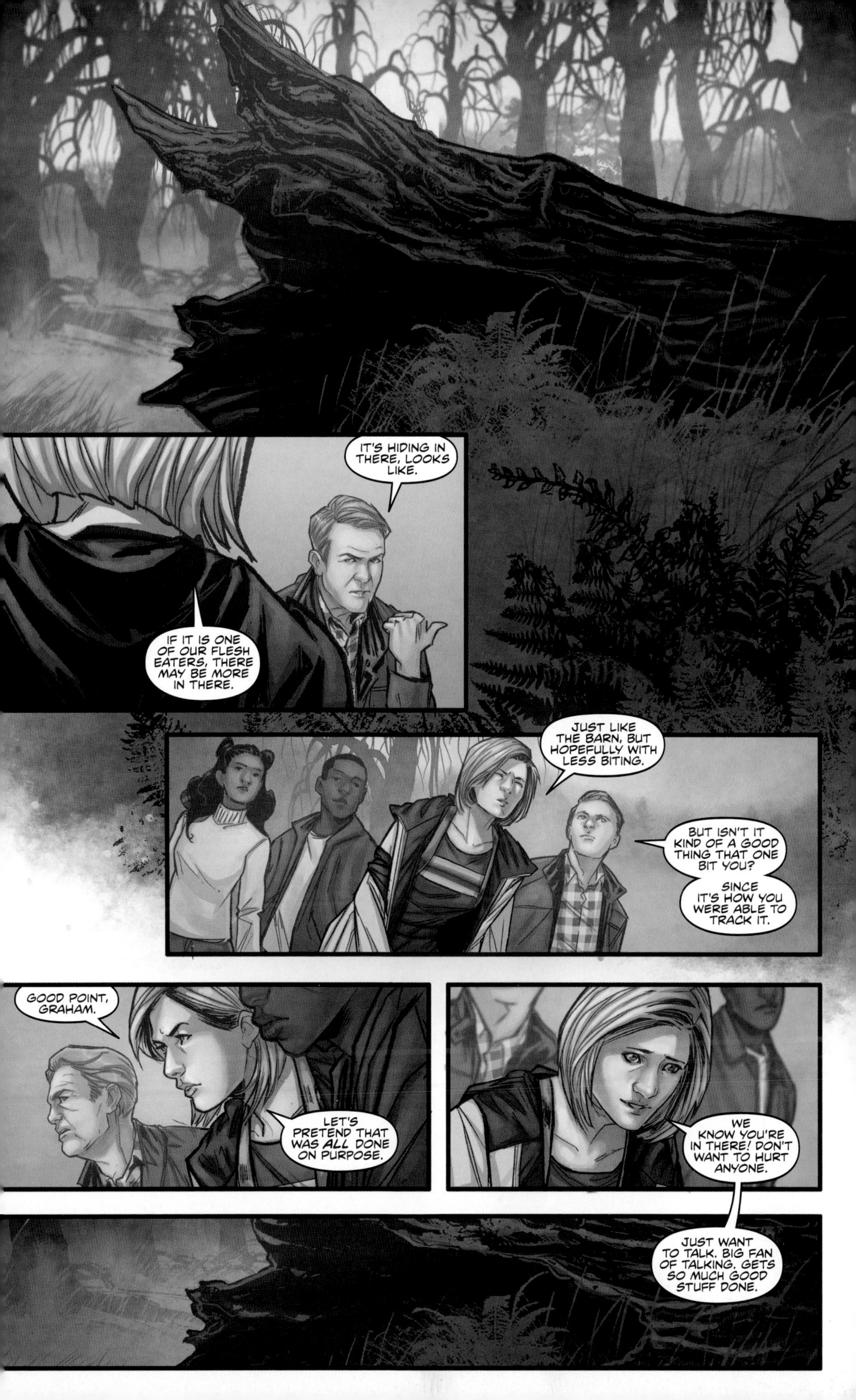
IT'S HIDING IN THERE, LOOKS LIKE.
IF IT IS ONE OF OUR FLESH EATERS, THERE MAY BE MORE IN THERE.
JUST LIKE THE BARN, BUT HOPEFULLY WITH LESS BITING.
BUT ISN'T IT KIND OF A GOOD THING THAT ONE BIT YOU?
SINCE IT'S HOW YOU WERE ABLE TO TRACK IT.
GOOD POINT, GRAHAM.
LET'S PRETEND THAT WAS ALL DONE ON PURPOSE.
WE KNOW YOU'RE IN THERE! DON'T WANT TO HURT ANYONE.
JUST WANT TO TALK. BIG FAN OF TALKING. GETS SO MUCH GOOD STUFF DONE.

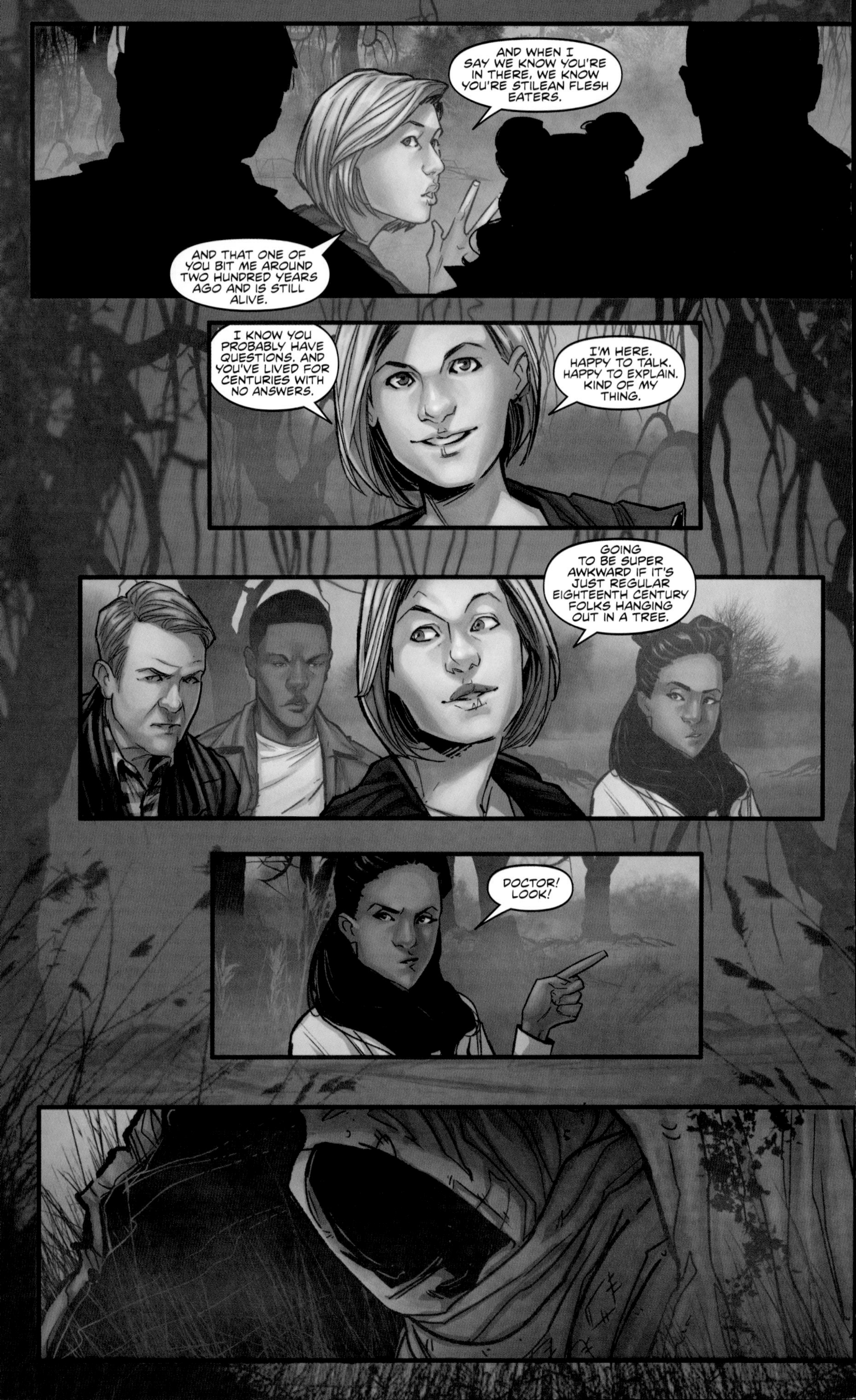
AND WHEN I SAY WE KNOW YOU'RE IN THERE, WE KNOW YOU'RE STILEAN FLESH EATERS.
AND THAT ONE OF YOU BIT ME AROUND TWO HUNDRED YEARS AGO AND IS STILL ALIVE.
I KNOW YOU PROBABLY HAVE QUESTIONS. AND YOU'VE LIVED FOR CENTURIES WITH NO ANSWERS.
I'M HERE. HAPPY TO TALK. HAPPY TO EXPLAIN. KIND OF MY THING.
GOING TO BE SUPER AWKWARD IF IT'S JUST REGULAR EIGHTEENTH CENTURY FOLKS HANGING OUT IN A TREE.
DOCTOR! LOOK!

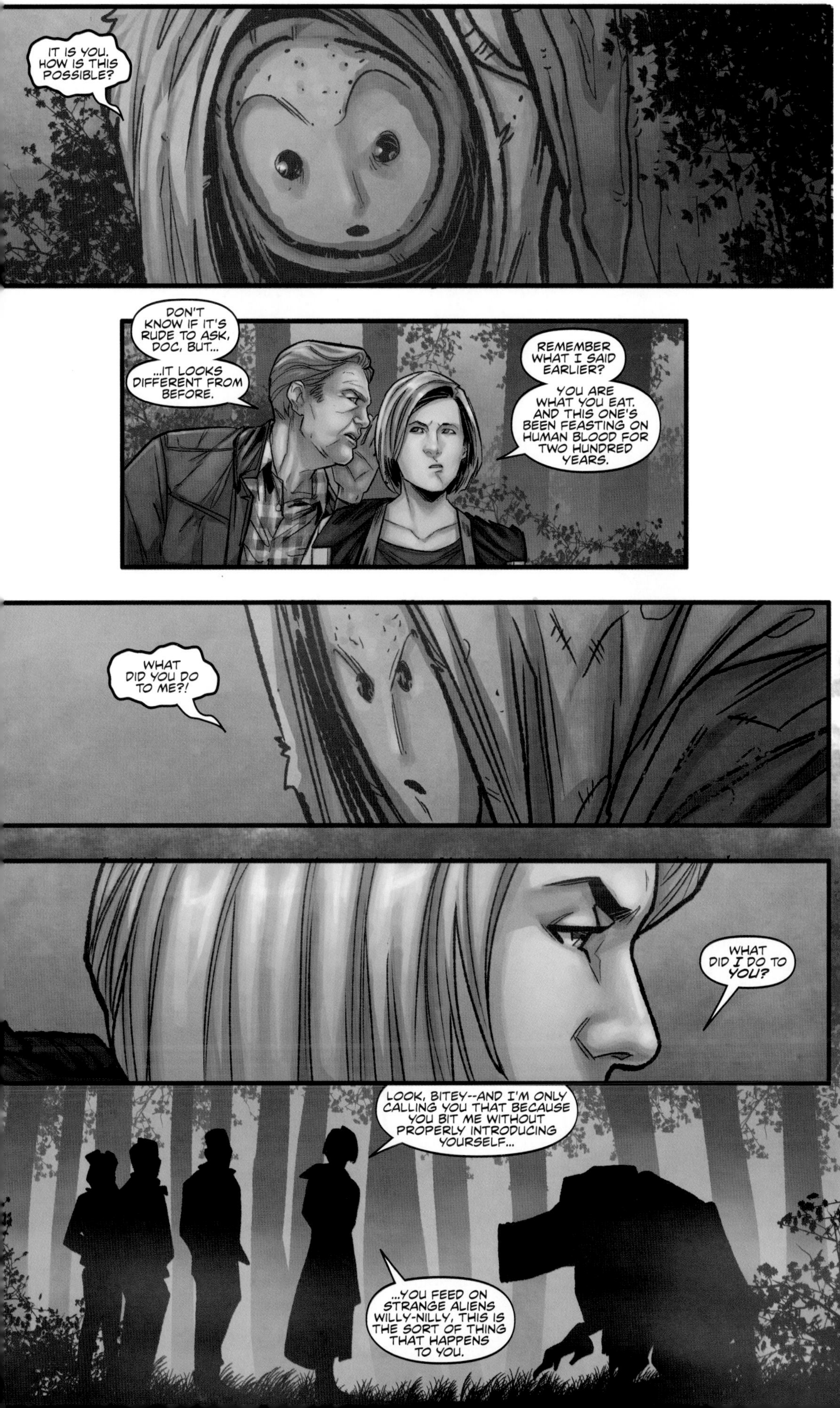
IT IS YOU. HOW IS THIS POSSIBLE?
DON'T KNOW IF IT'S RUDE TO ASK, DOC, BUT...
...IT LOOKS DIFFERENT FROM BEFORE.
REMEMBER WHAT I SAID EARLIER?
YOU ARE WHAT YOU EAT. AND THIS ONE'S BEEN FEASTING ON HUMAN BLOOD FOR TWO HUNDRED YEARS.
WHAT DID YOU DO TO ME?!
WHAT DID I DO TO YOU?
LOOK, BITEY--AND I'M ONLY CALLING YOU THAT BECAUSE YOU BIT ME WITHOUT PROPERLY INTRODUCING YOURSELF...
...YOU FEED ON STRANGE ALIENS WILLY-NILLY, THIS IS THE SORT OF THING THAT HAPPENS TO YOU.

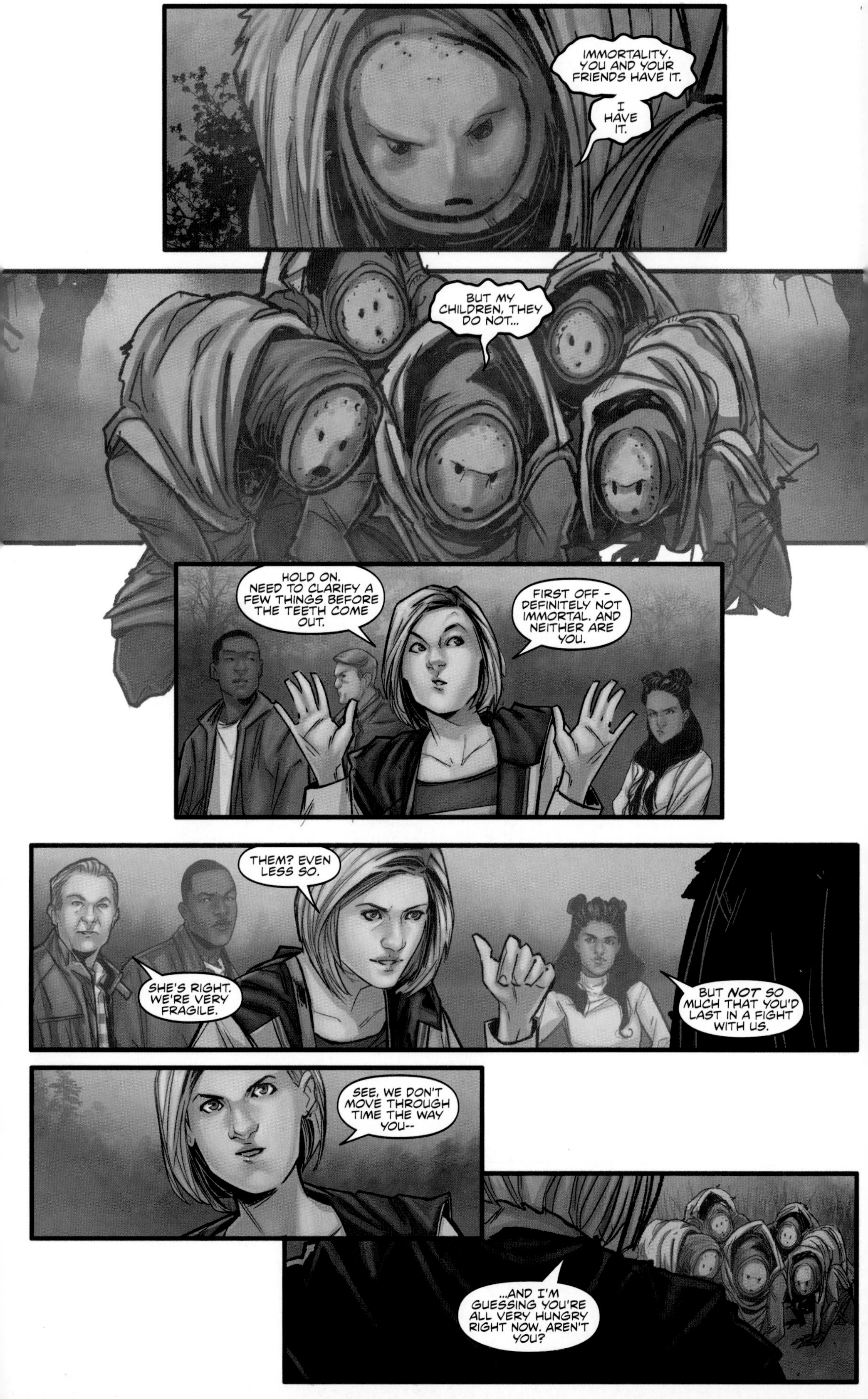
IMMORTALITY. YOU AND YOUR FRIENDS HAVE IT.
I HAVE IT.
BUT MY CHILDREN, THEY DO NOT...
HOLD ON. NEED TO CLARIFY A FEW THINGS BEFORE THE TEETH COME OUT.
FIRST OFF - DEFINITELY NOT IMMORTAL. AND NEITHER ARE YOU.
THEM? EVEN LESS SO.
SHE'S RIGHT. WE'RE VERY FRAGILE.
BUT NOT SO MUCH THAT YOU'D LAST IN A FIGHT WITH US.
SEE, WE DON'T MOVE THROUGH TIME THE WAY YOU--
...AND I'M GUESSING YOU'RE ALL VERY HUNGRY RIGHT NOW. AREN'T YOU?

DOCTOR! BE CAREFUL!

ALWAYS AM, RYAN. EXCEPT WHEN IT'S BORING.

WE'VE ALREADY DONE THE SCARY MONSTER CHASE BIT. DIDN'T REALLY WORK OUT.

SO LET'S TRY SOMETHING DIFFERENT.

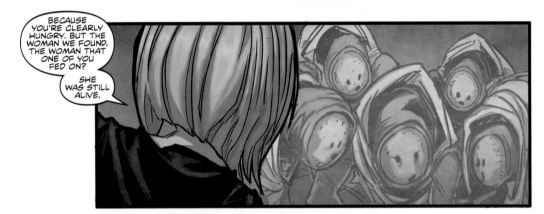

BECAUSE YOU'RE CLEARLY HUNGRY. BUT THE WOMAN WE FOUND, THE WOMAN THAT ONE OF YOU FED ON?

SHE WAS STILL ALIVE.

LAST TIME I SAW YOU, YOU WERE KILLING TO FEED.

STILL NOT A FAN OF THE LIVE VICTIMS, MIND YOU. BUT FULL MARKS FOR IMPROVEMENT.

SO WHAT CHANGED?

WE... WE FOUND THAT--

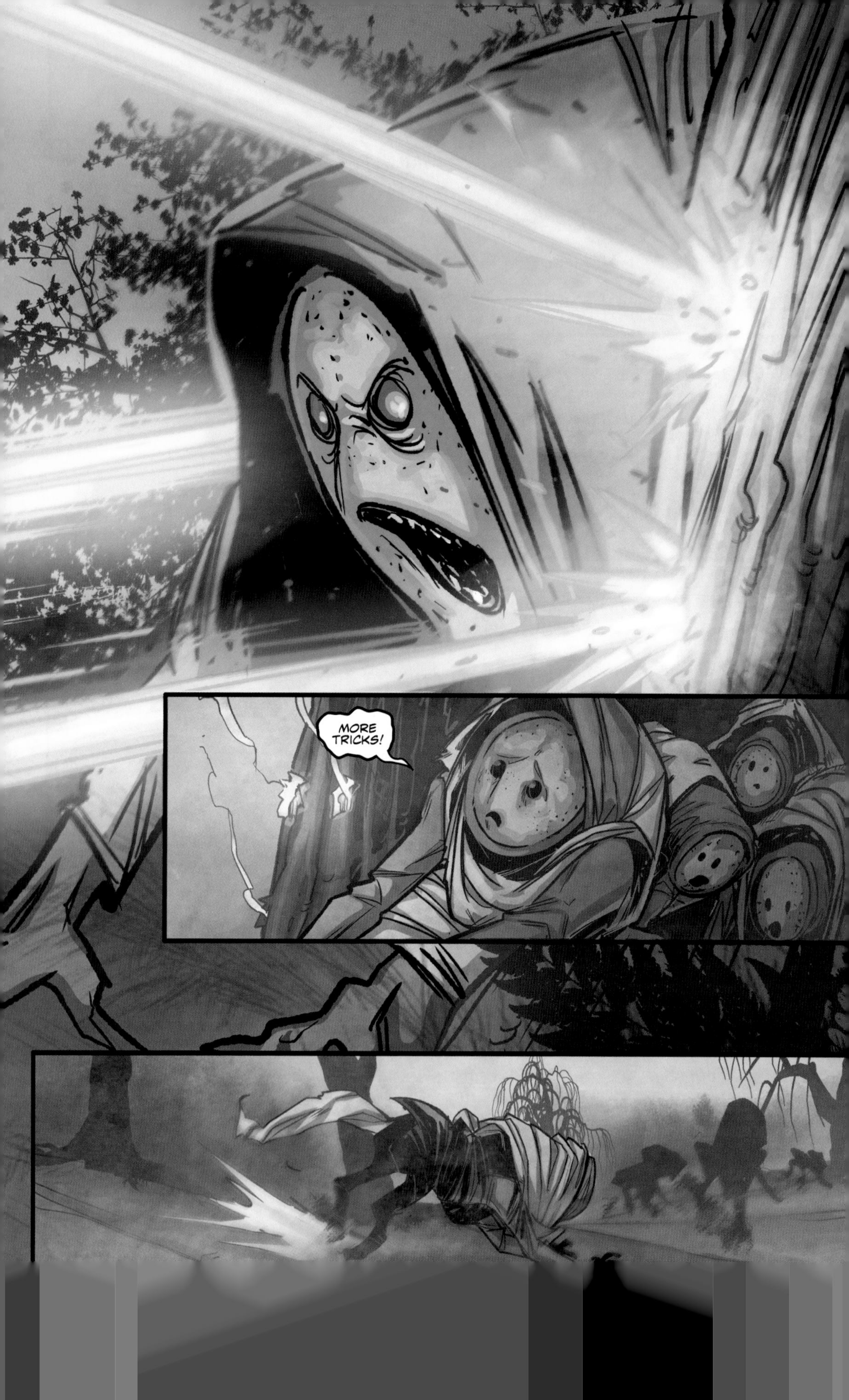
MORE TRICKS!

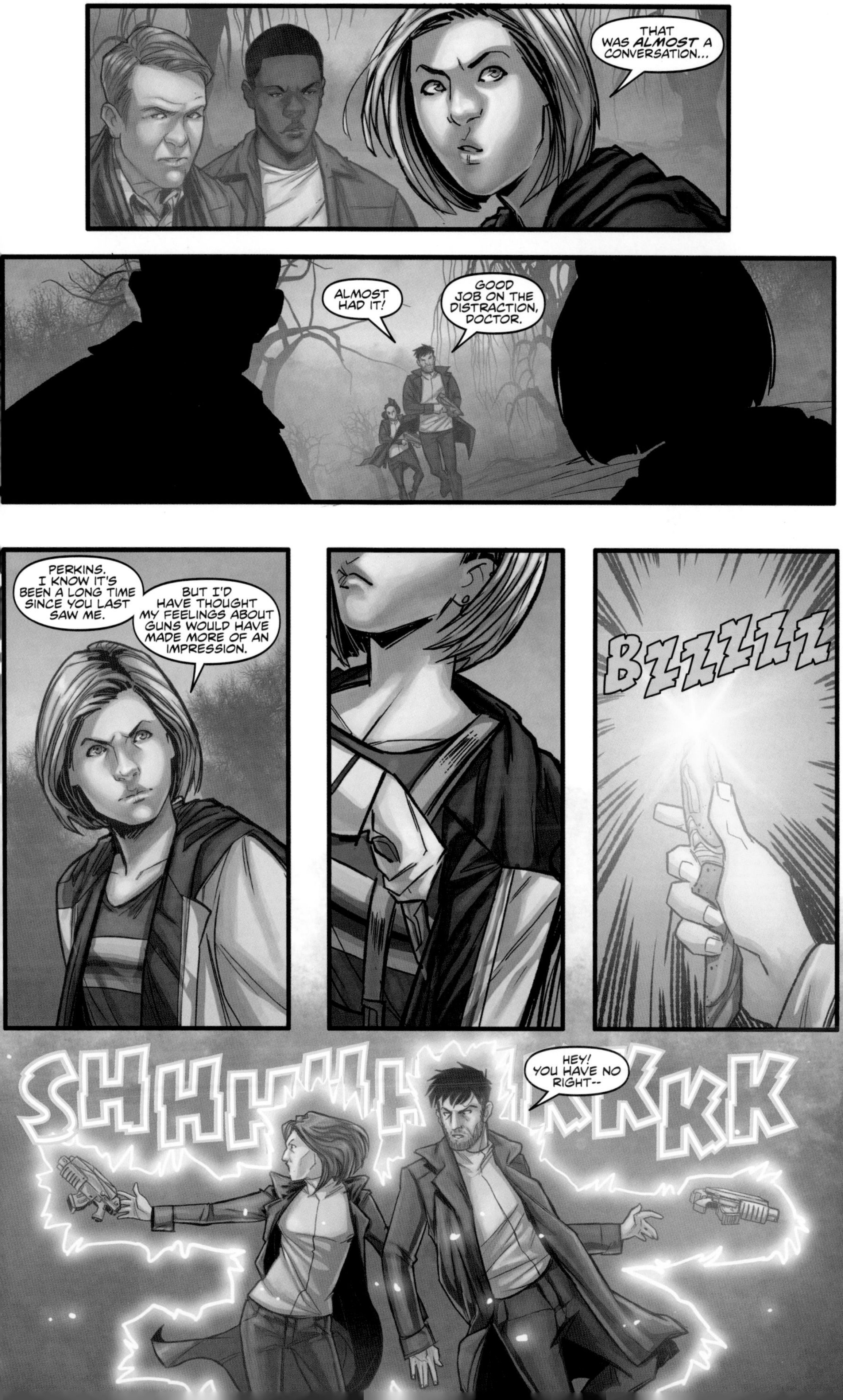
THAT WAS *ALMOST* A CONVERSATION...
ALMOST HAD IT!
GOOD JOB ON THE DISTRACTION, DOCTOR.
PERKINS. I KNOW IT'S BEEN A LONG TIME SINCE YOU LAST SAW ME.
BUT I'D HAVE THOUGHT MY FEELINGS ABOUT GUNS WOULD HAVE MADE MORE OF AN IMPRESSION.
BZZZZZ
HEY! YOU HAVE NO RIGHT--

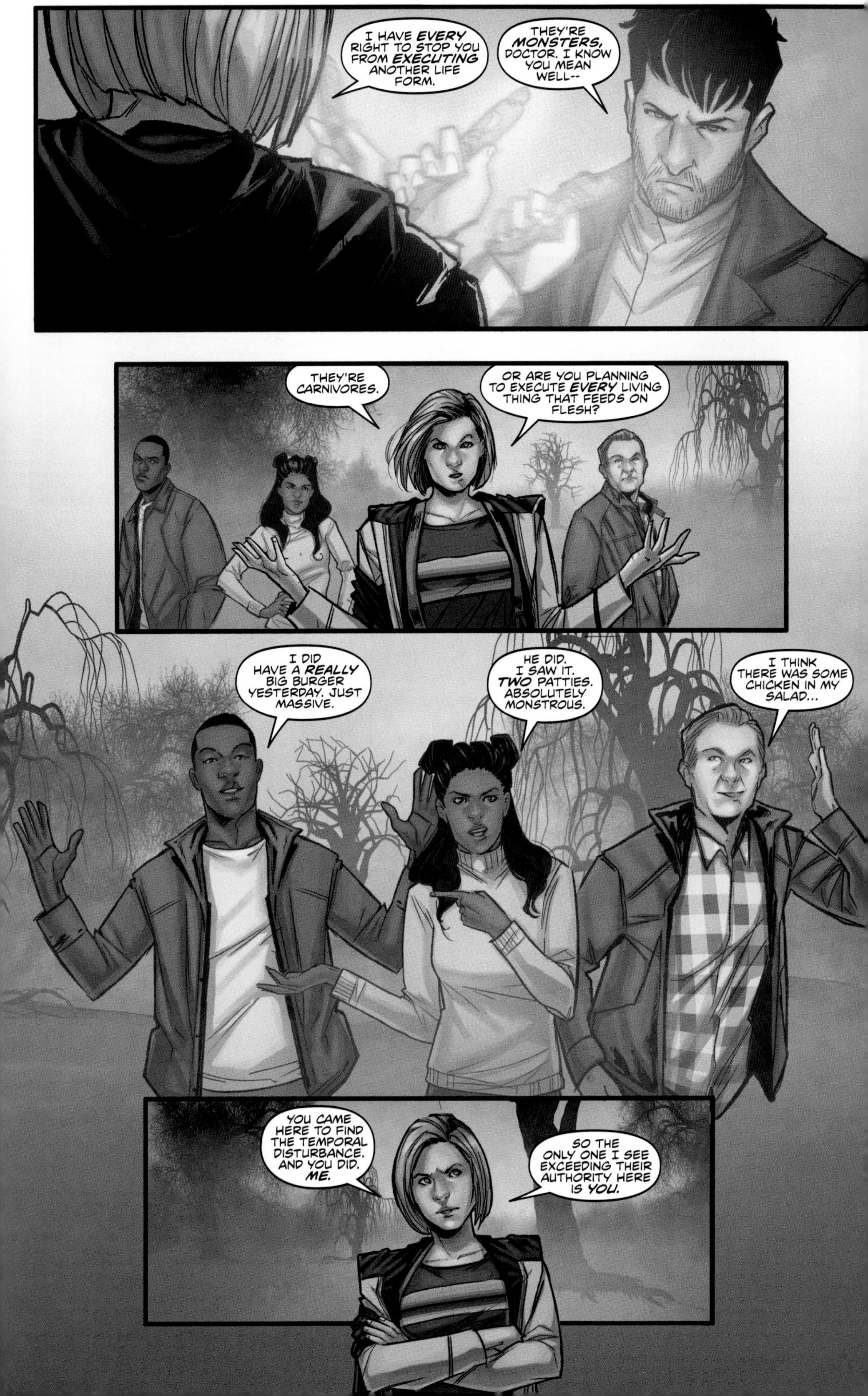
I HAVE EVERY RIGHT TO STOP YOU FROM EXECUTING ANOTHER LIFE FORM.
THEY'RE MONSTERS, DOCTOR. I KNOW YOU MEAN WELL--
THEY'RE CARNIVORES.
OR ARE YOU PLANNING TO EXECUTE EVERY LIVING THING THAT FEEDS ON FLESH?
I DID HAVE A REALLY BIG BURGER YESTERDAY. JUST MASSIVE.
HE DID. I SAW IT. TWO PATTIES. ABSOLUTELY MONSTROUS.
I THINK THERE WAS SOME CHICKEN IN MY SALAD...
YOU CAME HERE TO FIND THE TEMPORAL DISTURBANCE. AND YOU DID. ME.
SO THE ONLY ONE I SEE EXCEEDING THEIR AUTHORITY HERE IS YOU.

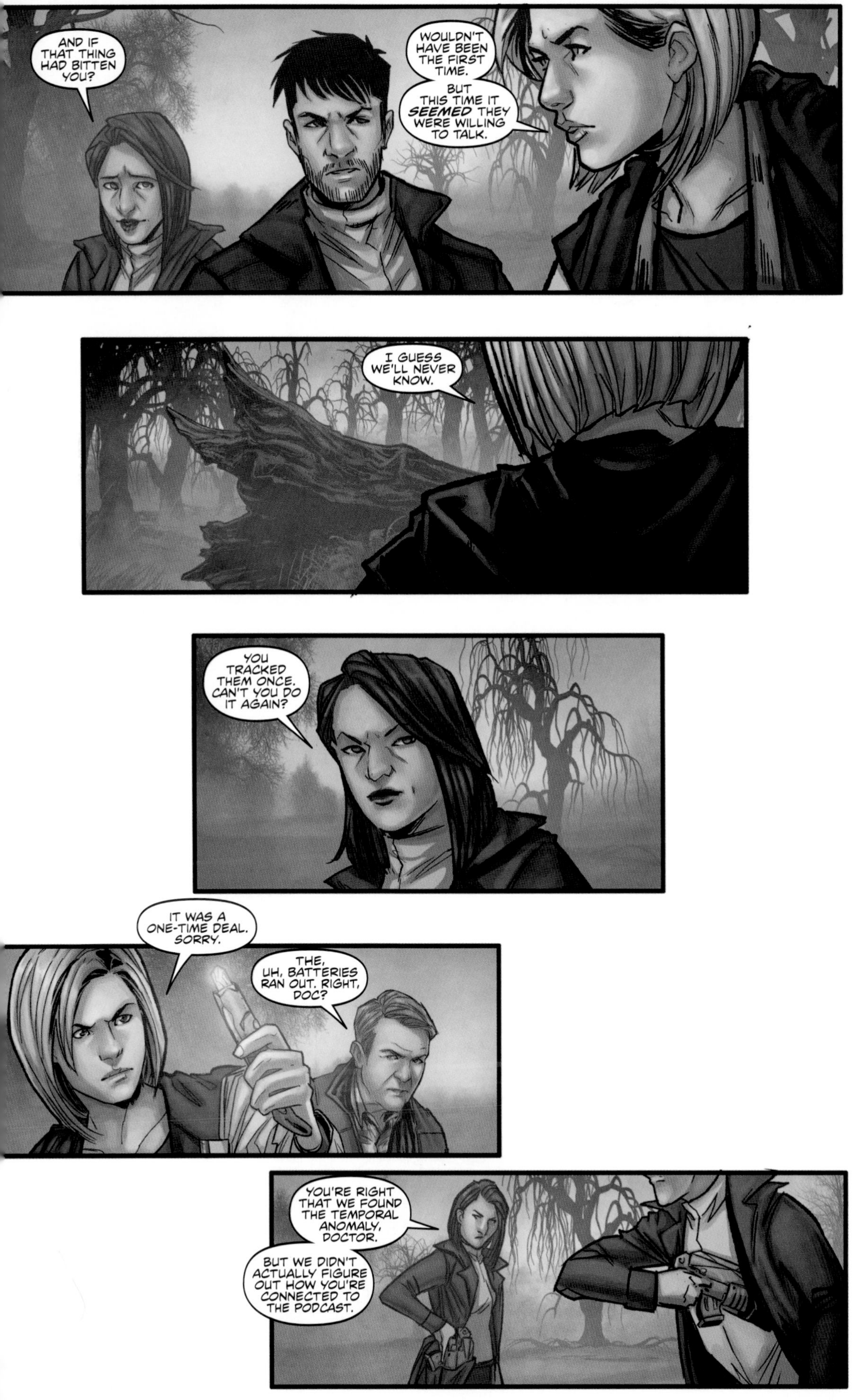
AND IF THAT THING HAD BITTEN YOU?
WOULDN'T HAVE BEEN THE FIRST TIME.
BUT THIS TIME IT *SEEMED* THEY WERE WILLING TO TALK.
I GUESS WE'LL NEVER KNOW.
YOU TRACKED THEM ONCE. CAN'T YOU DO IT AGAIN?
IT WAS A ONE-TIME DEAL. SORRY.
THE, UH, BATTERIES RAN OUT. RIGHT, DOC?
YOU'RE RIGHT THAT WE FOUND THE TEMPORAL ANOMALY, DOCTOR.
BUT WE DIDN'T ACTUALLY FIGURE OUT HOW YOU'RE CONNECTED TO THE PODCAST.

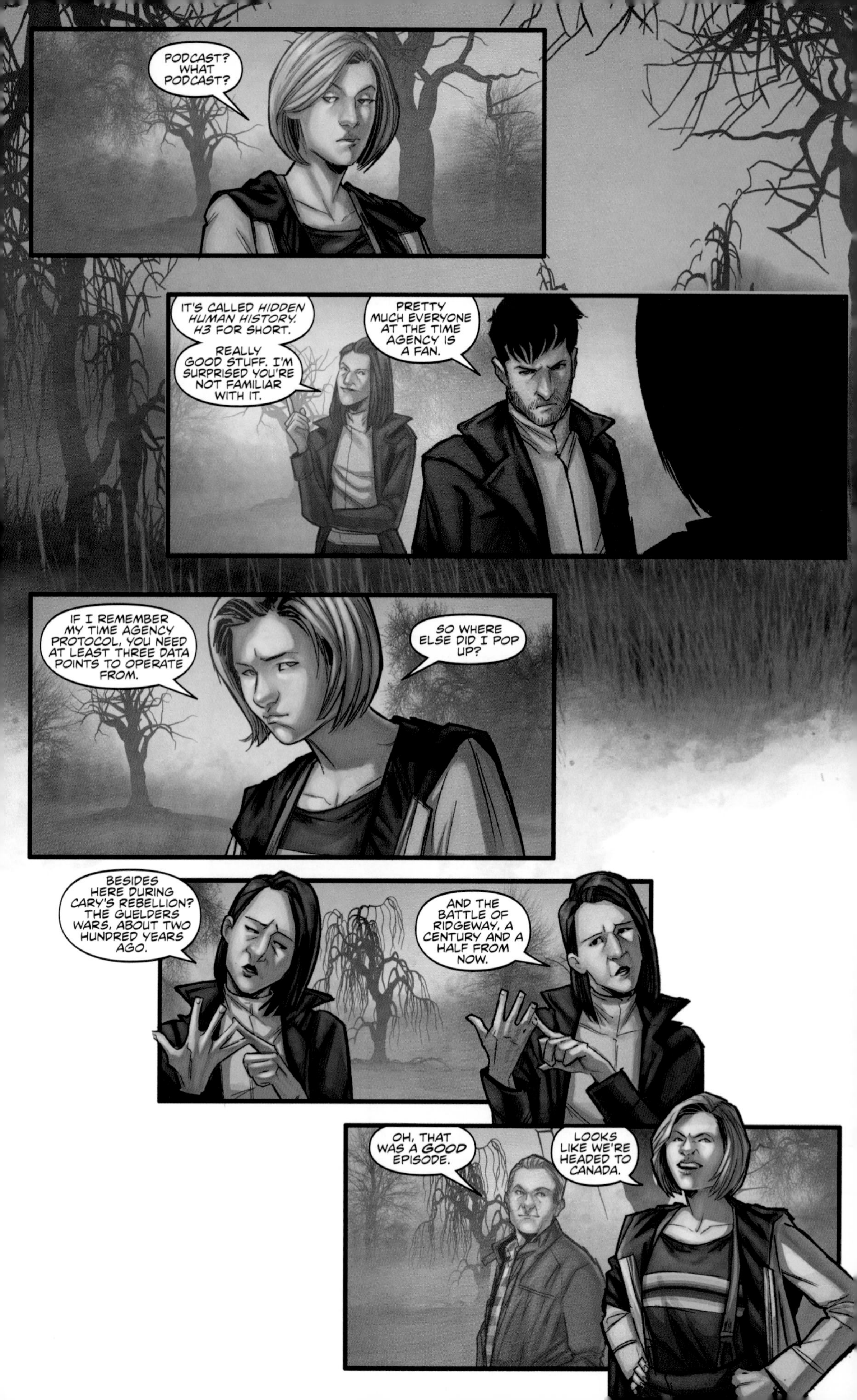
PODCAST? WHAT PODCAST?
IT'S CALLED *HIDDEN HUMAN HISTORY*. *H3* FOR SHORT.
REALLY GOOD STUFF. I'M SURPRISED YOU'RE NOT FAMILIAR WITH IT.
PRETTY MUCH EVERYONE AT THE TIME AGENCY IS A FAN.
IF I REMEMBER MY TIME AGENCY PROTOCOL, YOU NEED AT LEAST THREE DATA POINTS TO OPERATE FROM.
SO WHERE ELSE DID I POP UP?
BESIDES HERE DURING CARY'S REBELLION? THE GUELDERS WARS, ABOUT TWO HUNDRED YEARS AGO.
AND THE BATTLE OF RIDGEWAY, A CENTURY AND A HALF FROM NOW.
OH, THAT WAS A **GOOD** EPISODE.
LOOKS LIKE WE'RE HEADED TO CANADA.

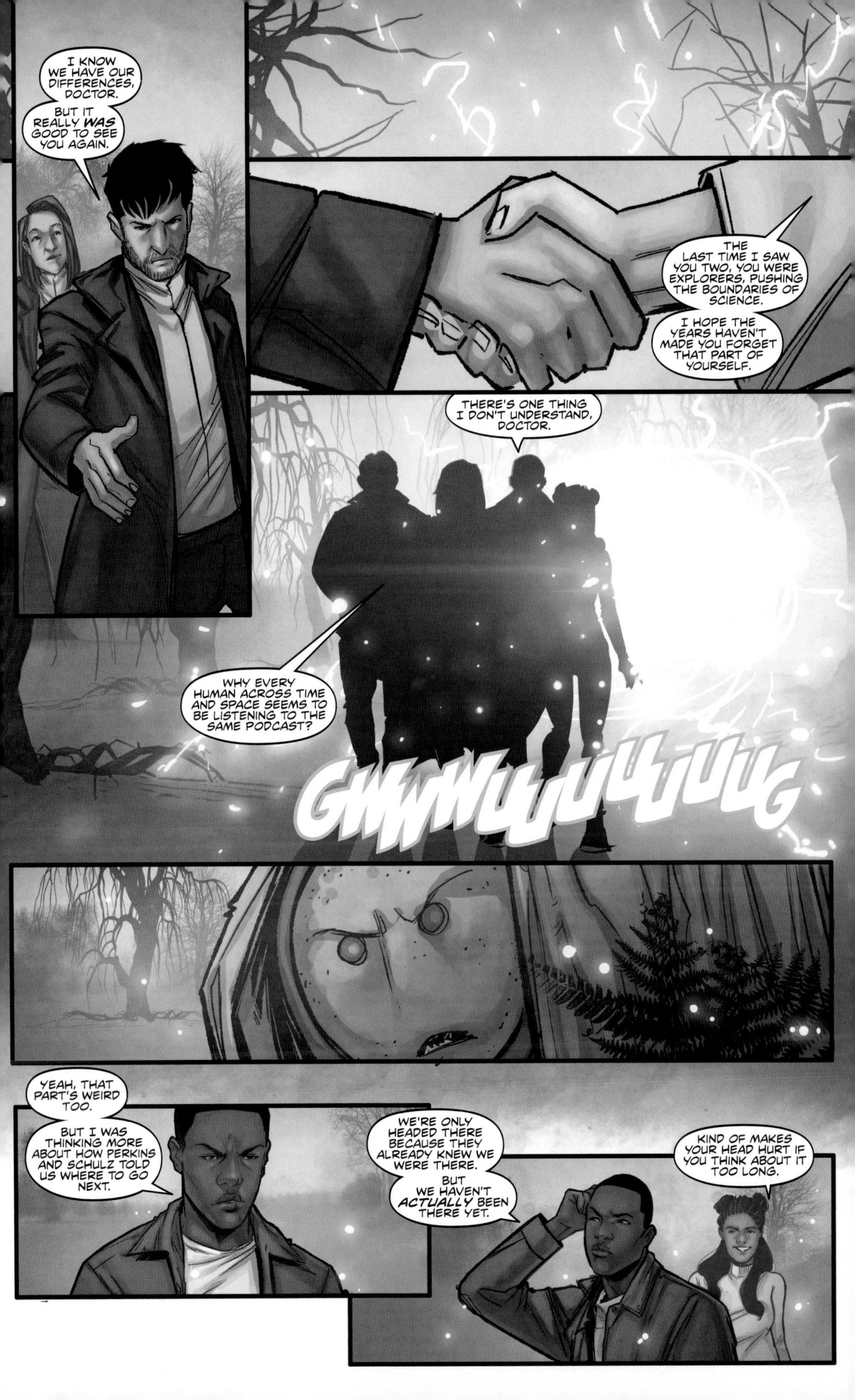
I KNOW WE HAVE OUR DIFFERENCES, DOCTOR.
BUT IT REALLY **WAS** GOOD TO SEE YOU AGAIN.
THE LAST TIME I SAW YOU TWO, YOU WERE EXPLORERS, PUSHING THE BOUNDARIES OF SCIENCE.
I HOPE THE YEARS HAVEN'T MADE YOU FORGET THAT PART OF YOURSELF.
THERE'S ONE THING I DON'T UNDERSTAND, DOCTOR.
WHY EVERY HUMAN ACROSS TIME AND SPACE SEEMS TO BE LISTENING TO THE SAME PODCAST?
GWWWUUUUUUUG
YEAH, THAT PART'S WEIRD TOO.
BUT I WAS THINKING MORE ABOUT HOW PERKINS AND SCHULZ TOLD US WHERE TO GO NEXT.
WE'RE ONLY HEADED THERE BECAUSE THEY ALREADY KNEW WE WERE THERE.
BUT WE HAVEN'T *ACTUALLY* BEEN THERE YET.
KIND OF MAKES YOUR HEAD HURT IF YOU THINK ABOUT IT TOO LONG.

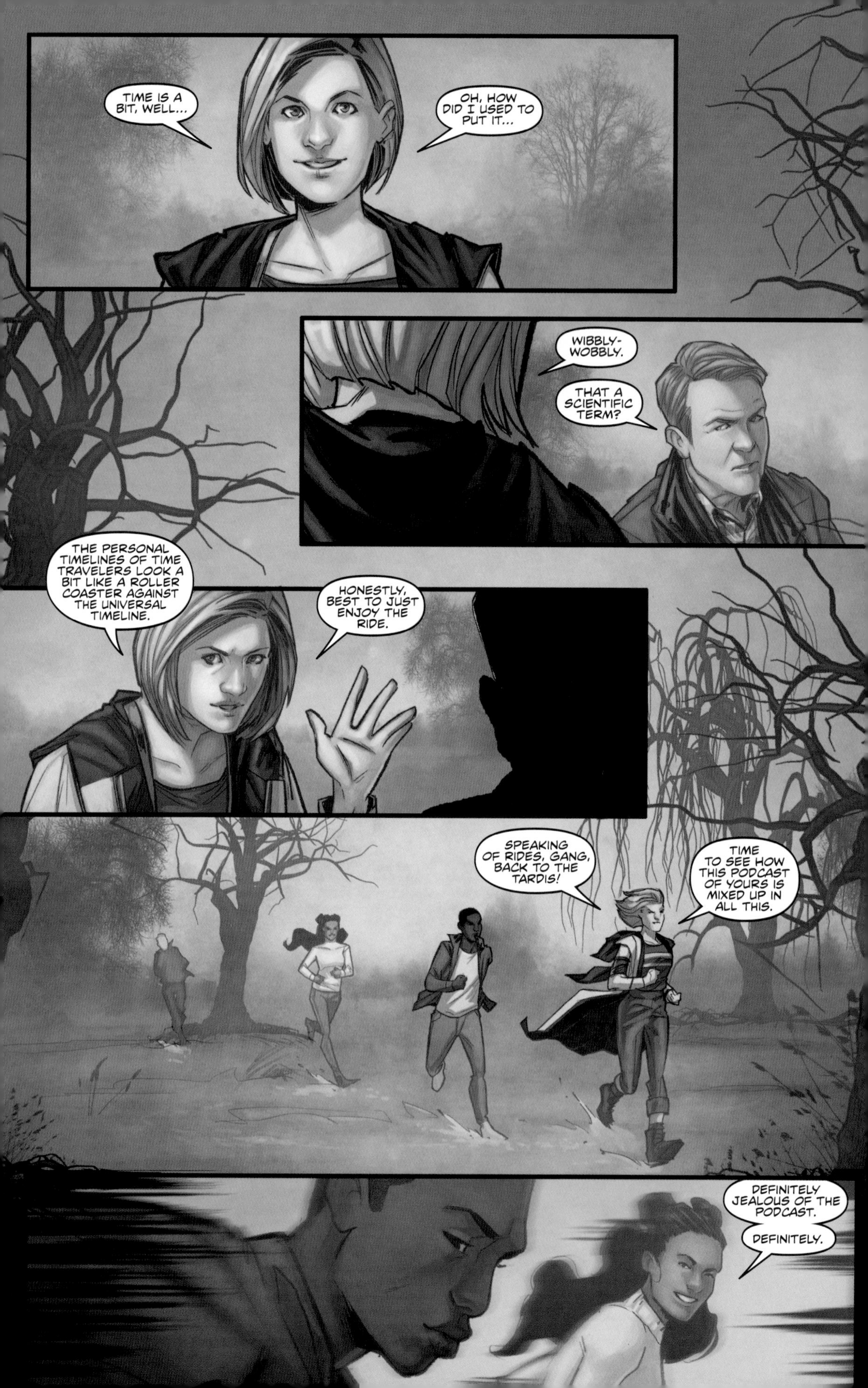
TIME IS A BIT, WELL...
OH, HOW DID I USED TO PUT IT...
WIBBLY-WOBBLY.
THAT A SCIENTIFIC TERM?
THE PERSONAL TIMELINES OF TIME TRAVELERS LOOK A BIT LIKE A ROLLER COASTER AGAINST THE UNIVERSAL TIMELINE.
HONESTLY, BEST TO JUST ENJOY THE RIDE.
SPEAKING OF RIDES, GANG, BACK TO THE TARDIS!
TIME TO SEE HOW THIS PODCAST OF YOURS IS MIXED UP IN ALL THIS.
DEFINITELY JEALOUS OF THE PODCAST.
DEFINITELY.

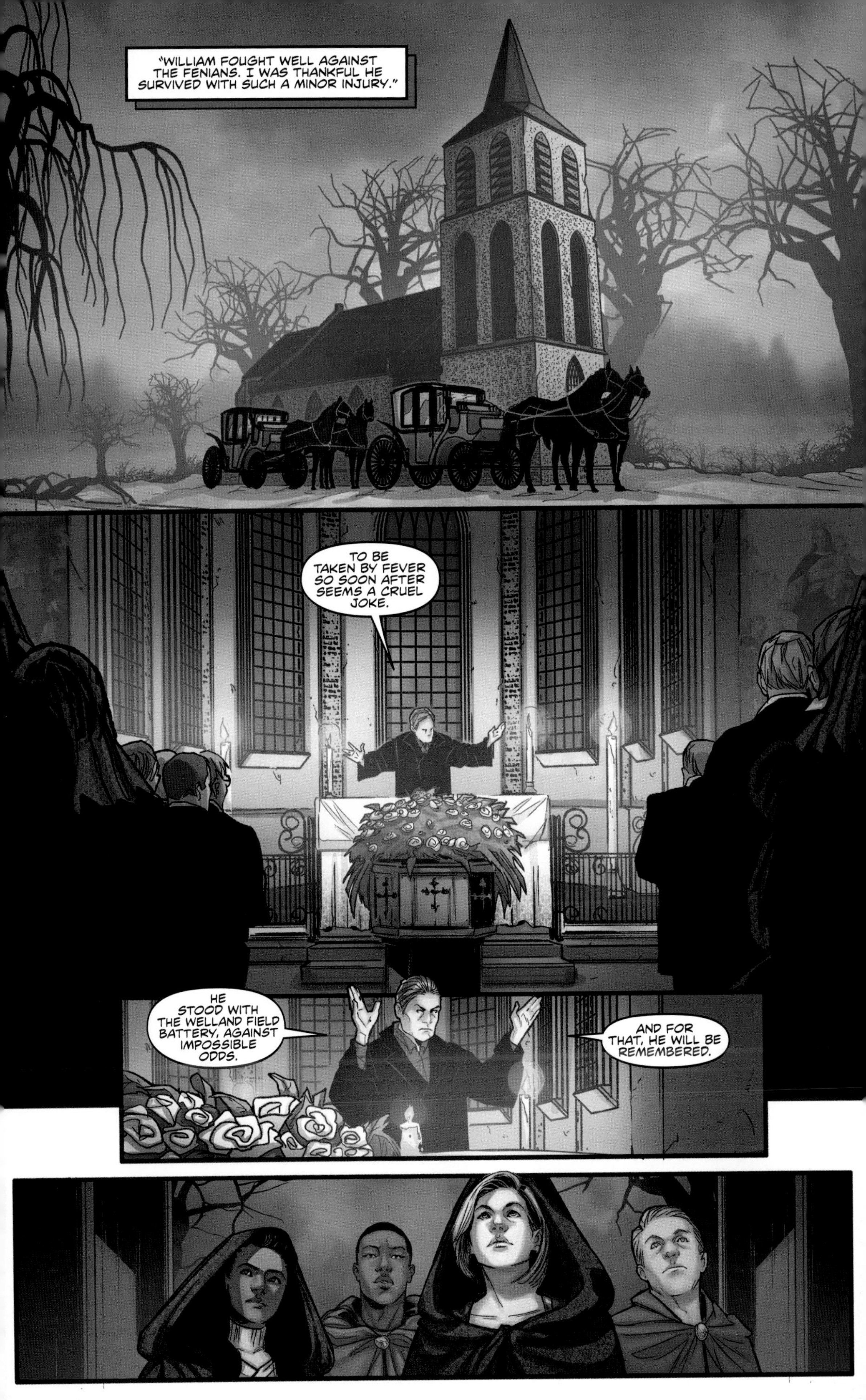
"WILLIAM FOUGHT WELL AGAINST THE FENIANS. I WAS THANKFUL HE SURVIVED WITH SUCH A MINOR INJURY."
TO BE TAKEN BY FEVER SO SOON AFTER SEEMS A CRUEL JOKE.
HE STOOD WITH THE WELLAND FIELD BATTERY, AGAINST IMPOSSIBLE ODDS.
AND FOR THAT, HE WILL BE REMEMBERED.

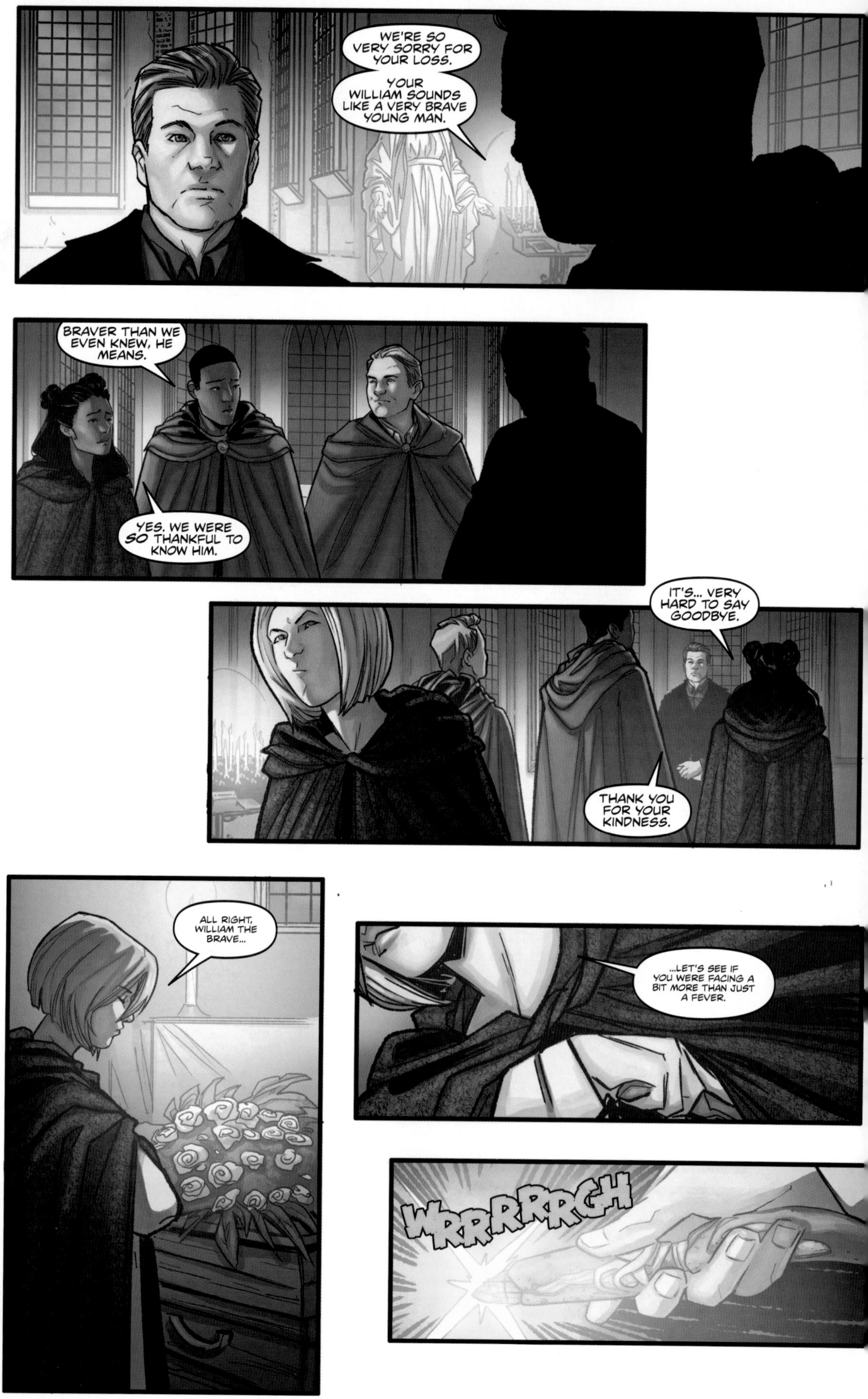
WE'RE SO VERY SORRY FOR YOUR LOSS.
YOUR WILLIAM SOUNDS LIKE A VERY BRAVE YOUNG MAN.
BRAVER THAN WE EVEN KNEW, HE MEANS.
YES. WE WERE SO THANKFUL TO KNOW HIM.
IT'S... VERY HARD TO SAY GOODBYE.
THANK YOU FOR YOUR KINDNESS.
ALL RIGHT, WILLIAM THE BRAVE...
...LET'S SEE IF YOU WERE FACING A BIT MORE THAN JUST A FEVER.
WRRRRRRGH

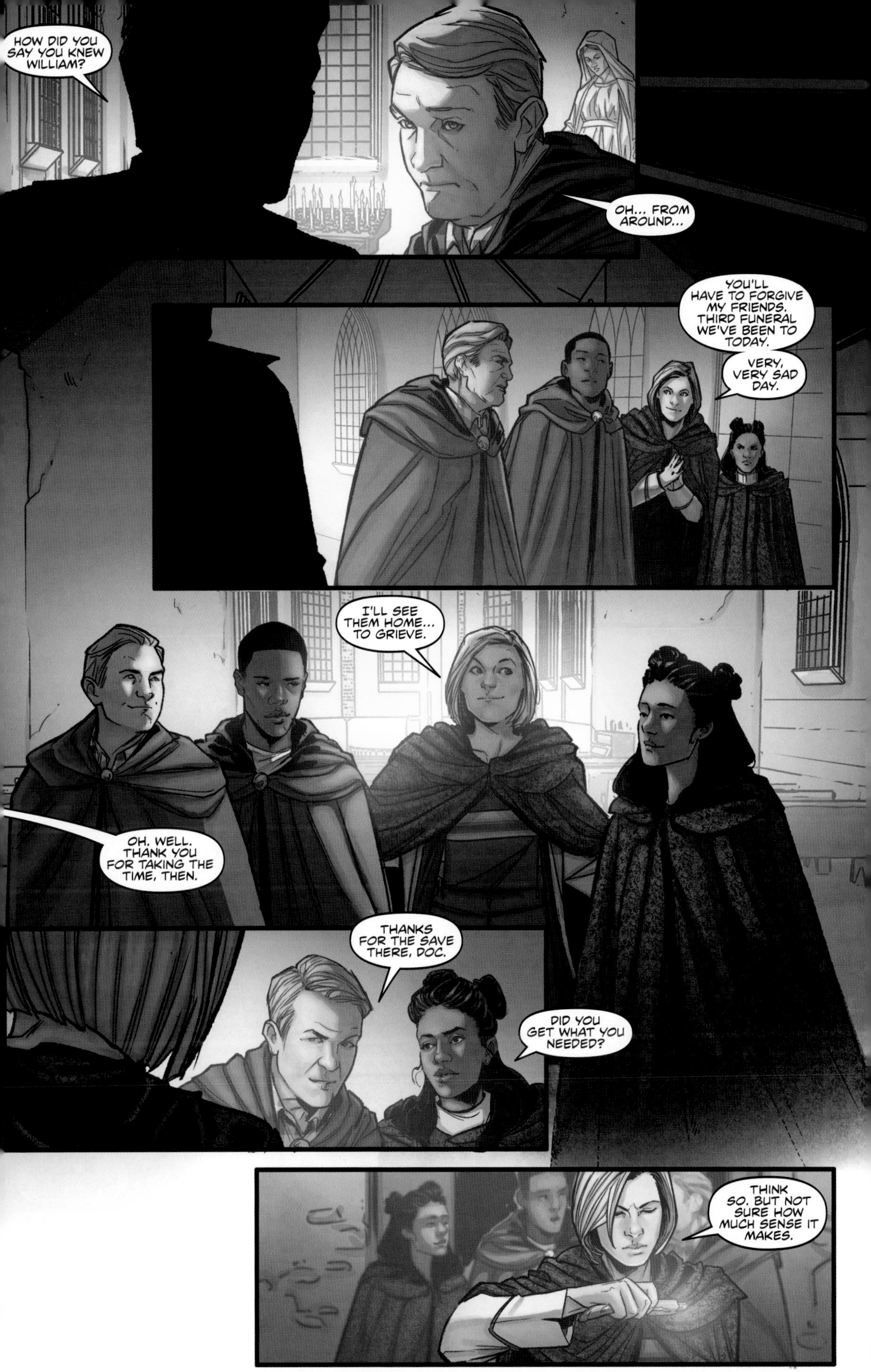
HOW DID YOU SAY YOU KNEW WILLIAM?
OH... FROM AROUND...
YOU'LL HAVE TO FORGIVE MY FRIENDS. THIRD FUNERAL WE'VE BEEN TO TODAY.
VERY, VERY SAD DAY.
I'LL SEE THEM HOME... TO GRIEVE.
OH. WELL. THANK YOU FOR TAKING THE TIME, THEN.
THANKS FOR THE SAVE THERE, DOC.
DID YOU GET WHAT YOU NEEDED?
THINK SO. BUT NOT SURE HOW MUCH SENSE IT MAKES.

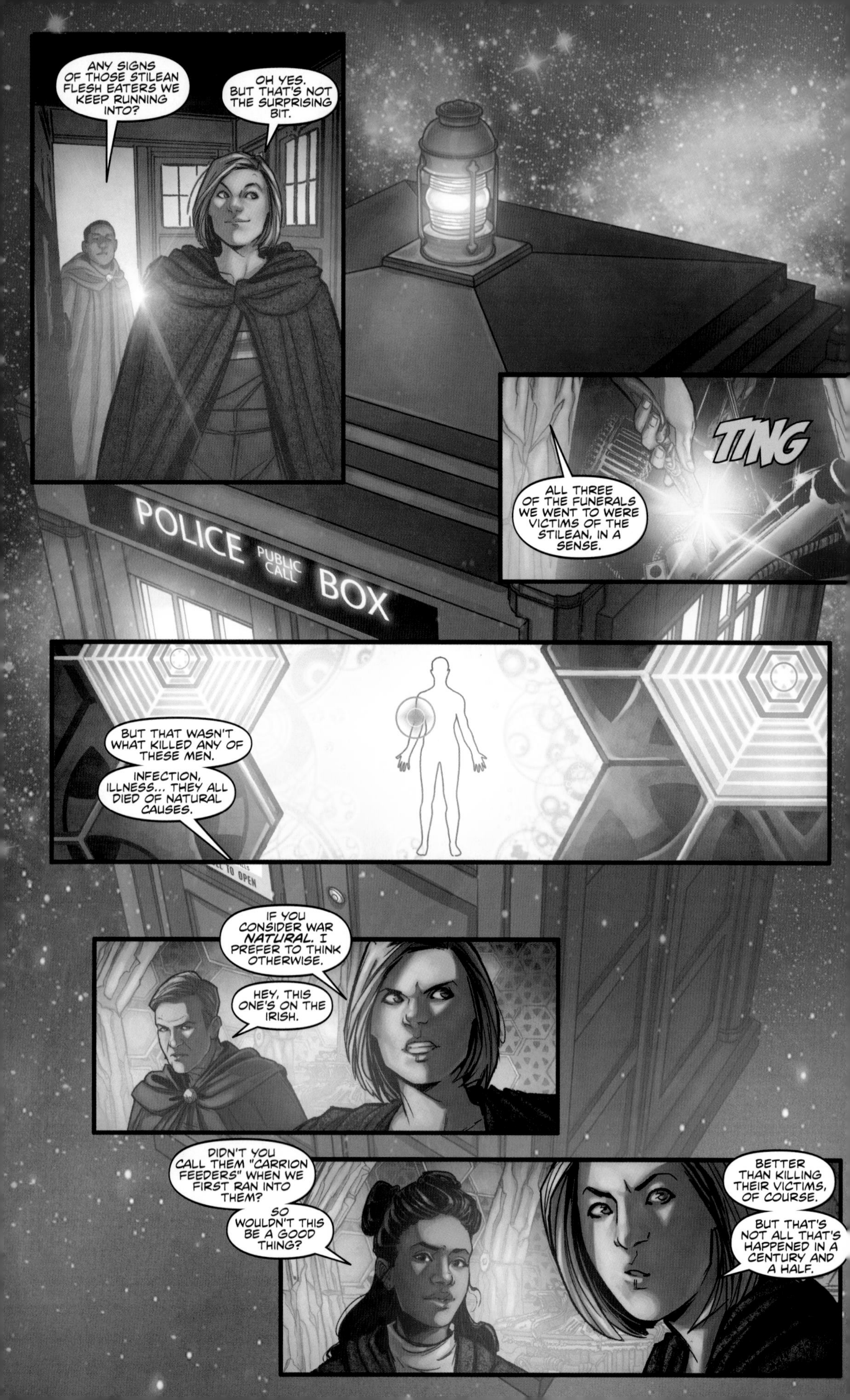
ANY SIGNS OF THOSE STILEAN FLESH EATERS WE KEEP RUNNING INTO?
OH YES. BUT THAT'S NOT THE SURPRISING BIT.
POLICE PUBLIC CALL BOX
TING
ALL THREE OF THE FUNERALS WE WENT TO WERE VICTIMS OF THE STILEAN, IN A SENSE.
BUT THAT WASN'T WHAT KILLED ANY OF THESE MEN.
INFECTION, ILLNESS... THEY ALL DIED OF NATURAL CAUSES.
IF YOU CONSIDER WAR NATURAL. I PREFER TO THINK OTHERWISE.
HEY, THIS ONE'S ON THE IRISH.
DIDN'T YOU CALL THEM "CARRION FEEDERS" WHEN WE FIRST RAN INTO THEM?
SO WOULDN'T THIS BE A GOOD THING?
BETTER THAN KILLING THEIR VICTIMS, OF COURSE.
BUT THAT'S NOT ALL THAT'S HAPPENED IN A CENTURY AND A HALF.

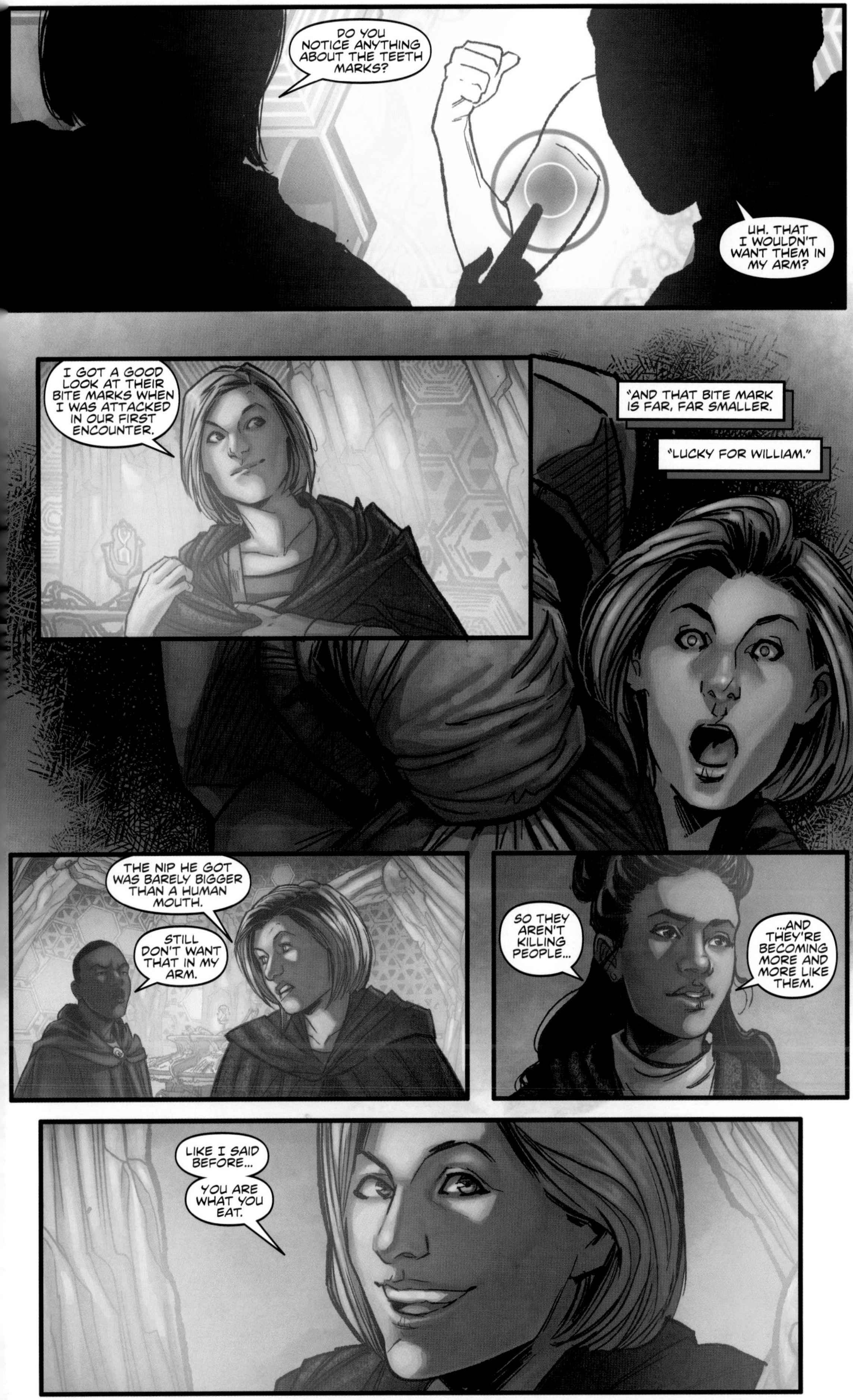
DO YOU NOTICE ANYTHING ABOUT THE TEETH MARKS?
UH. THAT I WOULDN'T WANT THEM IN MY ARM?
I GOT A GOOD LOOK AT THEIR BITE MARKS WHEN I WAS ATTACKED IN OUR FIRST ENCOUNTER.
"AND THAT BITE MARK IS FAR, FAR SMALLER.
"LUCKY FOR WILLIAM."
THE NIP HE GOT WAS BARELY BIGGER THAN A HUMAN MOUTH.
STILL DON'T WANT THAT IN MY ARM.
SO THEY AREN'T KILLING PEOPLE...
...AND THEY'RE BECOMING MORE AND MORE LIKE THEM.
LIKE I SAID BEFORE...
YOU ARE WHAT YOU EAT.

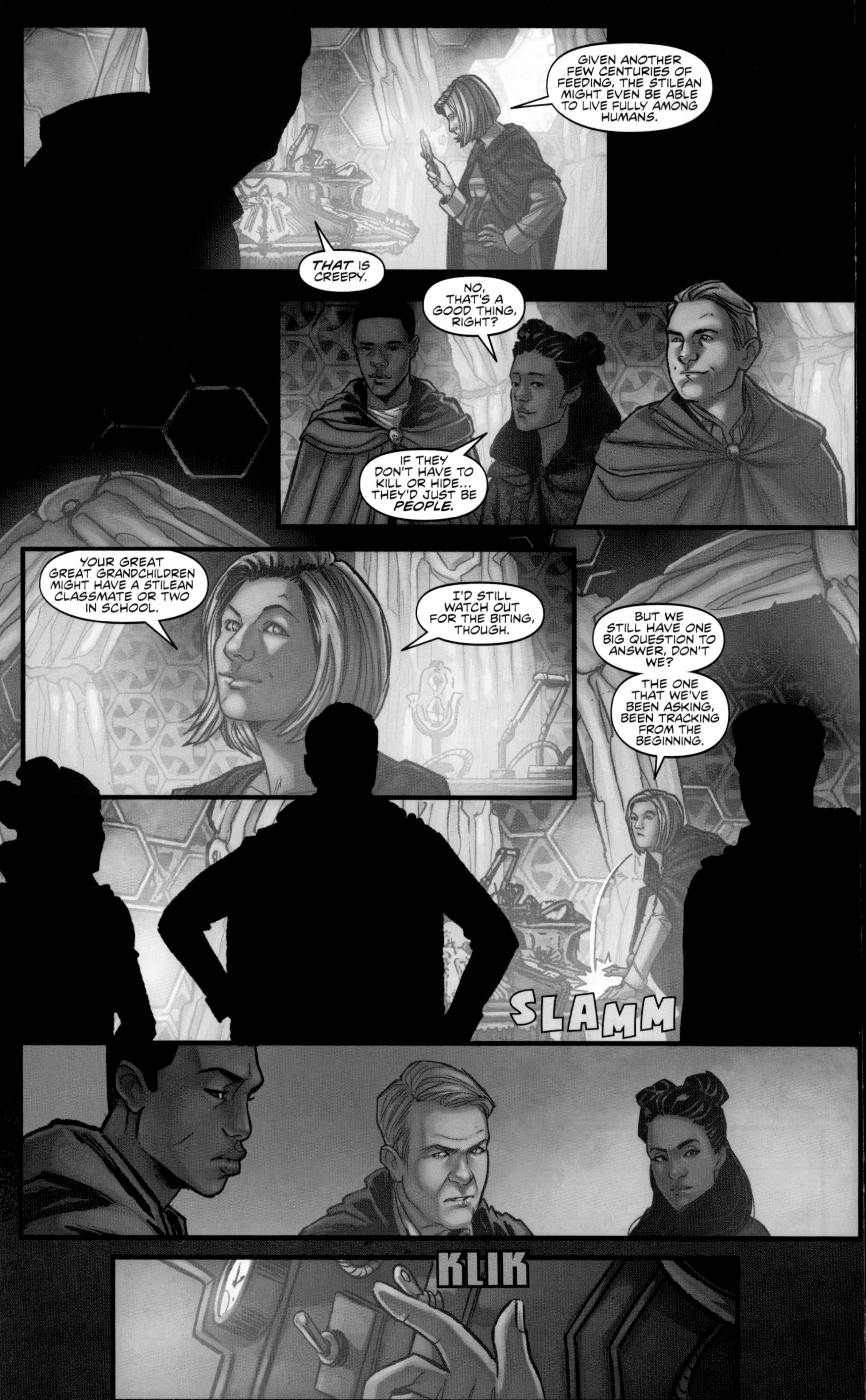

GIVEN ANOTHER FEW CENTURIES OF FEEDING, THE STILEAN MIGHT EVEN BE ABLE TO LIVE FULLY AMONG HUMANS.
THAT IS CREEPY.
NO, THAT'S A GOOD THING, RIGHT?
IF THEY DON'T HAVE TO KILL OR HIDE... THEY'D JUST BE PEOPLE.
YOUR GREAT GREAT GRANDCHILDREN MIGHT HAVE A STILEAN CLASSMATE OR TWO IN SCHOOL.
I'D STILL WATCH OUT FOR THE BITING, THOUGH.
BUT WE STILL HAVE ONE BIG QUESTION TO ANSWER, DON'T WE?
THE ONE THAT WE'VE BEEN ASKING, BEEN TRACKING FROM THE BEGINNING.
SLAMM
KLIK

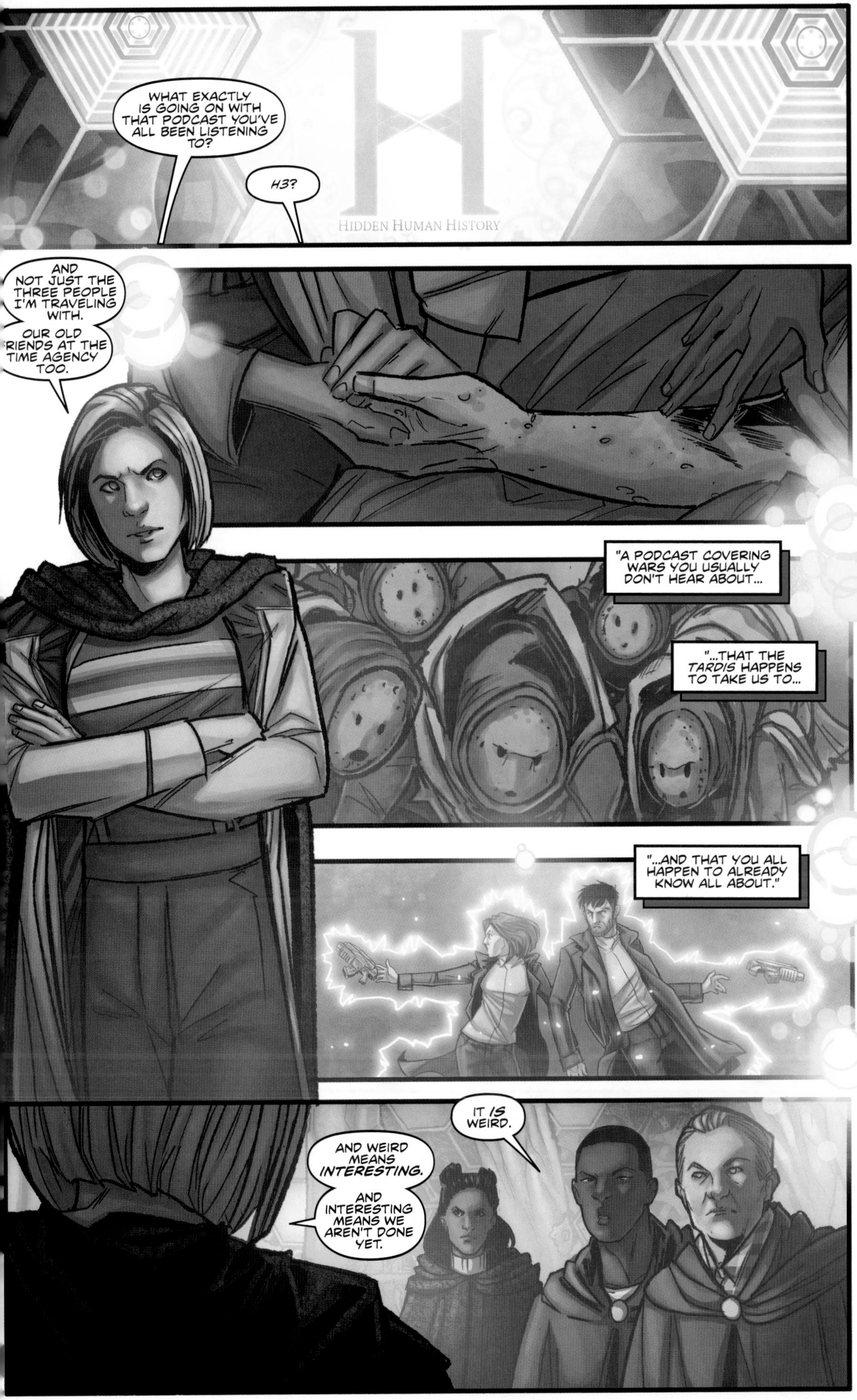
WHAT EXACTLY IS GOING ON WITH THAT PODCAST YOU'VE ALL BEEN LISTENING TO?
H3?
HIDDEN HUMAN HISTORY
AND NOT JUST THE THREE PEOPLE I'M TRAVELING WITH.
OUR OLD FRIENDS AT THE TIME AGENCY TOO.
"A PODCAST COVERING WARS YOU USUALLY DON'T HEAR ABOUT...
"...THAT THE TARDIS HAPPENS TO TAKE US TO...
"...AND THAT YOU ALL HAPPEN TO ALREADY KNOW ALL ABOUT."
IT IS WEIRD.
AND WEIRD MEANS INTERESTING.
AND INTERESTING MEANS WE AREN'T DONE YET.

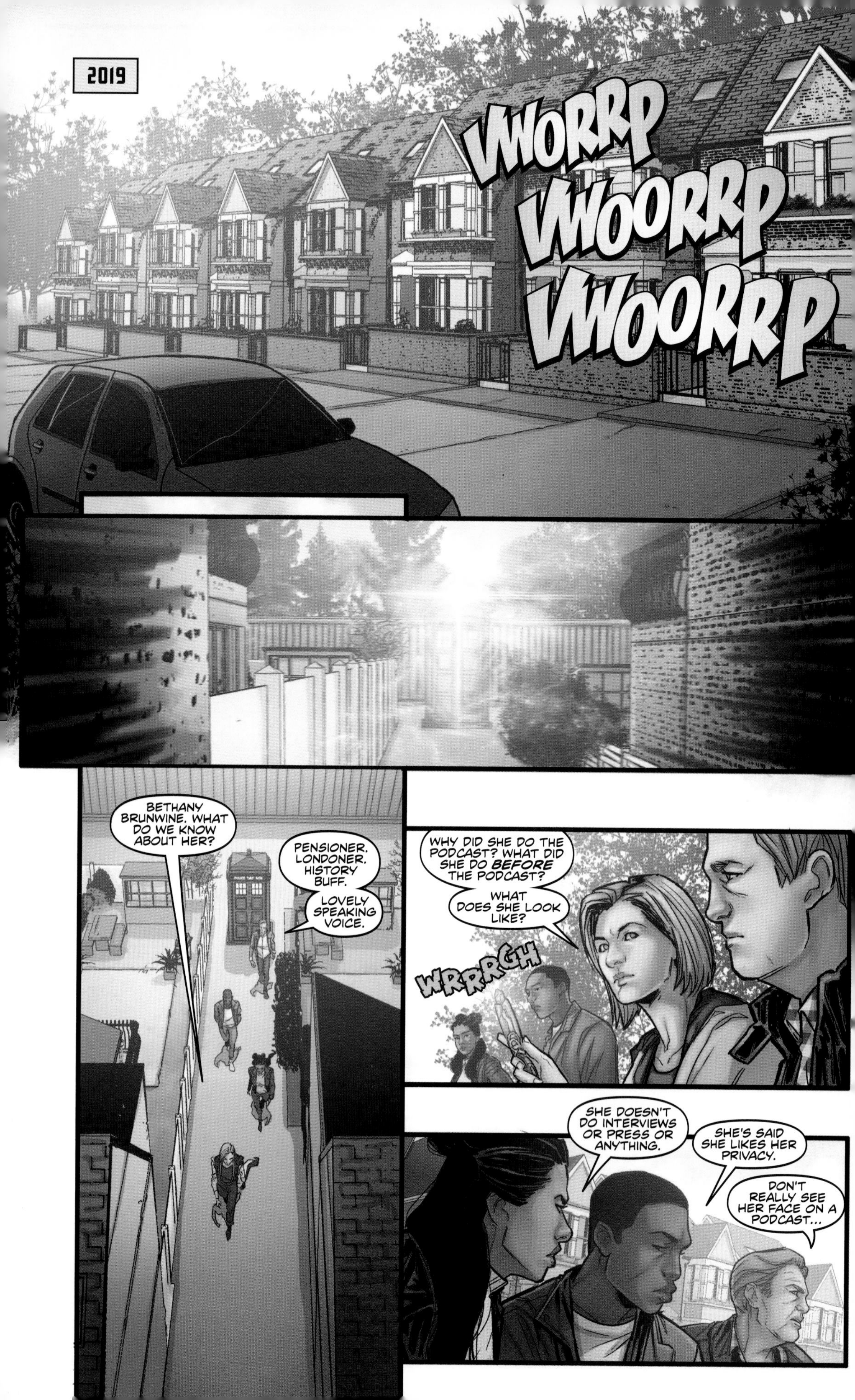
2019
VWORRP
VWOORRP
VWOORRP
BETHANY BRUNWINE. WHAT DO WE KNOW ABOUT HER?
PENSIONER. LONDONER. HISTORY BUFF.
LOVELY SPEAKING VOICE.
WHY DID SHE DO THE PODCAST? WHAT DID SHE DO BEFORE THE PODCAST?
WHAT DOES SHE LOOK LIKE?
WRRRGH
SHE DOESN'T DO INTERVIEWS OR PRESS OR ANYTHING.
SHE'S SAID SHE LIKES HER PRIVACY.
DON'T REALLY SEE HER FACE ON A PODCAST...

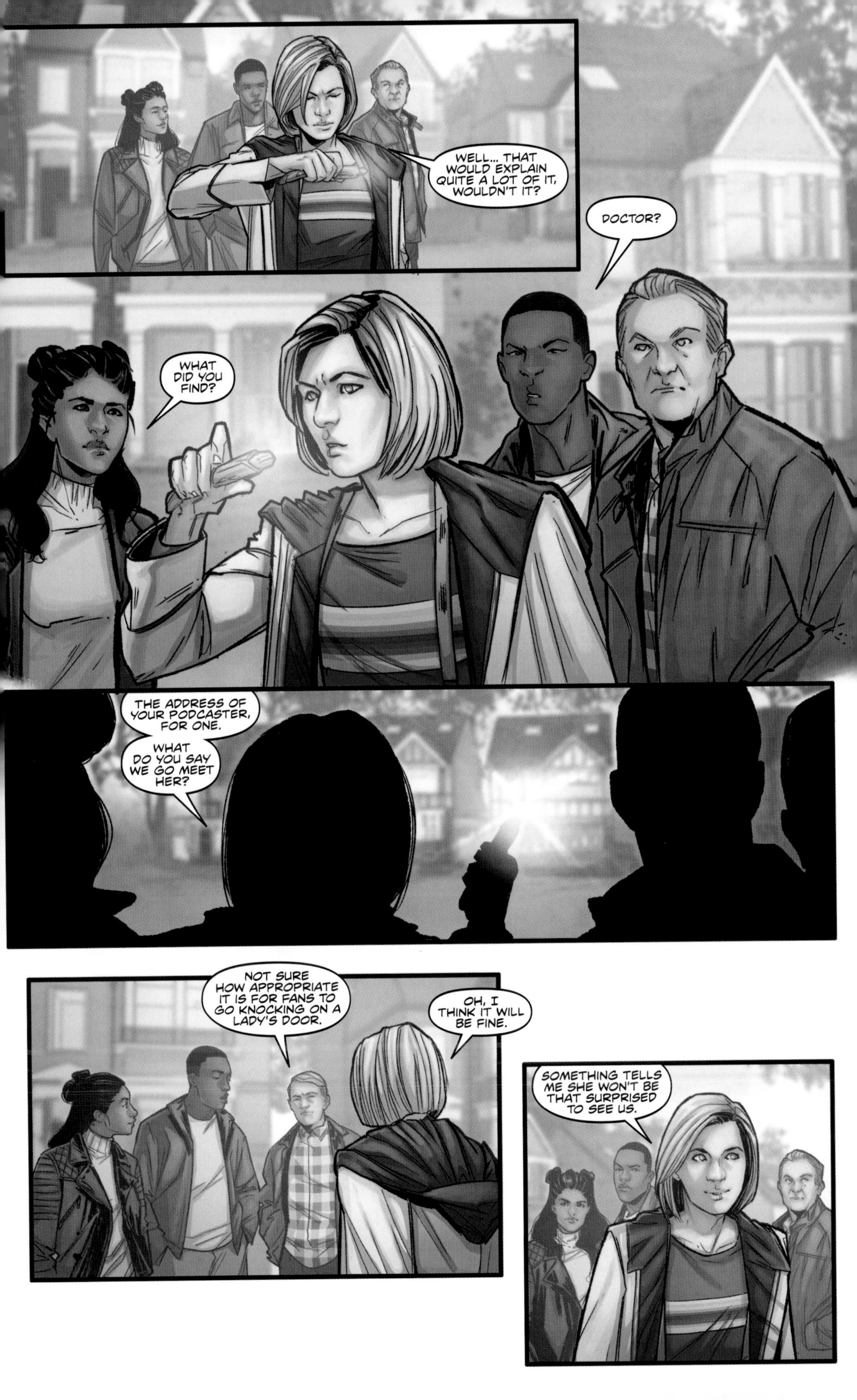
WELL... THAT WOULD EXPLAIN QUITE A LOT OF IT, WOULDN'T IT?
DOCTOR?
WHAT DID YOU FIND?
THE ADDRESS OF YOUR PODCASTER, FOR ONE.
WHAT DO YOU SAY WE GO MEET HER?
NOT SURE HOW APPROPRIATE IT IS FOR FANS TO GO KNOCKING ON A LADY'S DOOR.
OH, I THINK IT WILL BE FINE.
SOMETHING TELLS ME SHE WON'T BE THAT SURPRISED TO SEE US.

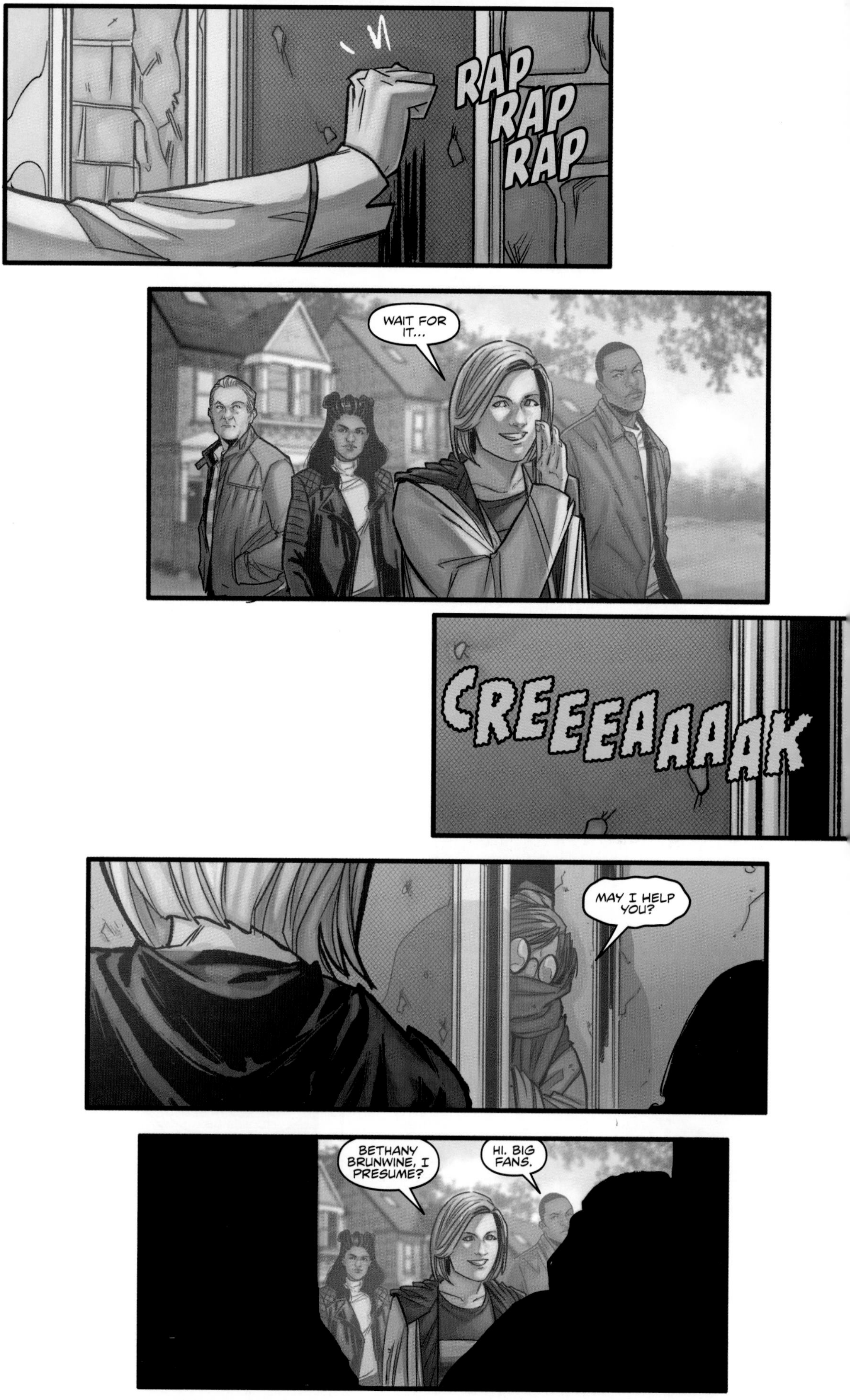
RAP
RAP
RAP
WAIT FOR IT...
CREEEAAAAK
MAY I HELP YOU?
BETHANY BRUNWINE, I PRESUME?
HI. BIG FANS.

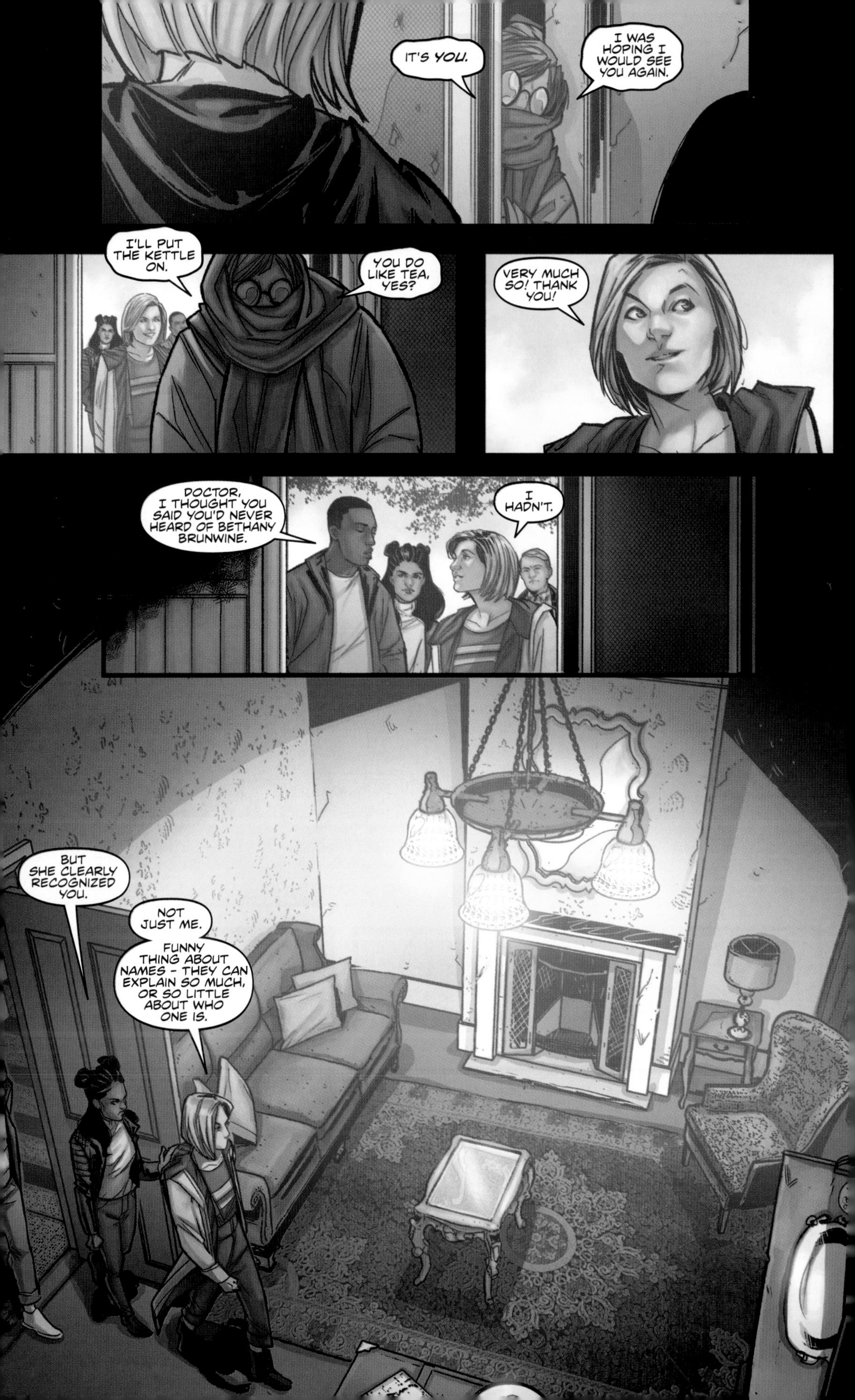
IT'S YOU.
I WAS HOPING I WOULD SEE YOU AGAIN.
I'LL PUT THE KETTLE ON.
YOU DO LIKE TEA, YES?
VERY MUCH SO! THANK YOU!
DOCTOR, I THOUGHT YOU SAID YOU'D NEVER HEARD OF BETHANY BRUNWINE.
I HADN'T.
BUT SHE CLEARLY RECOGNIZED YOU.
NOT JUST ME.
FUNNY THING ABOUT NAMES - THEY CAN EXPLAIN SO MUCH, OR SO LITTLE ABOUT WHO ONE IS.

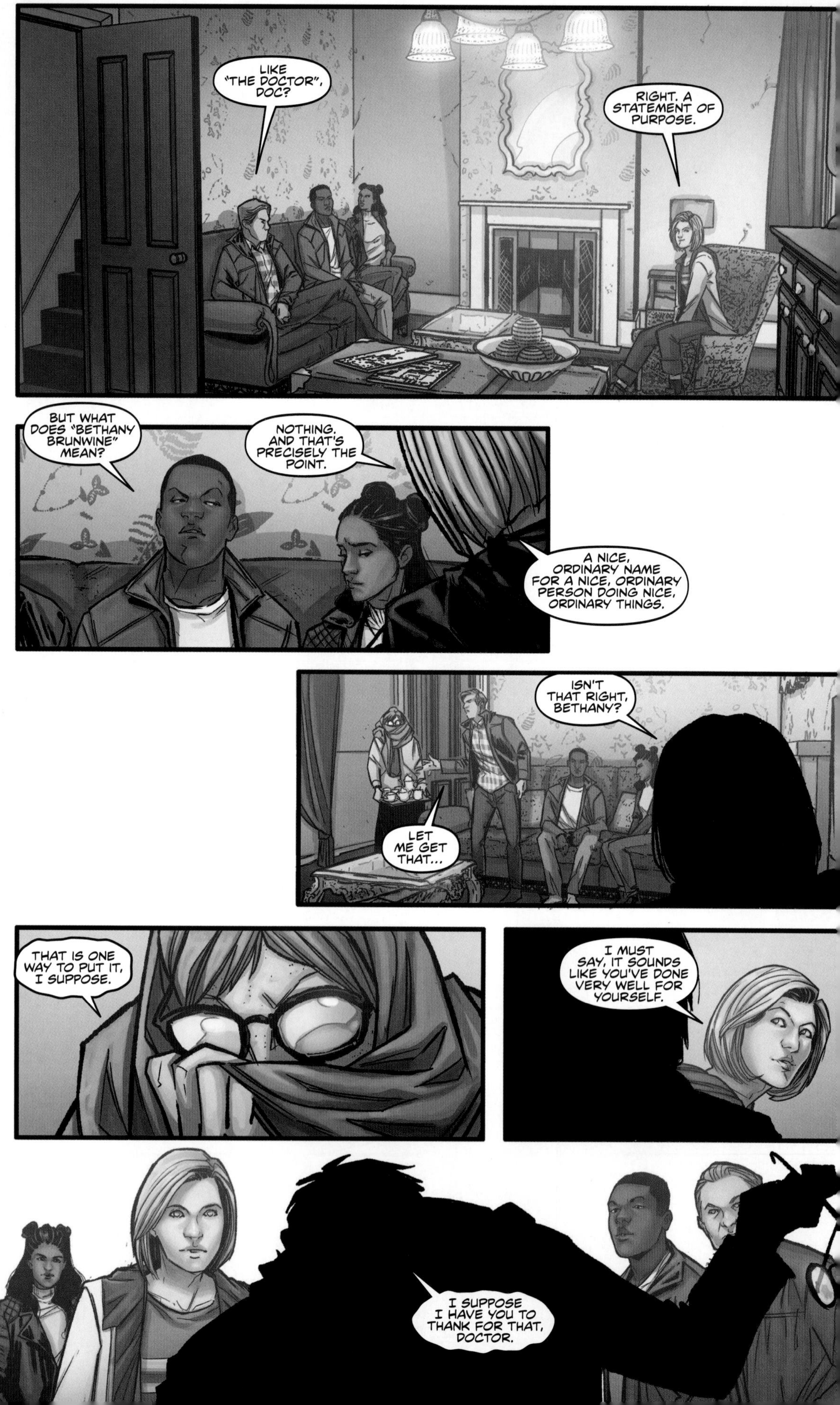
LIKE "THE DOCTOR", DOC?
RIGHT. A STATEMENT OF PURPOSE.
BUT WHAT DOES "BETHANY BRUNWINE" MEAN?
NOTHING. AND THAT'S PRECISELY THE POINT.
A NICE, ORDINARY NAME FOR A NICE, ORDINARY PERSON DOING NICE, ORDINARY THINGS.
ISN'T THAT RIGHT, BETHANY?
LET ME GET THAT...
THAT IS ONE WAY TO PUT IT, I SUPPOSE.
I MUST SAY, IT SOUNDS LIKE YOU'VE DONE VERY WELL FOR YOURSELF.
I SUPPOSE I HAVE YOU TO THANK FOR THAT, DOCTOR.

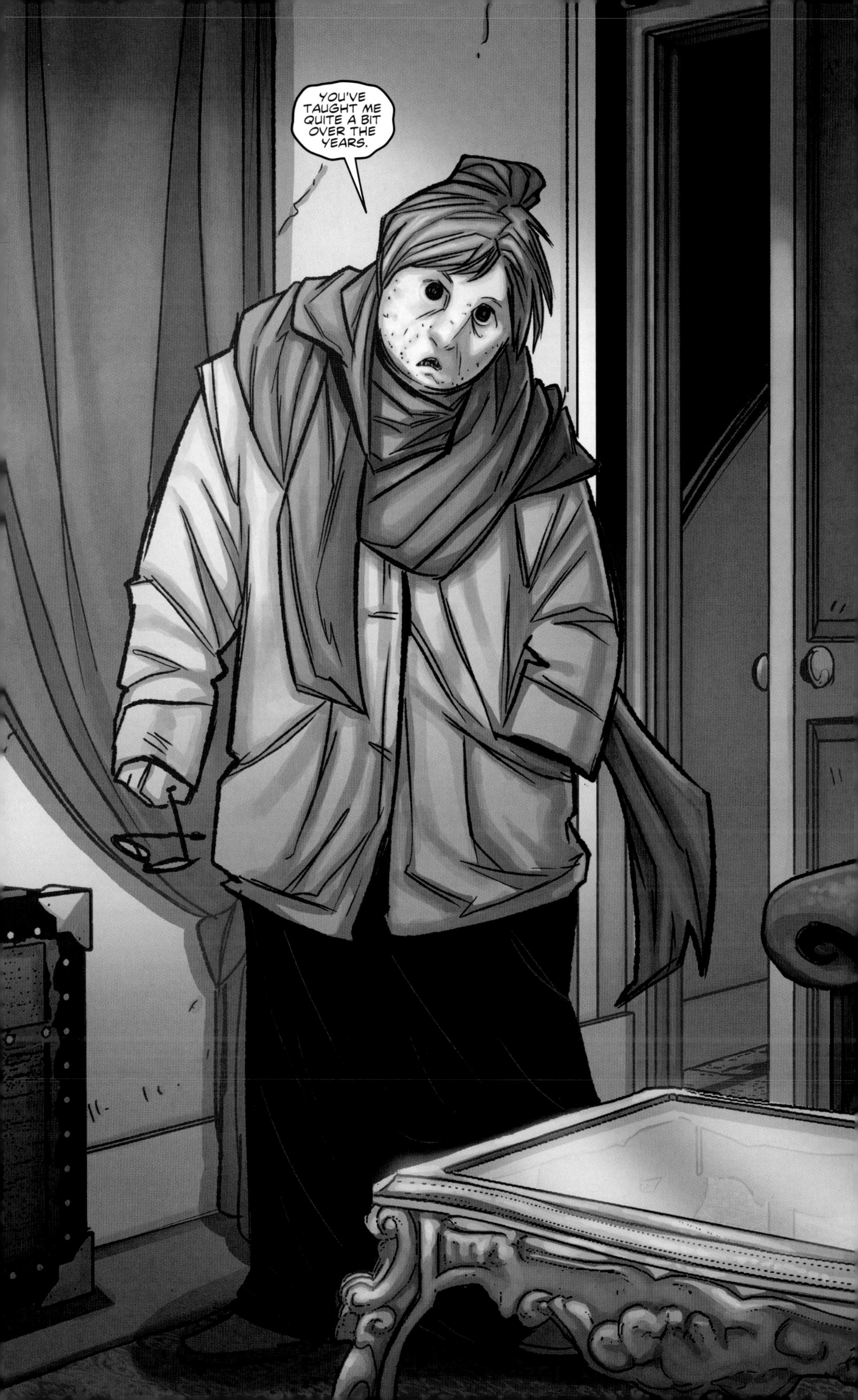
YOU'VE TAUGHT ME QUITE A BIT OVER THE YEARS.

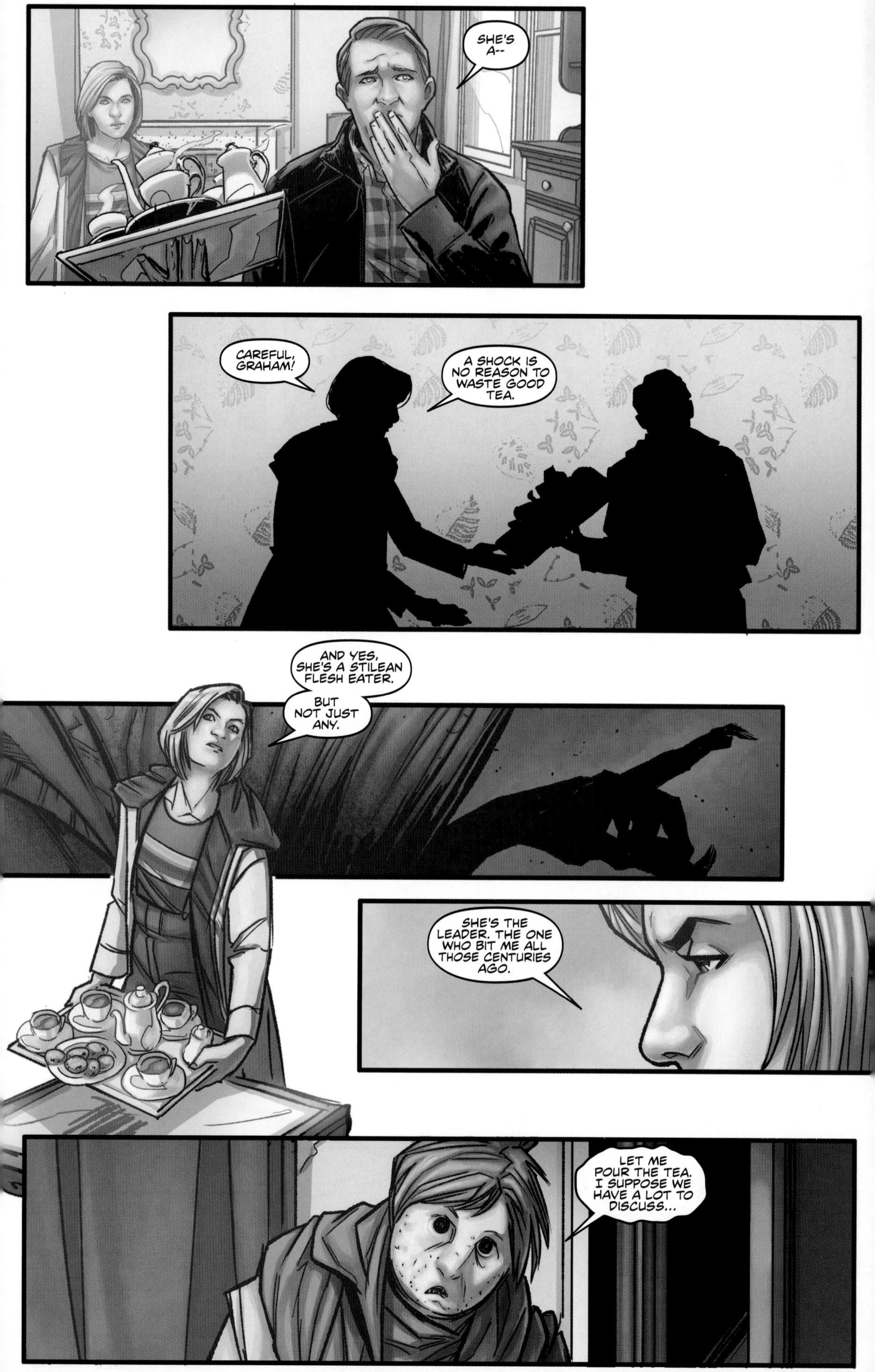
SHE'S A--
CAREFUL, GRAHAM!
A SHOCK IS NO REASON TO WASTE GOOD TEA.
AND YES, SHE'S A STILEAN FLESH EATER.
BUT NOT JUST ANY.
SHE'S THE LEADER. THE ONE WHO BIT ME ALL THOSE CENTURIES AGO.
LET ME POUR THE TEA. I SUPPOSE WE HAVE A LOT TO DISCUSS...

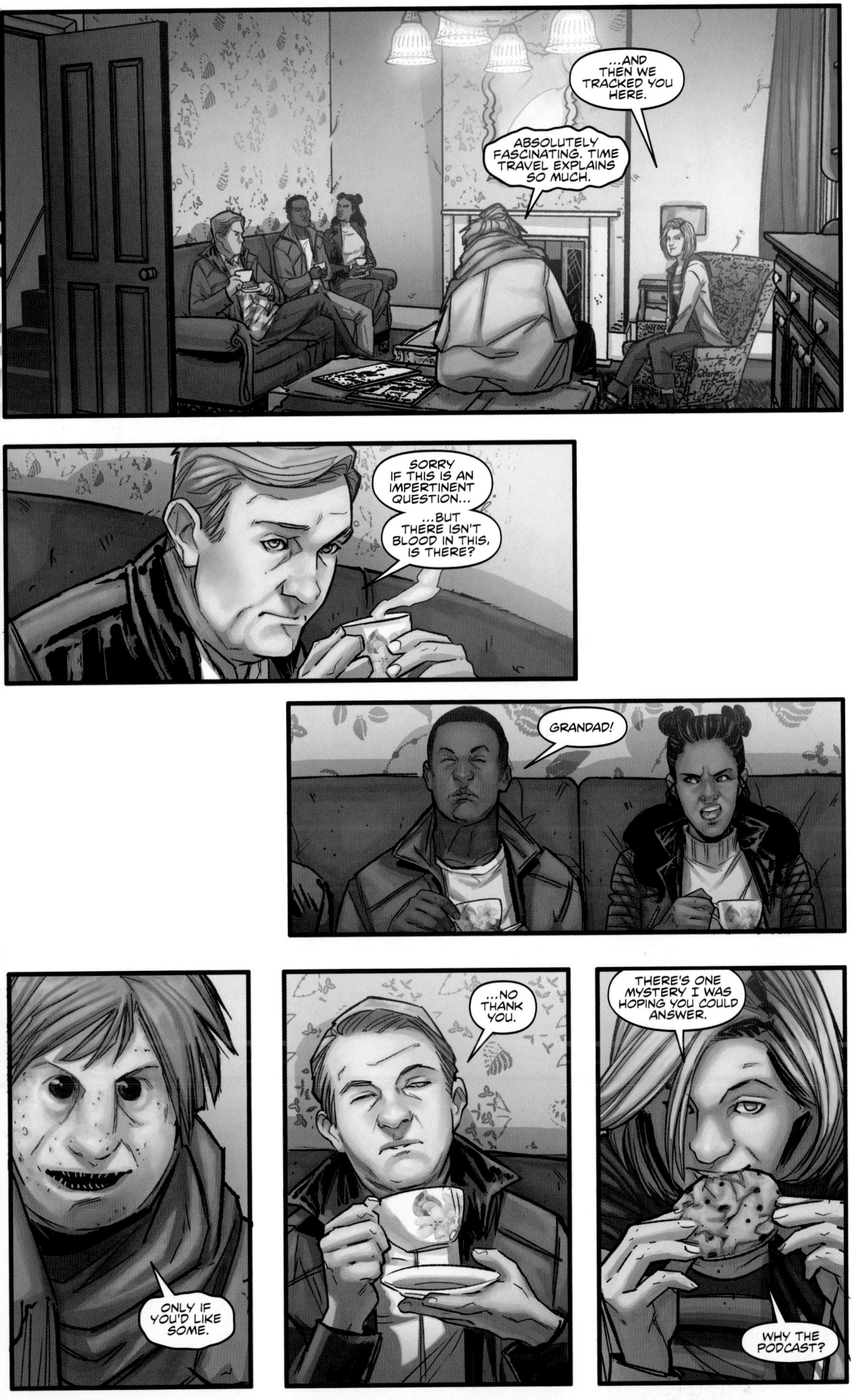
...AND THEN WE TRACKED YOU HERE.
ABSOLUTELY FASCINATING. TIME TRAVEL EXPLAINS SO MUCH.
SORRY IF THIS IS AN IMPERTINENT QUESTION...
...BUT THERE ISN'T BLOOD IN THIS, IS THERE?
GRANDAD!
ONLY IF YOU'D LIKE SOME.
...NO THANK YOU.
THERE'S ONE MYSTERY I WAS HOPING YOU COULD ANSWER.
WHY THE PODCAST?

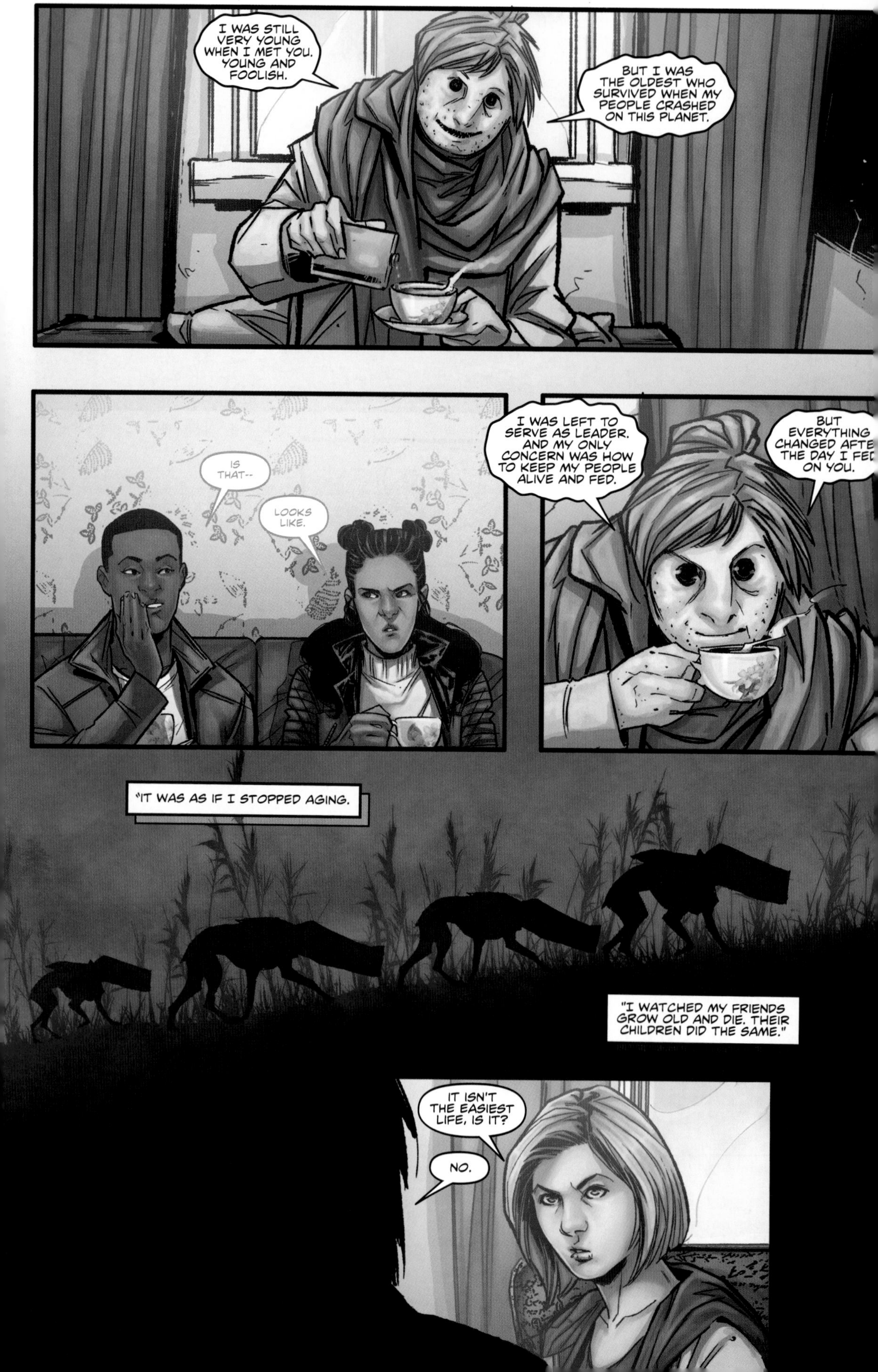
I WAS STILL VERY YOUNG WHEN I MET YOU. YOUNG AND FOOLISH.
BUT I WAS THE OLDEST WHO SURVIVED WHEN MY PEOPLE CRASHED ON THIS PLANET.
IS THAT--
LOOKS LIKE.
I WAS LEFT TO SERVE AS LEADER. AND MY ONLY CONCERN WAS HOW TO KEEP MY PEOPLE ALIVE AND FED.
BUT EVERYTHING CHANGED AFTE THE DAY I FED ON YOU.
"IT WAS AS IF I STOPPED AGING.
"I WATCHED MY FRIENDS GROW OLD AND DIE. THEIR CHILDREN DID THE SAME."
IT ISN'T THE EASIEST LIFE, IS IT?
NO.

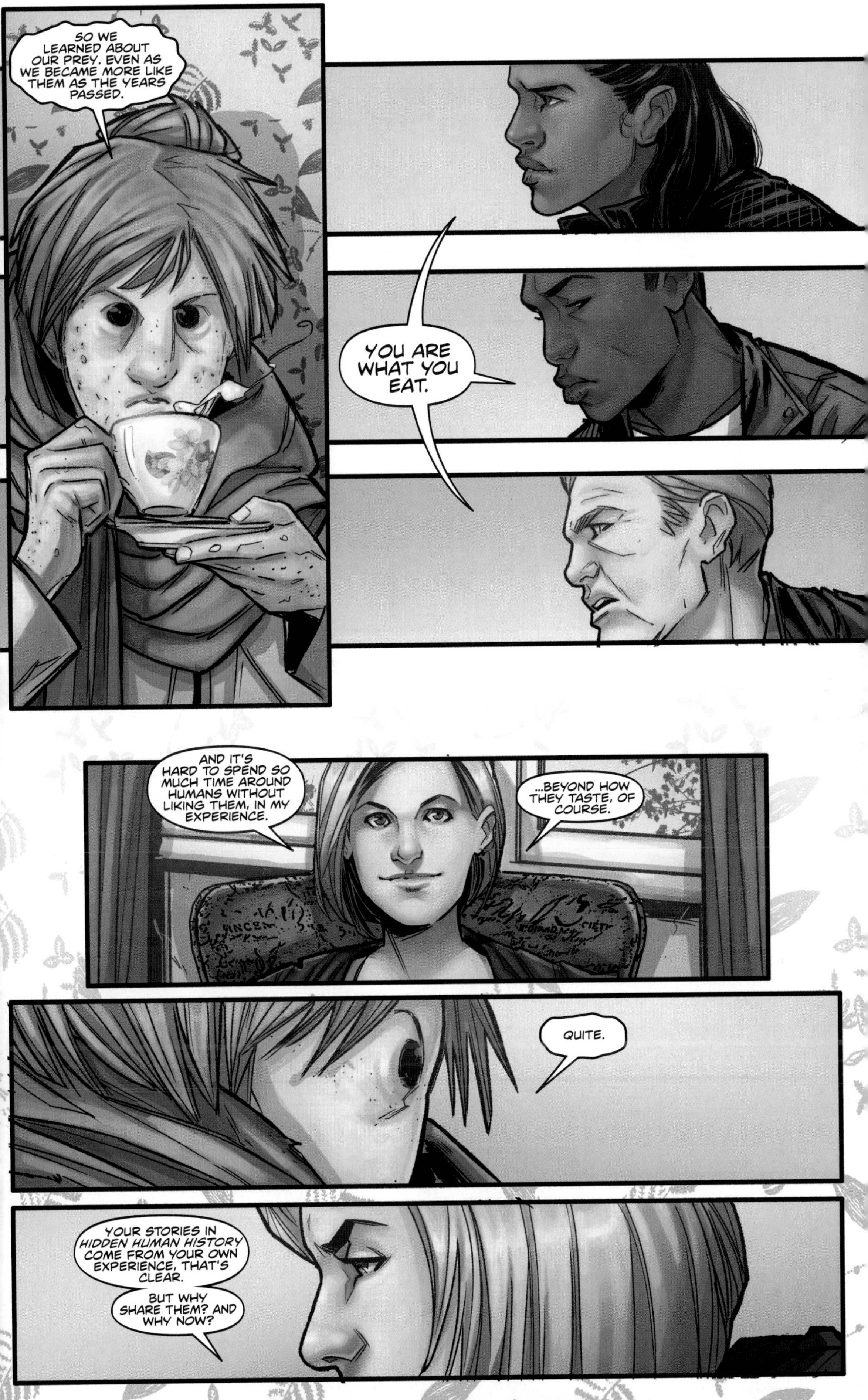
SO WE LEARNED ABOUT OUR PREY. EVEN AS WE BECAME MORE LIKE THEM AS THE YEARS PASSED.
YOU ARE WHAT YOU EAT.
AND IT'S HARD TO SPEND SO MUCH TIME AROUND HUMANS WITHOUT LIKING THEM, IN MY EXPERIENCE.
...BEYOND HOW THEY TASTE, OF COURSE.
QUITE.
YOUR STORIES IN *HIDDEN HUMAN HISTORY* COME FROM YOUR OWN EXPERIENCE, THAT'S CLEAR.
BUT WHY SHARE THEM? AND WHY NOW?

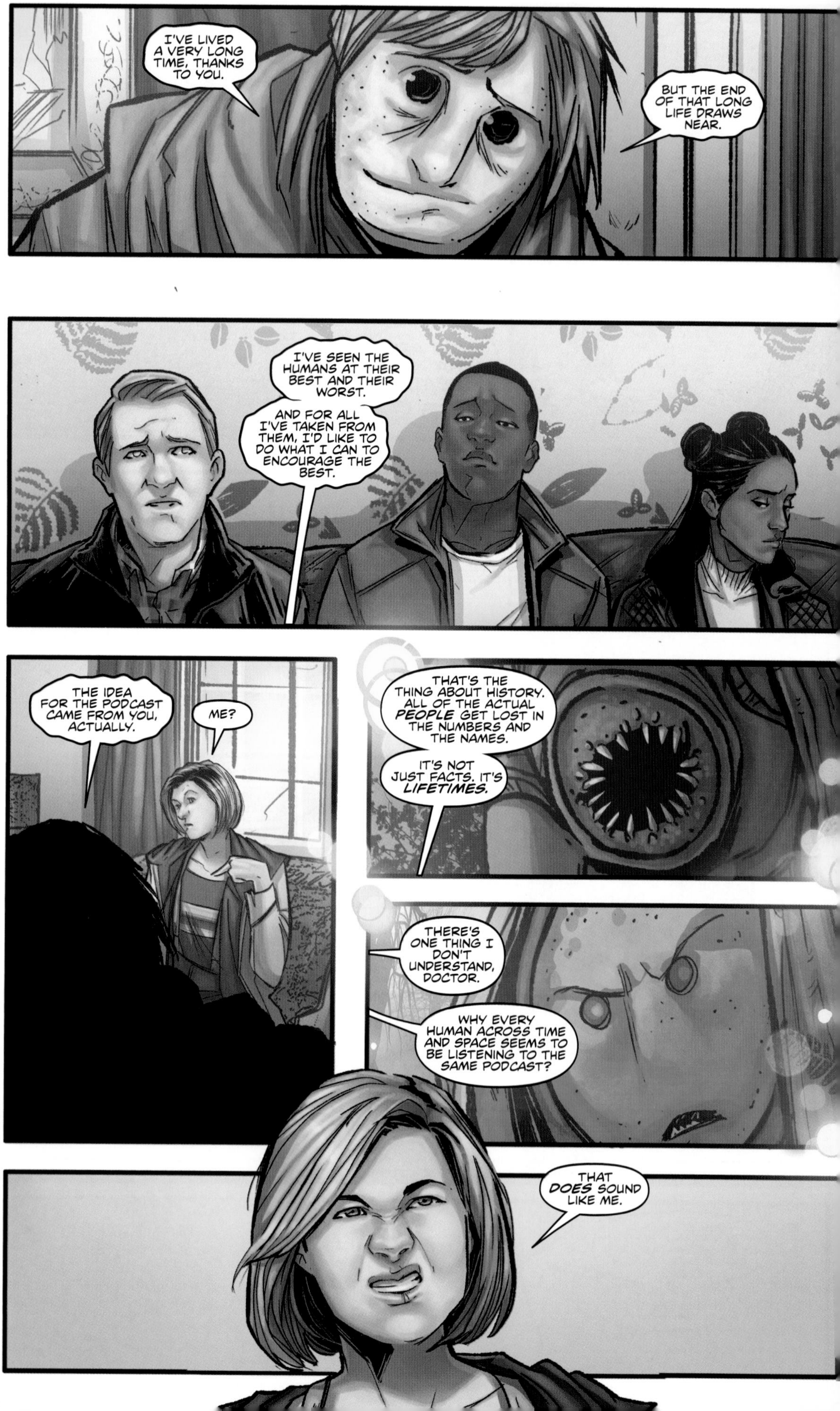
I'VE LIVED A VERY LONG TIME, THANKS TO YOU.
BUT THE END OF THAT LONG LIFE DRAWS NEAR.
I'VE SEEN THE HUMANS AT THEIR BEST AND THEIR WORST.
AND FOR ALL I'VE TAKEN FROM THEM, I'D LIKE TO DO WHAT I CAN TO ENCOURAGE THE BEST.
THE IDEA FOR THE PODCAST CAME FROM YOU, ACTUALLY.
ME?
THAT'S THE THING ABOUT HISTORY. ALL OF THE ACTUAL PEOPLE GET LOST IN THE NUMBERS AND THE NAMES.
IT'S NOT JUST FACTS. IT'S LIFETIMES.
THERE'S ONE THING I DON'T UNDERSTAND, DOCTOR.
WHY EVERY HUMAN ACROSS TIME AND SPACE SEEMS TO BE LISTENING TO THE SAME PODCAST?
THAT DOES SOUND LIKE ME.

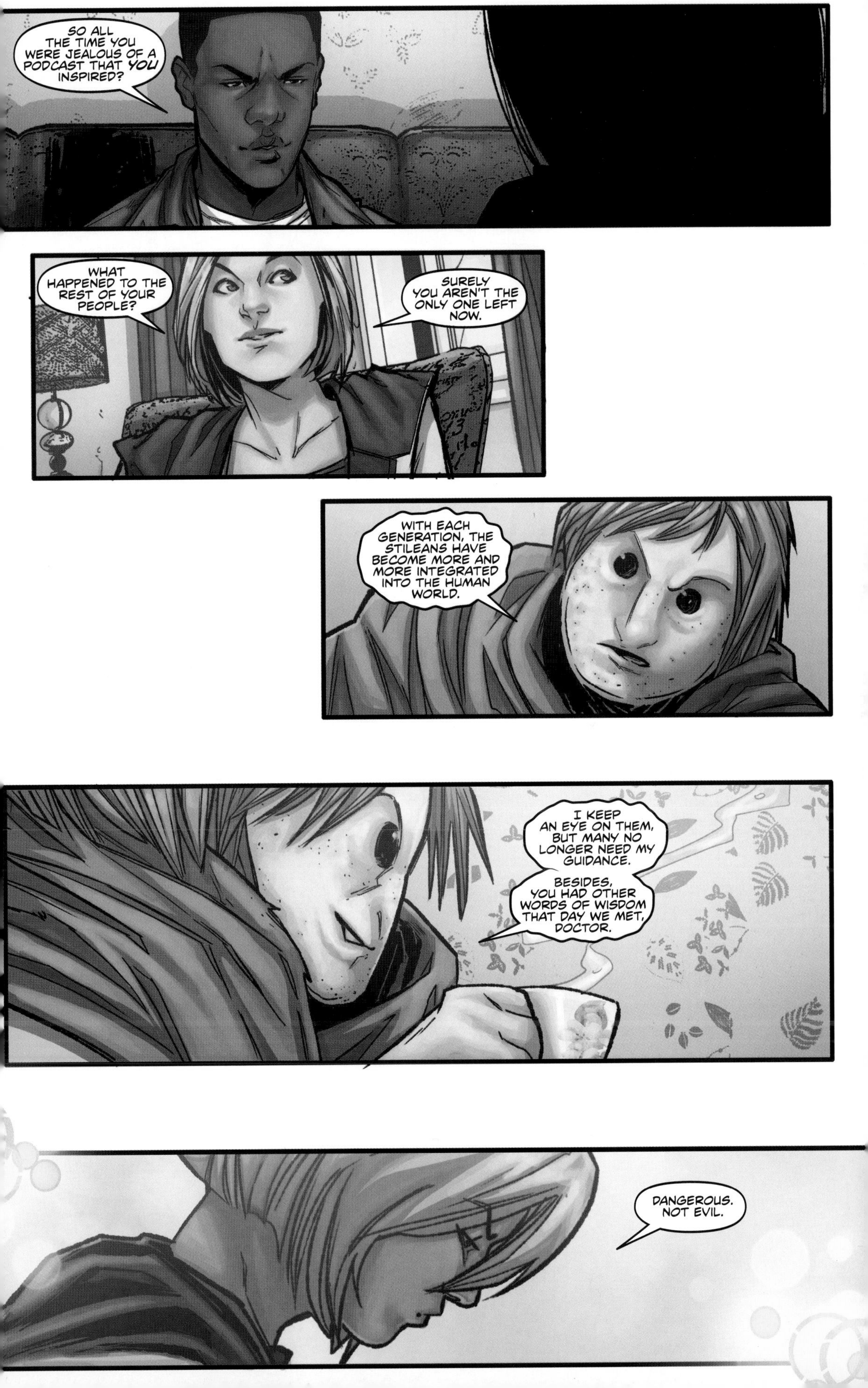
SO ALL THE TIME YOU WERE JEALOUS OF A PODCAST THAT YOU INSPIRED?
WHAT HAPPENED TO THE REST OF YOUR PEOPLE?
SURELY YOU AREN'T THE ONLY ONE LEFT NOW.
WITH EACH GENERATION, THE STILEANS HAVE BECOME MORE AND MORE INTEGRATED INTO THE HUMAN WORLD.
I KEEP AN EYE ON THEM, BUT MANY NO LONGER NEED MY GUIDANCE.
BESIDES, YOU HAD OTHER WORDS OF WISDOM THAT DAY WE MET, DOCTOR.
DANGEROUS. NOT EVIL.

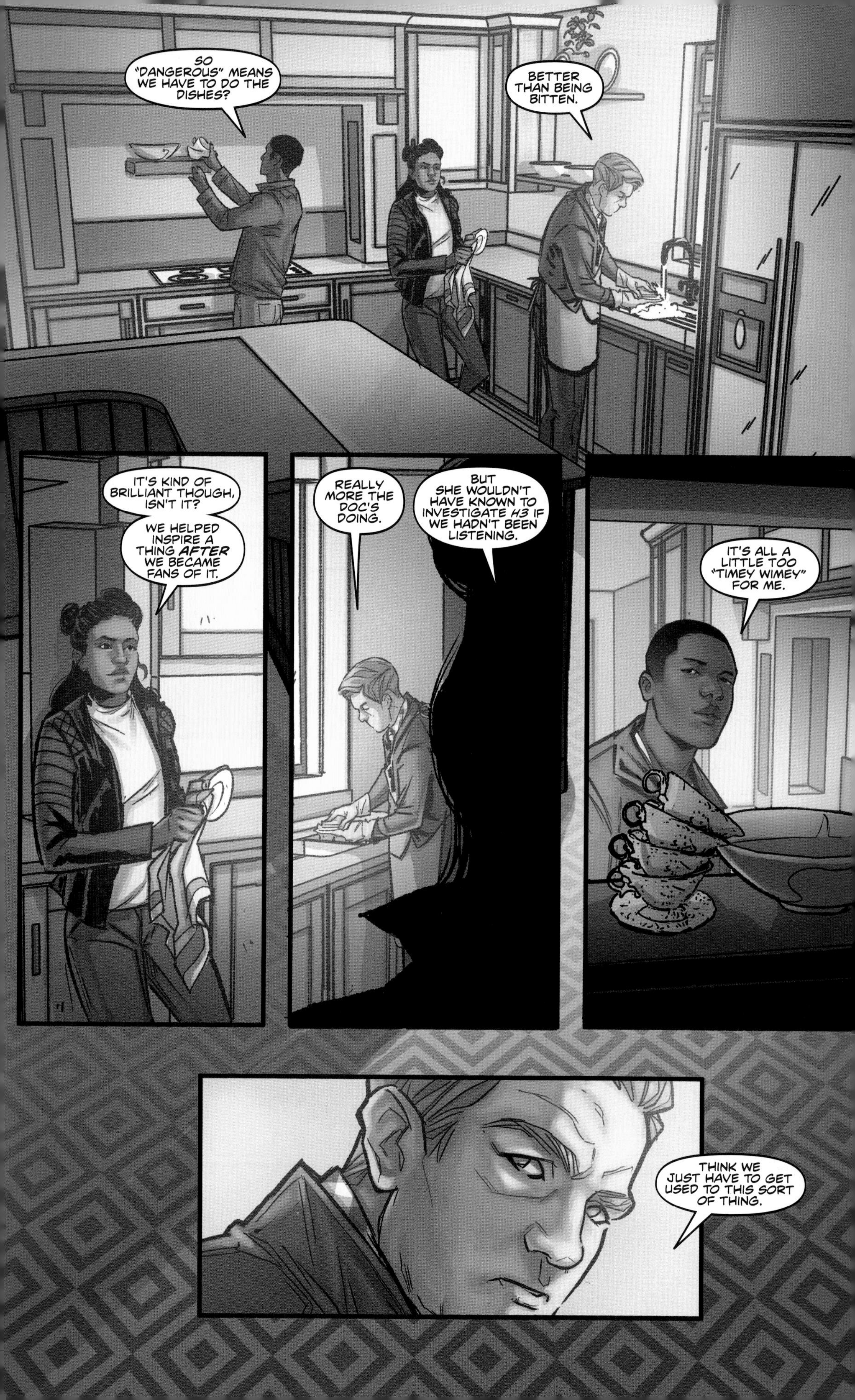
SO "DANGEROUS" MEANS WE HAVE TO DO THE DISHES?
BETTER THAN BEING BITTEN.
IT'S KIND OF BRILLIANT THOUGH, ISN'T IT?
WE HELPED INSPIRE A THING *AFTER* WE BECAME FANS OF IT.
REALLY MORE THE DOC'S DOING.
BUT SHE WOULDN'T HAVE KNOWN TO INVESTIGATE *H3* IF WE HADN'T BEEN LISTENING.
IT'S ALL A LITTLE TOO "TIMEY WIMEY" FOR ME.
THINK WE JUST HAVE TO GET USED TO THIS SORT OF THING.

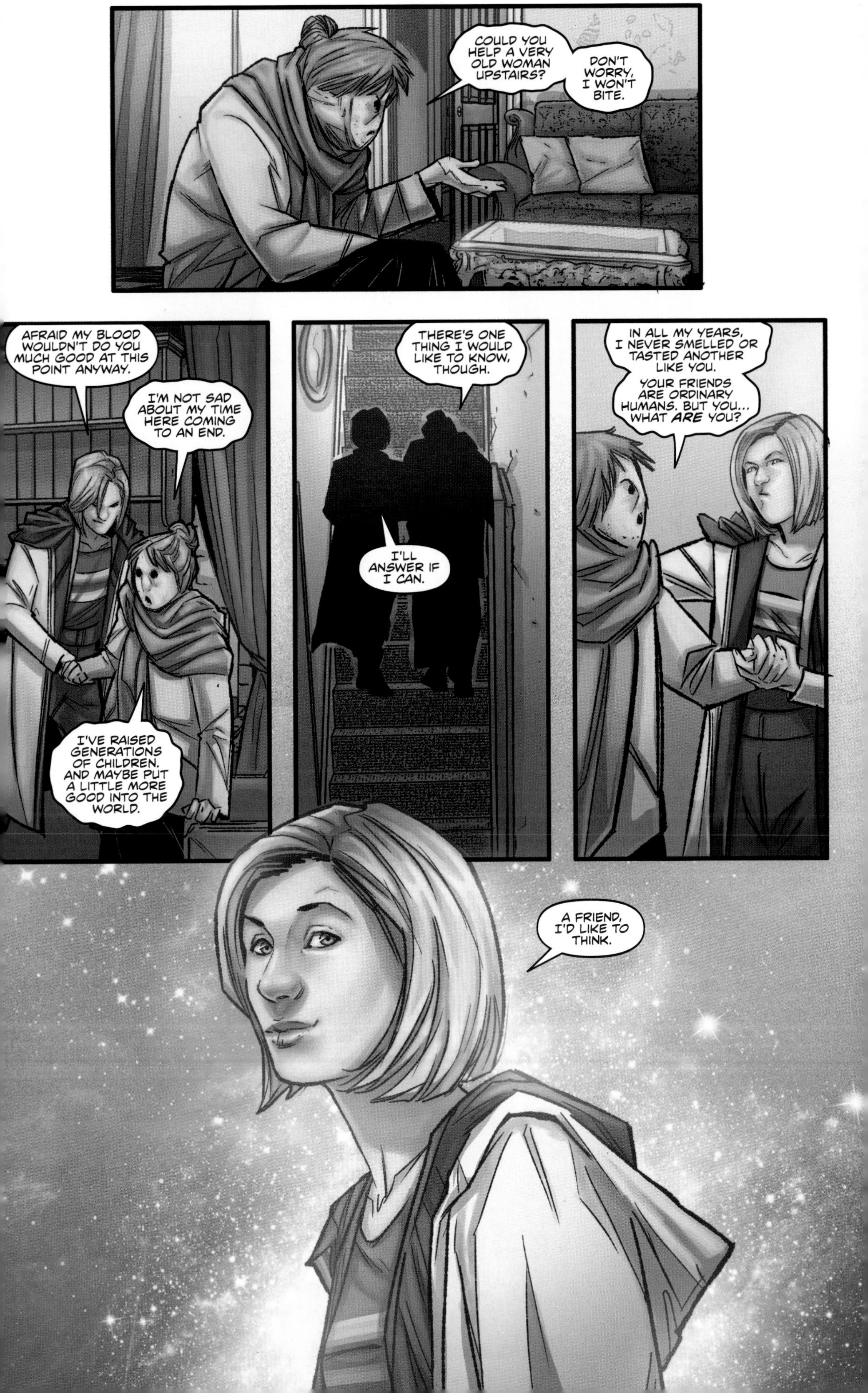
COULD YOU HELP A VERY OLD WOMAN UPSTAIRS?
DON'T WORRY, I WON'T BITE.
AFRAID MY BLOOD WOULDN'T DO YOU MUCH GOOD AT THIS POINT ANYWAY.
I'M NOT SAD ABOUT MY TIME HERE COMING TO AN END.
I'VE RAISED GENERATIONS OF CHILDREN. AND MAYBE PUT A LITTLE MORE GOOD INTO THE WORLD.
THERE'S ONE THING I WOULD LIKE TO KNOW, THOUGH.
I'LL ANSWER IF I CAN.
IN ALL MY YEARS, I NEVER SMELLED OR TASTED ANOTHER LIKE YOU.
YOUR FRIENDS ARE ORDINARY HUMANS. BUT YOU... WHAT ARE YOU?
A FRIEND, I'D LIKE TO THINK.

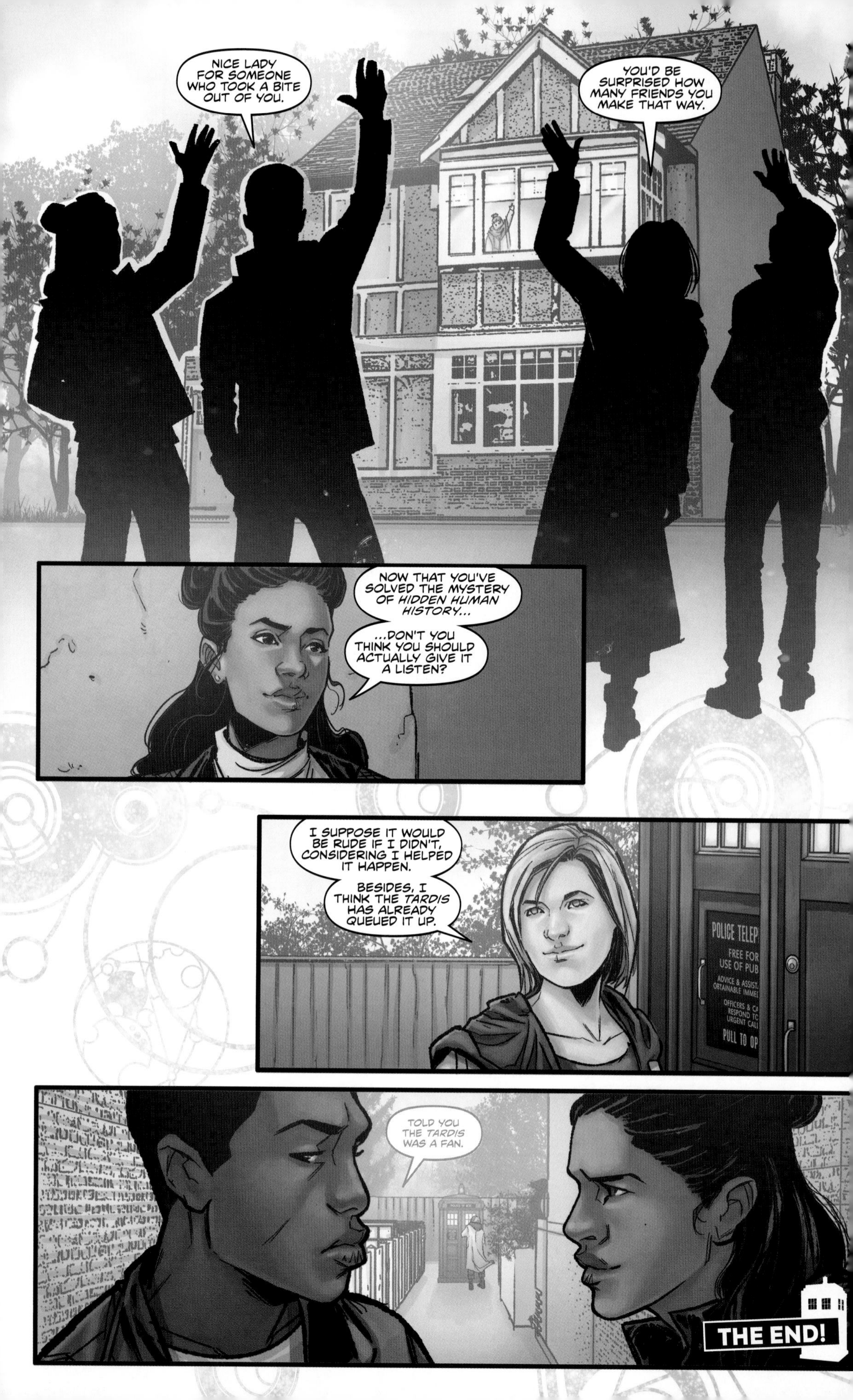
NICE LADY FOR SOMEONE WHO TOOK A BITE OUT OF YOU.
YOU'D BE SURPRISED HOW MANY FRIENDS YOU MAKE THAT WAY.
NOW THAT YOU'VE SOLVED THE MYSTERY OF *HIDDEN HUMAN HISTORY*...
...DON'T YOU THINK YOU SHOULD ACTUALLY GIVE IT A LISTEN?
I SUPPOSE IT WOULD BE RUDE IF I DIDN'T, CONSIDERING I HELPED IT HAPPEN.
BESIDES, I THINK THE *TARDIS* HAS ALREADY QUEUED IT UP.
TOLD YOU THE *TARDIS* WAS A FAN.
THE END!

BBC

DOCTOR WHO

THE THIRTEENTH DOCTOR

Covers Gallery

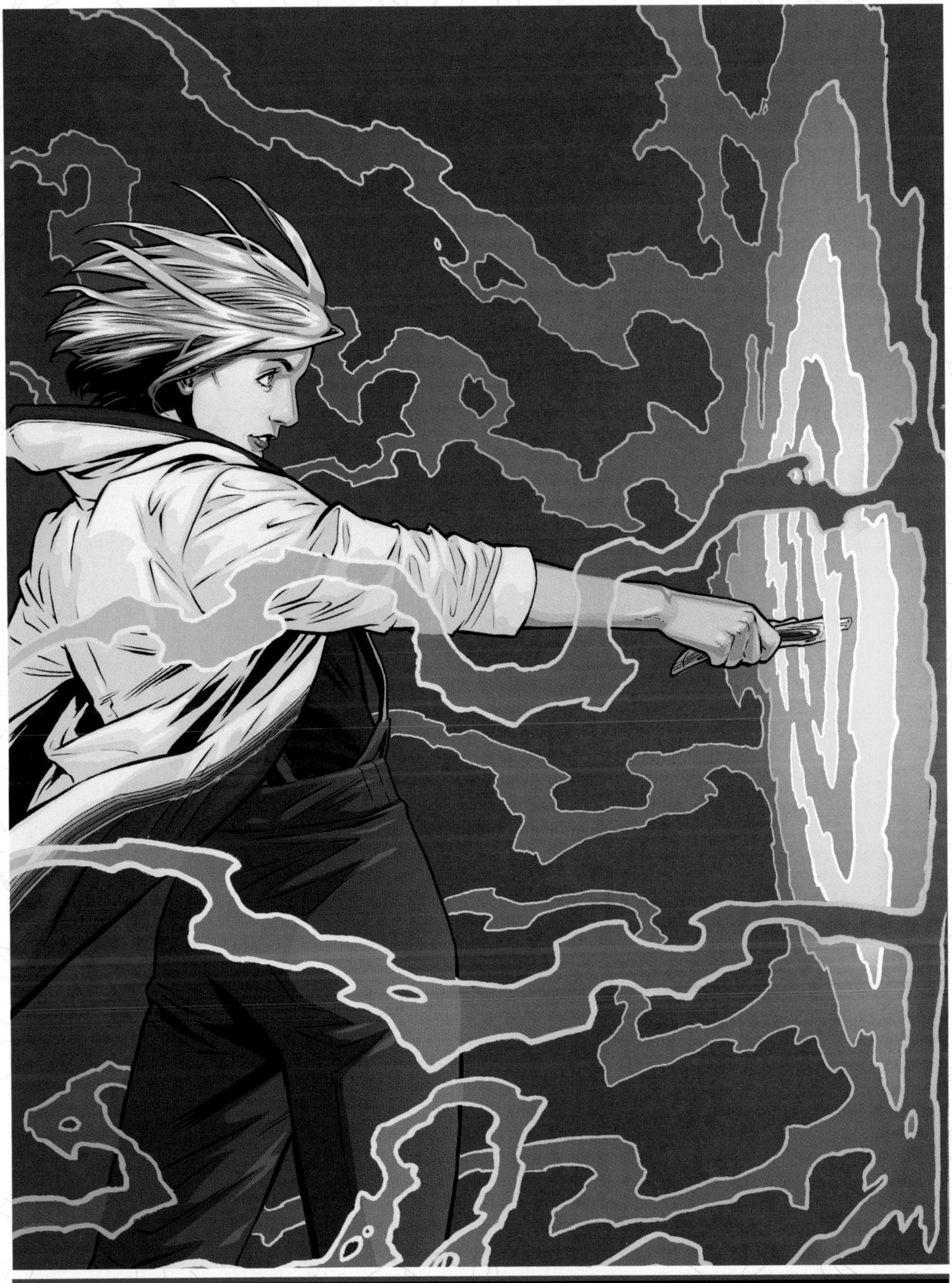

ISSUE #5 COVER A • REBEKAH ISAACS & DAN JACKSON

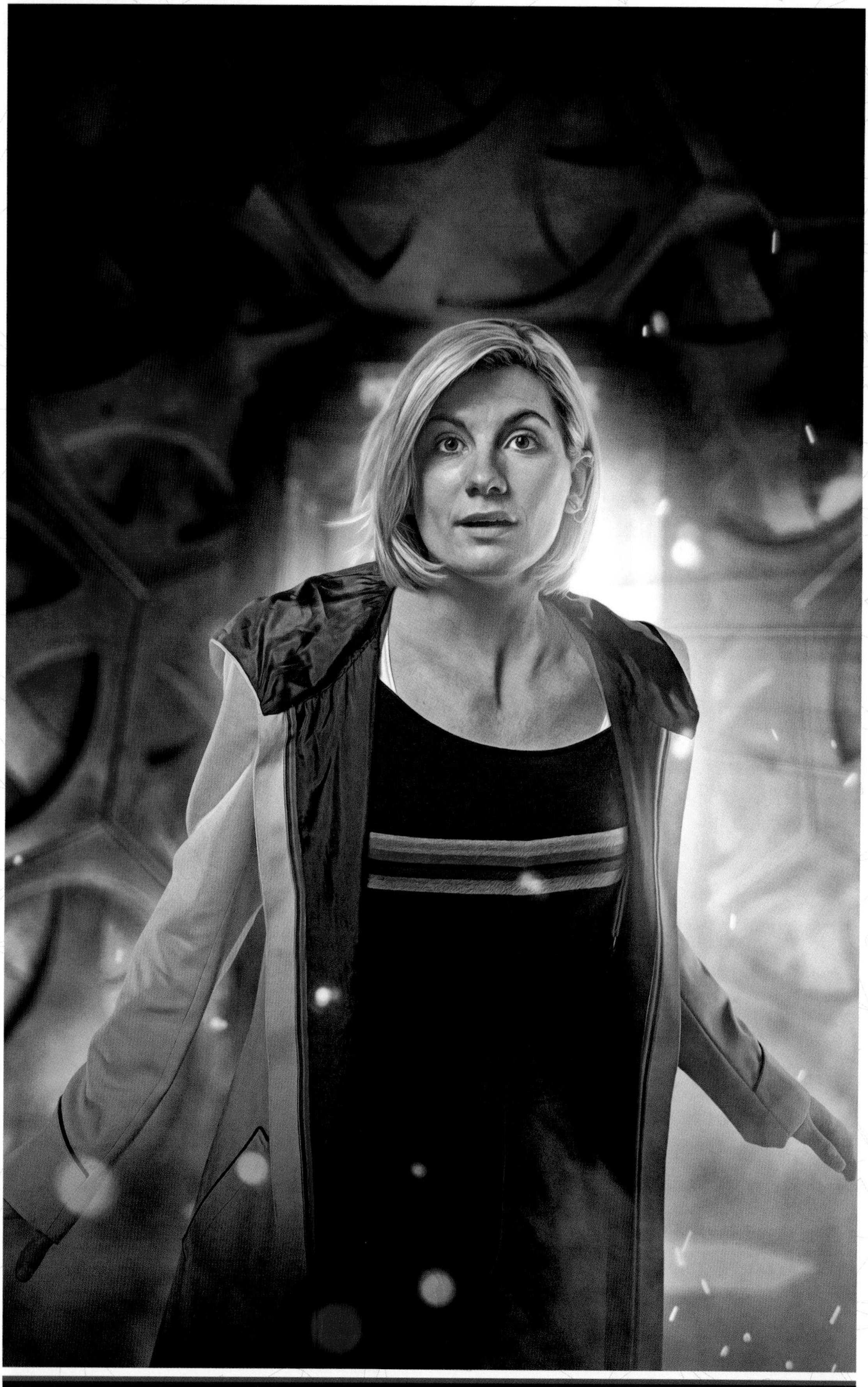

ISSUE #5 COVER B • WILL BROOKS

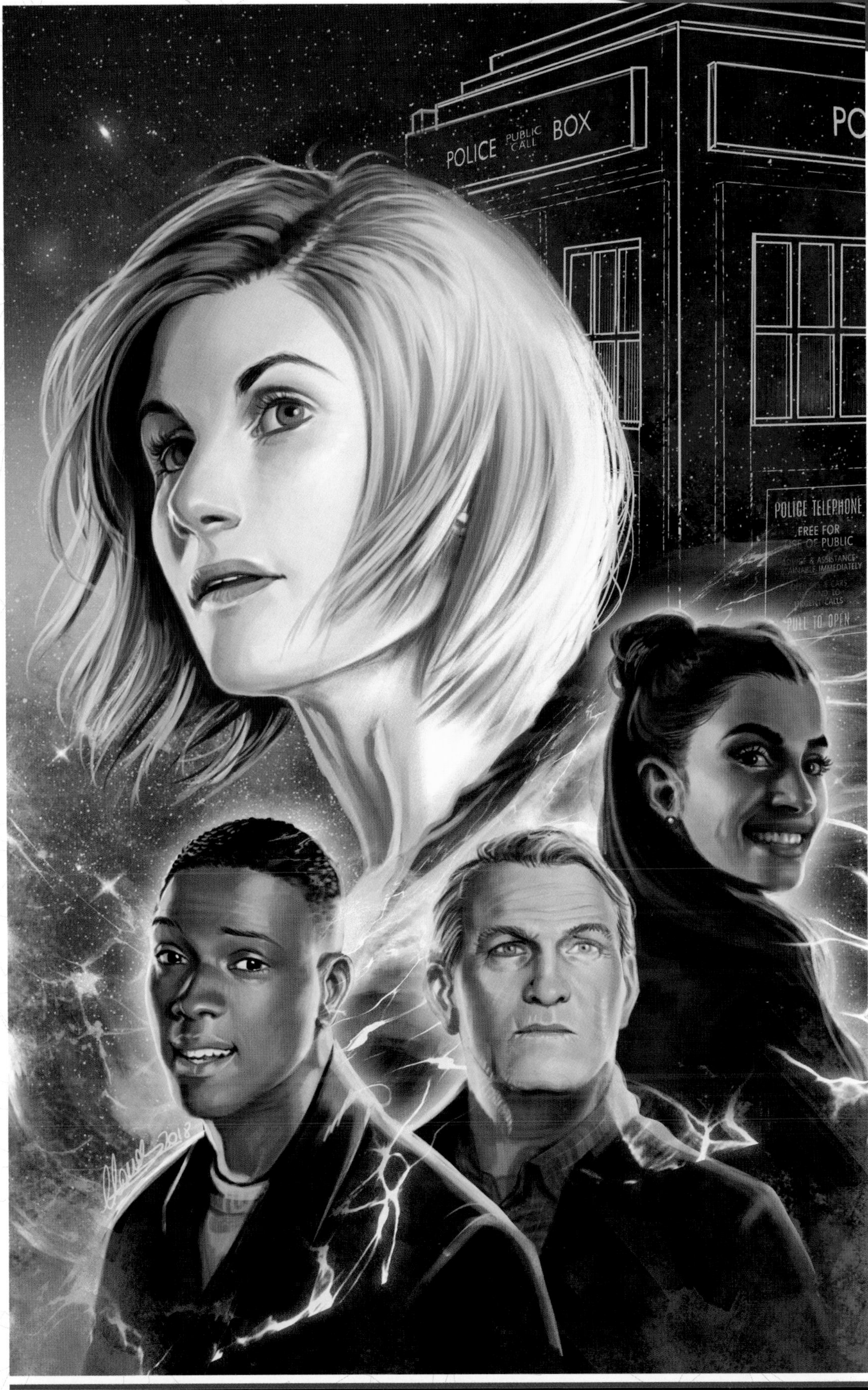
POLICE PUBLIC CALL BOX
POLICE TELEPHONE
FREE FOR
PULL TO OPEN

ISSUE #5 COVER C • CLAUDIA IANNICIELLO

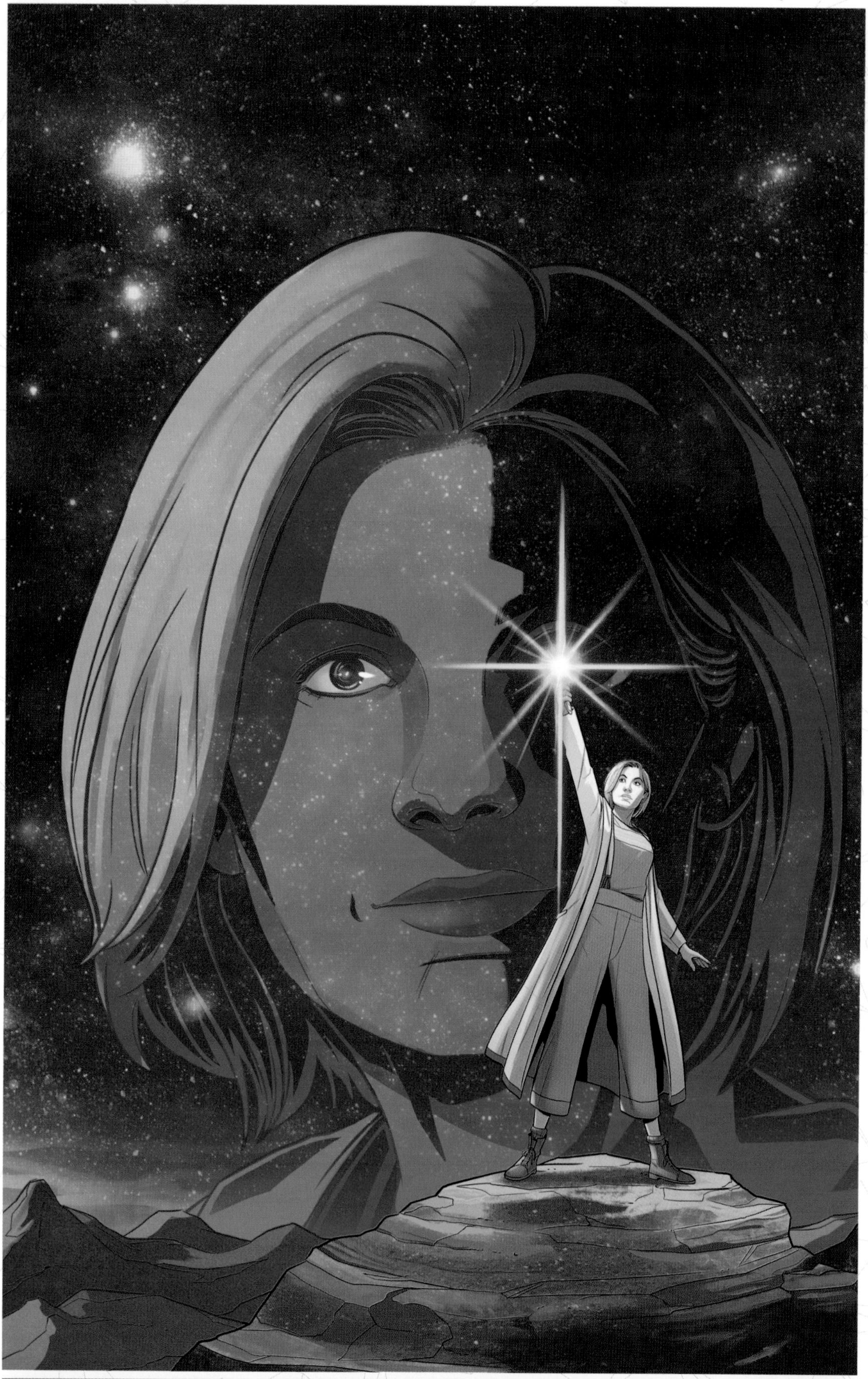

ISSUE #6 COVER A • GIORGIA SPOSITO & ADELE MATERA

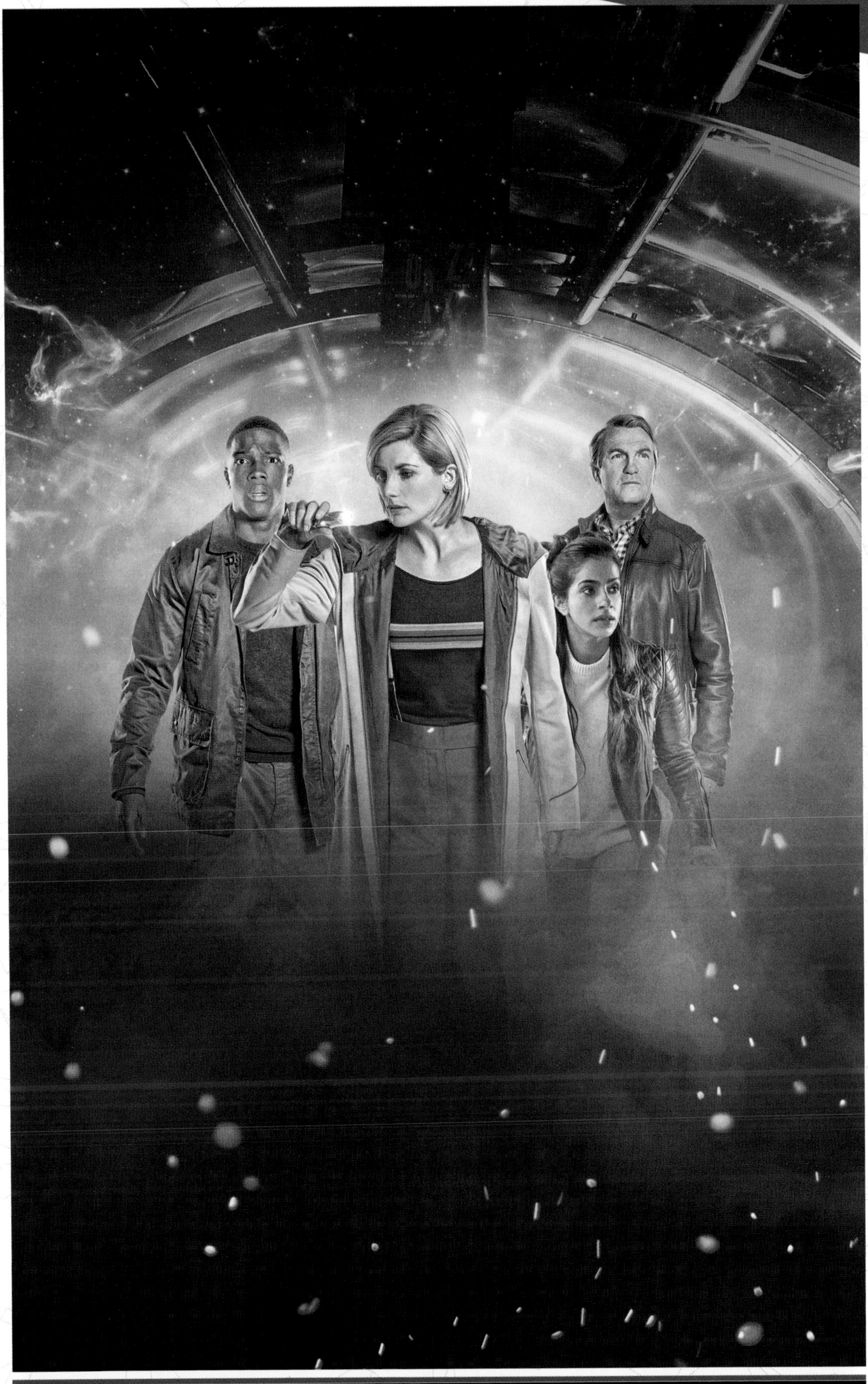

ISSUE #6 COVER B • WILL BROOKS

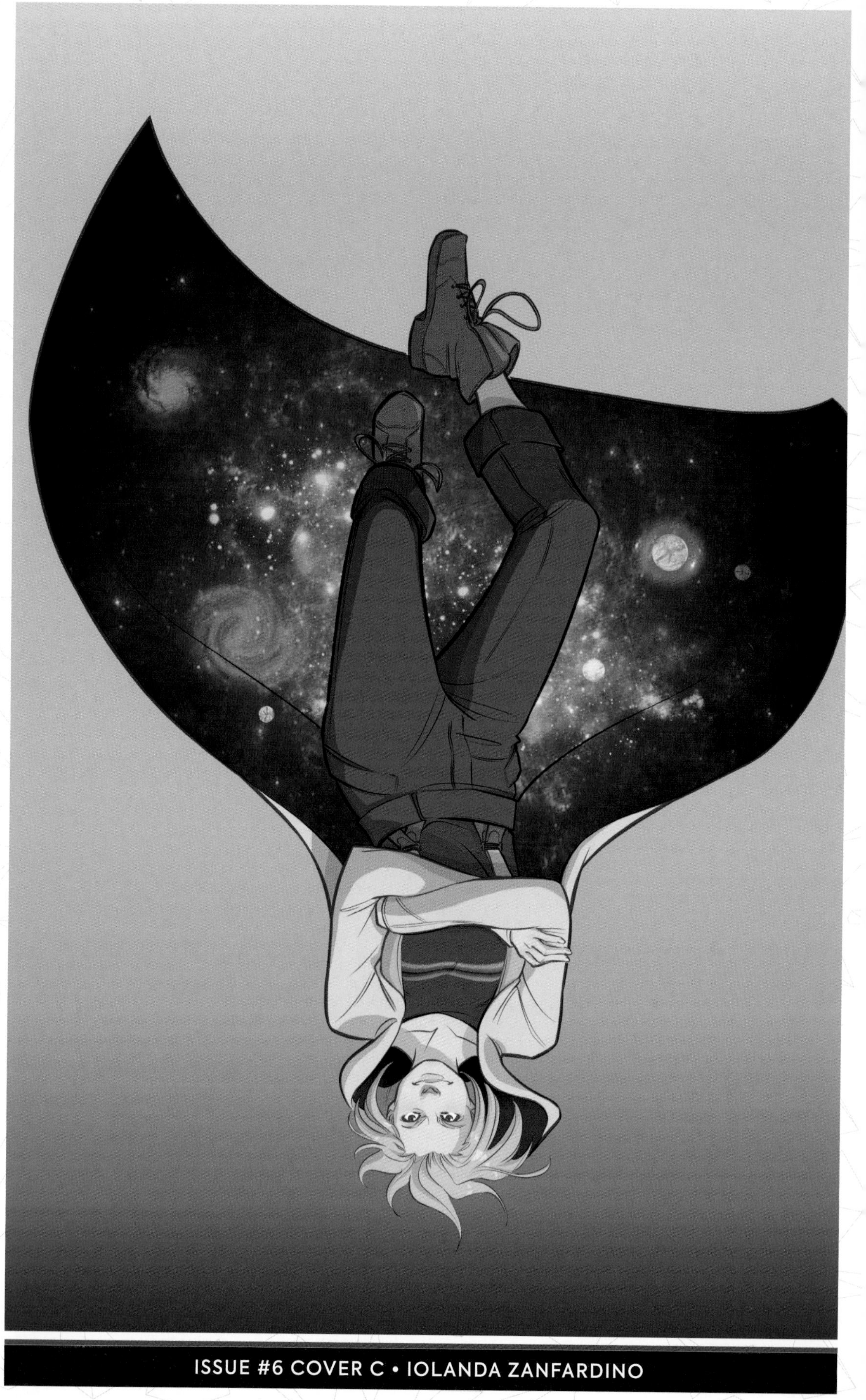

ISSUE #6 COVER C • IOLANDA ZANFARDINO

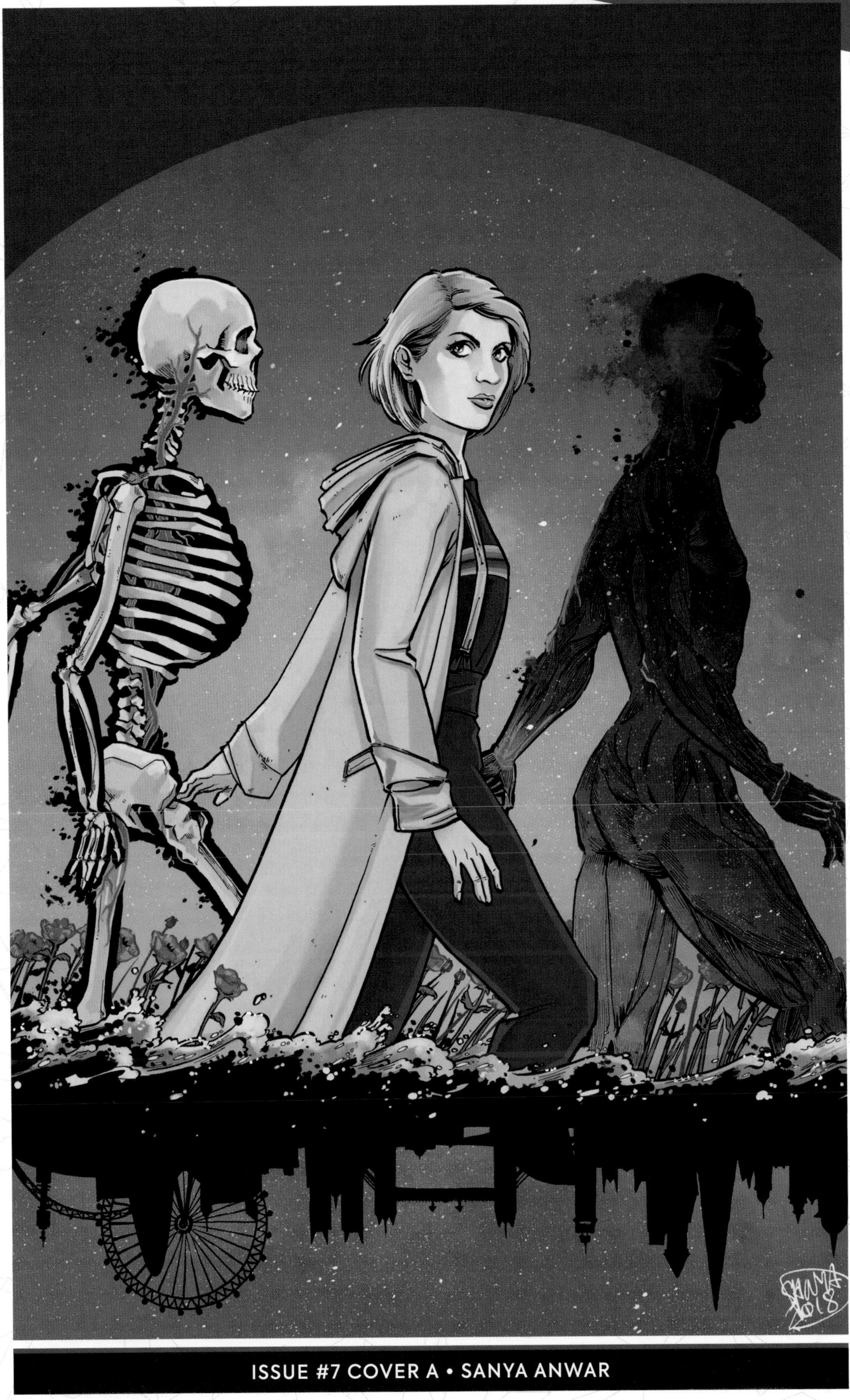

ISSUE #7 COVER A • SANYA ANWAR

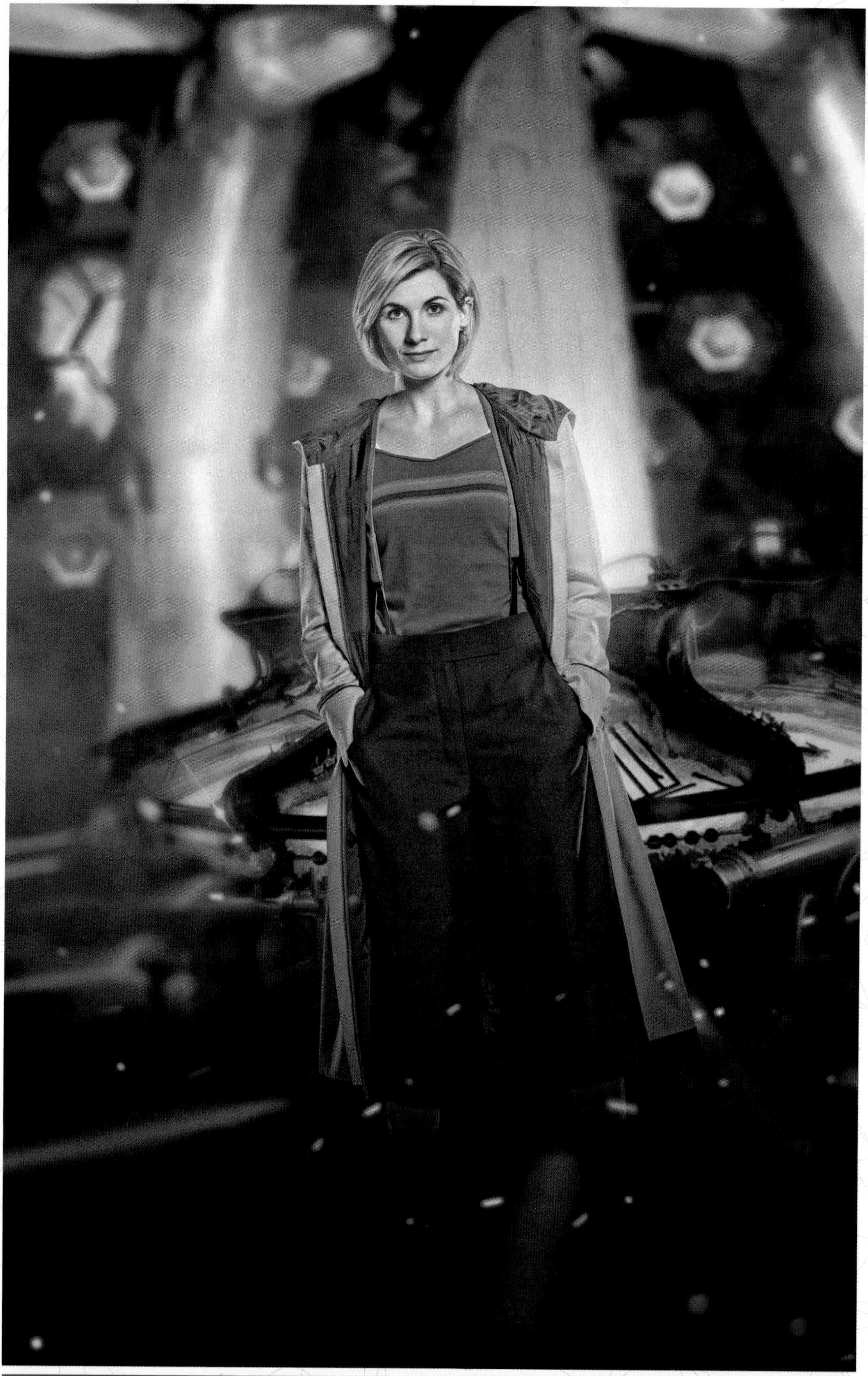

ISSUE #7 COVER B • WILL BROOKS

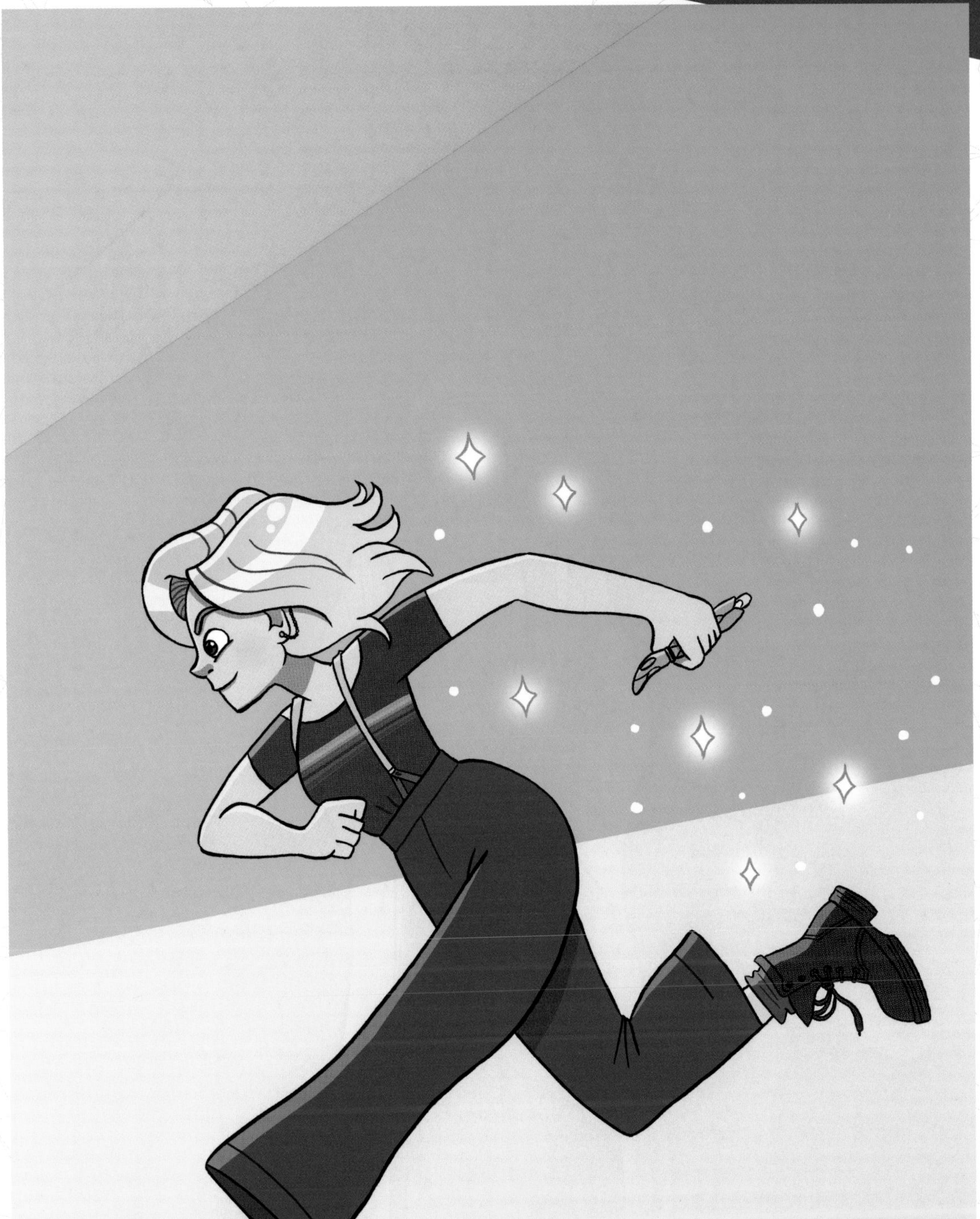

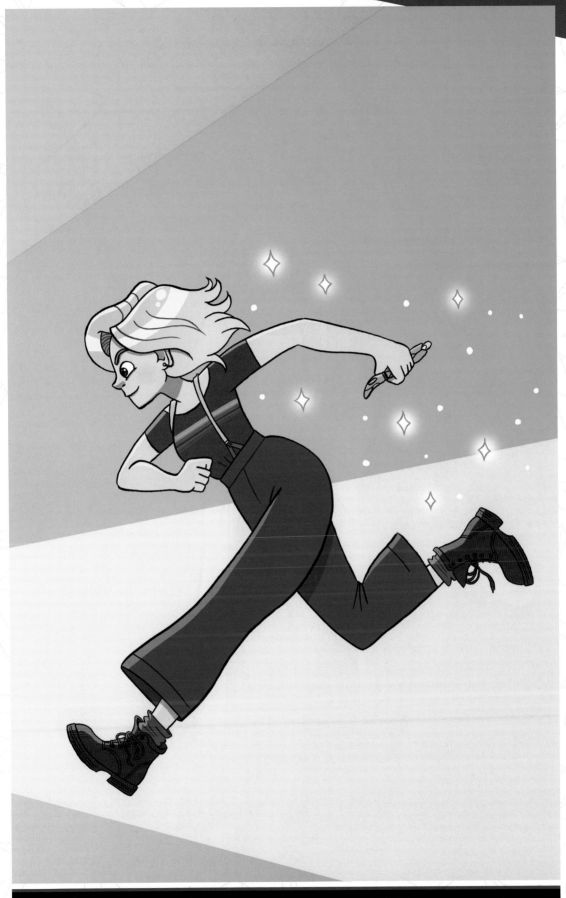

ISSUE #7 COVER C • RACHAEL SMITH

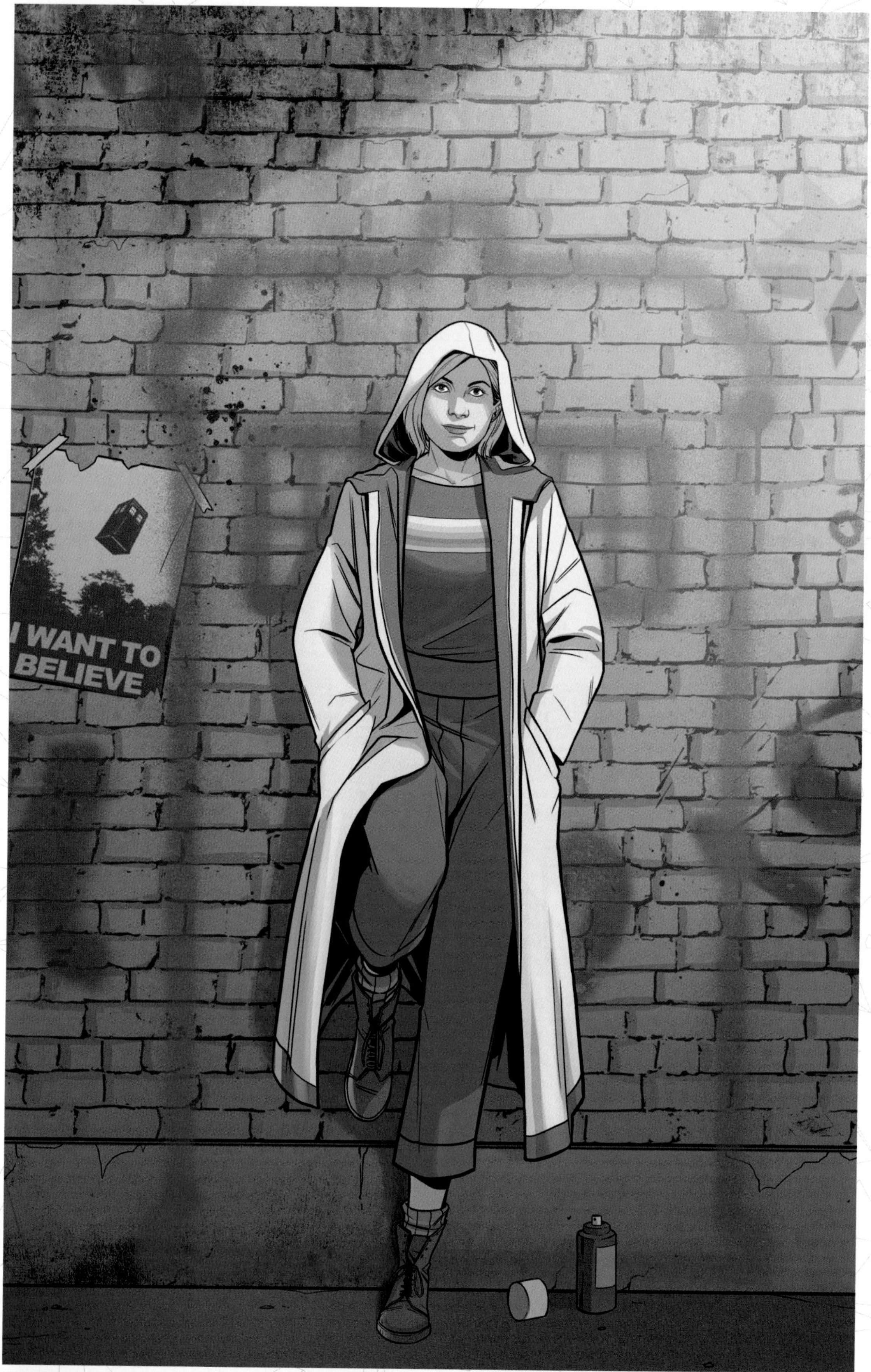
WANT TO
BELIEVE

ISSUE #8 COVER A • GIORGIA SPOSITO & ADELE MATERA

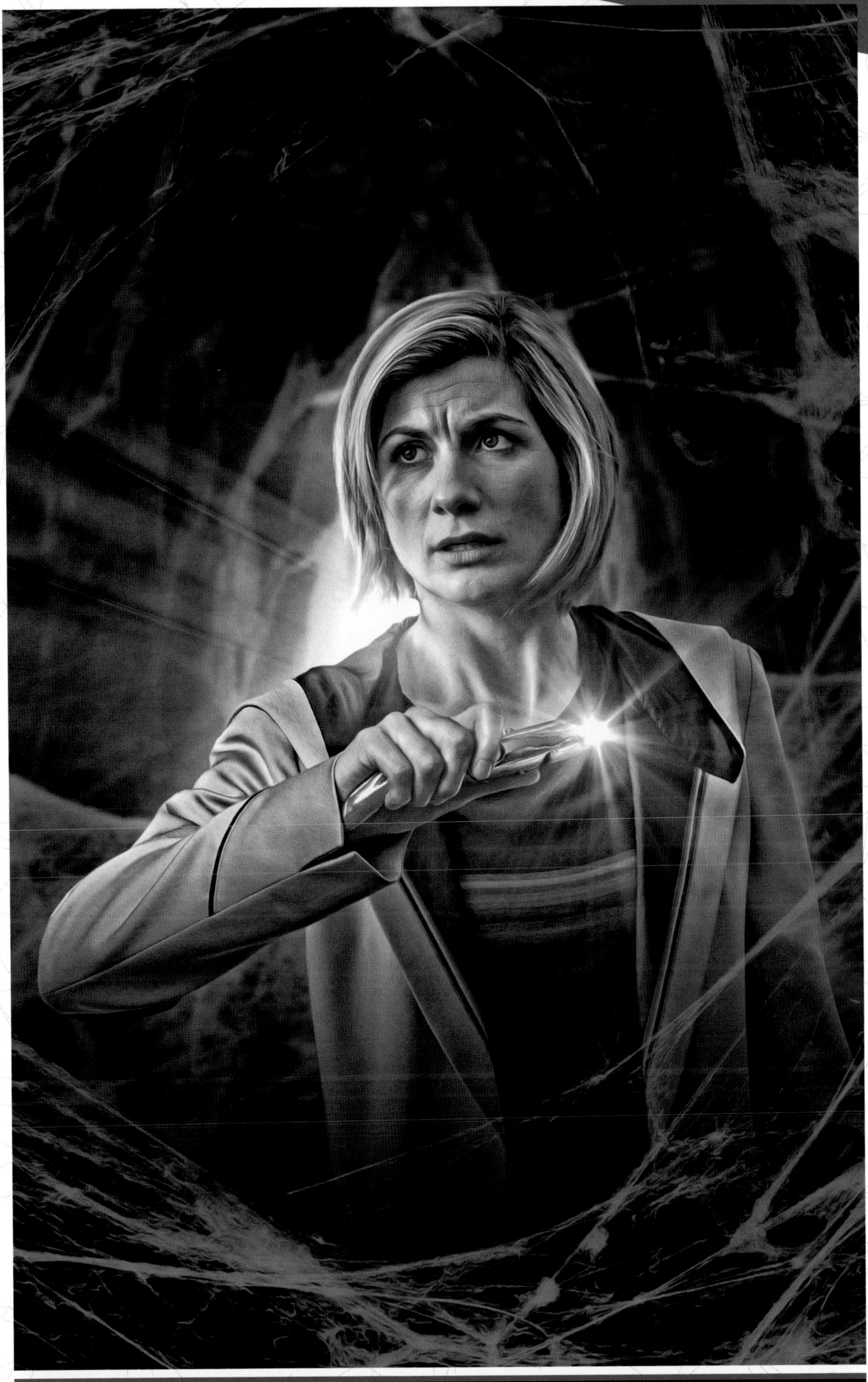

ISSUE #8 COVER B • WILL BROOKS

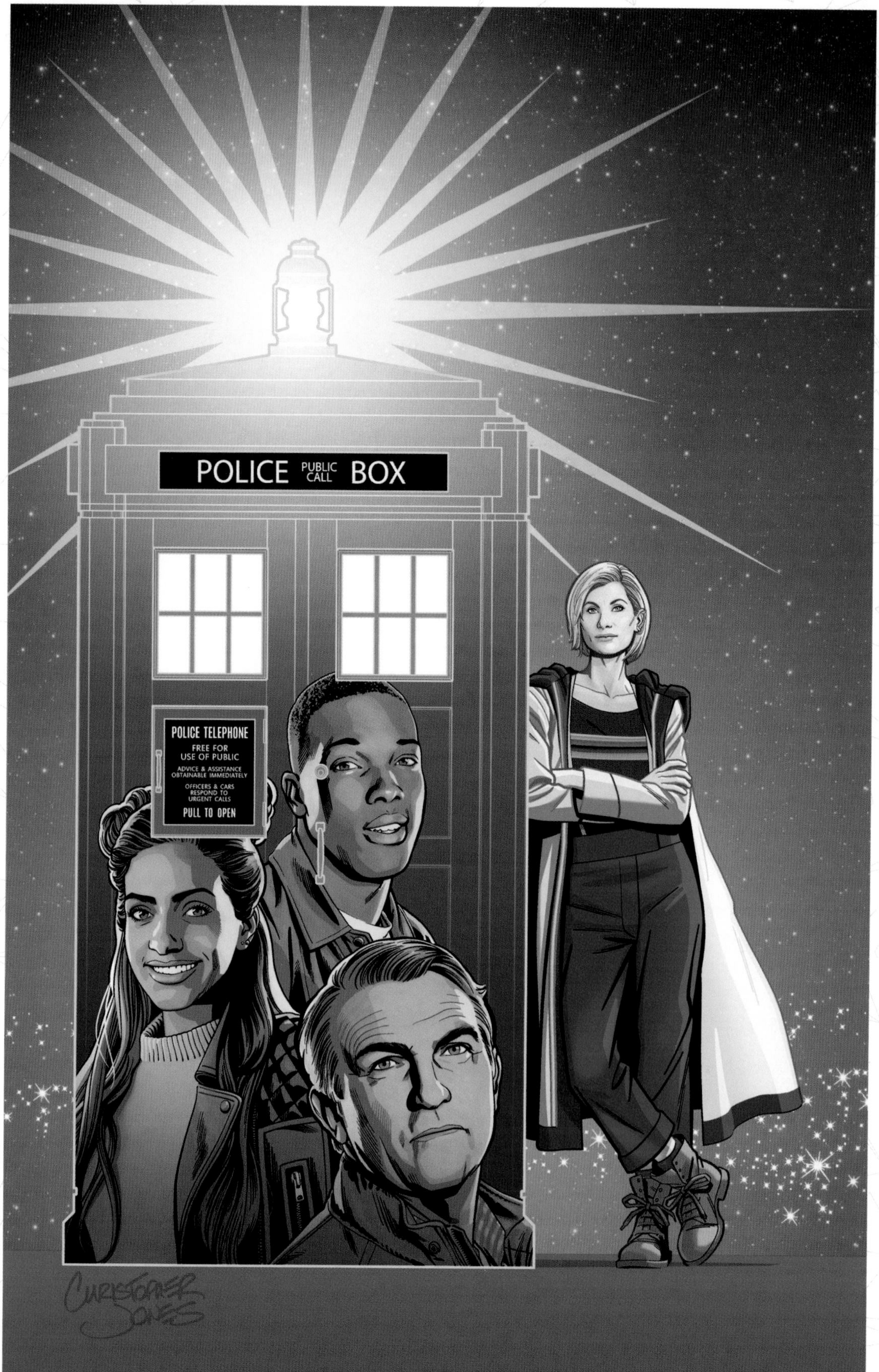
POLICE PUBLIC CALL BOX
POLICE TELEPHONE
FREE FOR USE OF PUBLIC
ADVICE & ASSISTANCE OBTAINABLE IMMEDIATELY
OFFICERS & CARS RESPOND TO URGENT CALLS
PULL TO OPEN
CHRISTOPHER JONES

ISSUE #8 COVER C • CHRISTOPHER JONES

The Doctor And I
By Jody Houser

Why do I like *Doctor Who*?

For many people, the answer to that goes back to the very beginning. There's a reason "Who was your first Doctor?" is such a popular question. For me, it's always fun to see people's reactions when I say that my first Doctor was the Eighth Doctor. I was an American kid who never watched classic *Who* on PBS, making the TV movie airing on Fox my first exposure to the madman with a box.

I can't say I loved the movie, but the character at the center of it? He fascinated me enough that I was already sold when the new series hit this side of the Atlantic.

But that's the how, not the why.

The cheeky answer is that a show that makes me cry is generally a show I'm hooked on for life. I enjoyed those first few episodes with Nine and Rose, but "Father's Day" was the gut punch. It's the episode I generally credit with making me a Whovian (thanks Paul!).

There's also the writer answer. As a professional storyteller, seeing a series that has reinvention and evolution built-in as a feature going back to its earliest days is brilliant. *Doctor Who* persists because the Doctor can be who and what we need them to be in that moment in time. As a writer playing in the world, weaving together the threads of the old and new is a delightful challenge.

And then there's the heartfelt answer. That, at the end of the day, we need to be reminded that there is still goodness and adventure out there in the universe.

As children, we read and watch stories of kids just like us going on mystical journeys. Through the closet to Narnia. On a magical train ride to Hogwarts. But as we grow up, it can seem like the age to have that magical life-changing adventure has passed us by. We may all know our Hogwarts house, but we're too old to expect that an owl with a letter will find its way to us.

But the Doctor? The Doctor is several thousand years old (or several billion, depending on if we're counting confession dials). And who has more adventures than the Doctor? The Doctor shows us that no matter the mileage, there are still new things to discover and admire and run from. And that's before we take a look at the Doctor's companions, which include multiple grandparents.

You would think that, at some point, the Doctor will have seen it all, done it all. But there are still more stories to write. More adventures to be had. And as long as that can hold true for the Doctor, perhaps the universe holds the same promise for all of us.

BBC
DOCTOR WHO

READER'S GUIDE

With so many amazing *Doctor Who* collections already on the shelves, it c
be difficult to know where to start. That's where this handy guide comes in
And don't be overwhelmed – every collection is designed to be welcoming
whatever your knowledge of *Doctor Who*.

THE TWELFTH DOCTOR

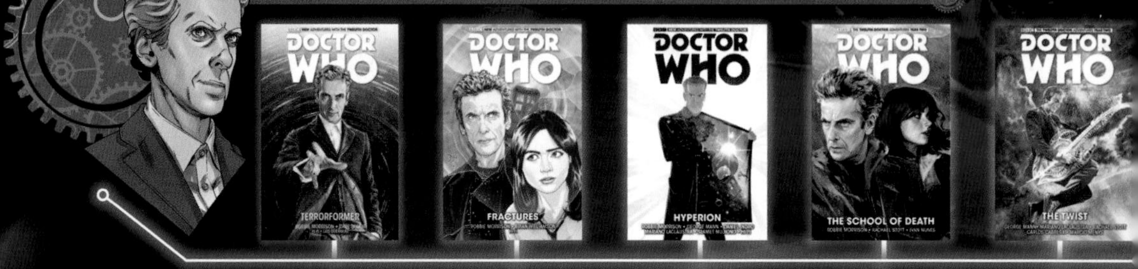

VOL. 1: TERRORFORMER

VOL. 2: FRACTURES

VOL. 3: HYPERION

YEAR TWO BEGINS! VOL. 4: SCHOOL OF DEATH

VOL. 5: THE TWIST

THE ELEVENTH DOCTOR

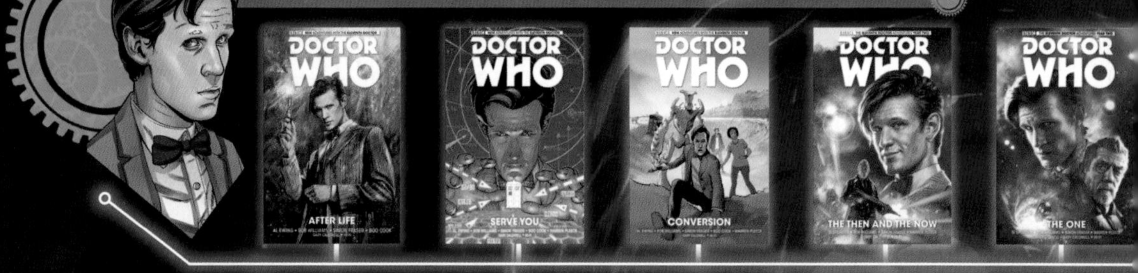

VOL. 1: AFTER LIFE

VOL. 2: SERVE YOU

VOL. 3: CONVERSION

YEAR TWO BEGINS! VOL. 4: THE THEN AND THE NOW

VOL. 5: THE ONE

THE TENTH DOCTOR

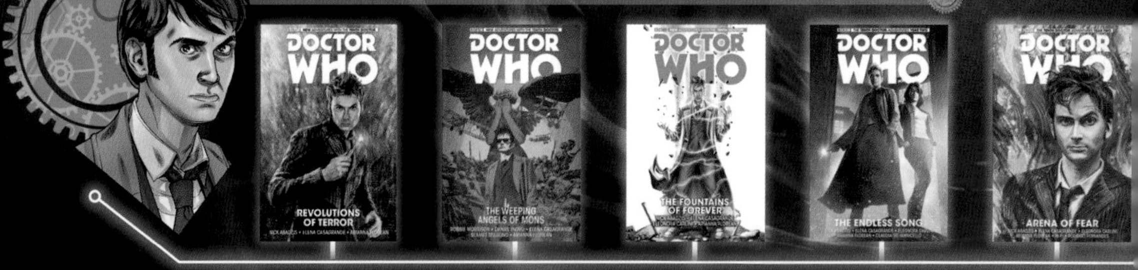

VOL. 1: REVOLUTIONS OF TERROR

VOL. 2: THE WEEPING ANGELS OF MONS

VOL. 3: THE FOUNTAINS OF FOREVER

YEAR TWO BEGINS! VOL. 4: THE ENDLESS SONG

VOL. 5: ARENA OF FEAR

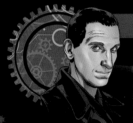

THE NINTH DOCTOR

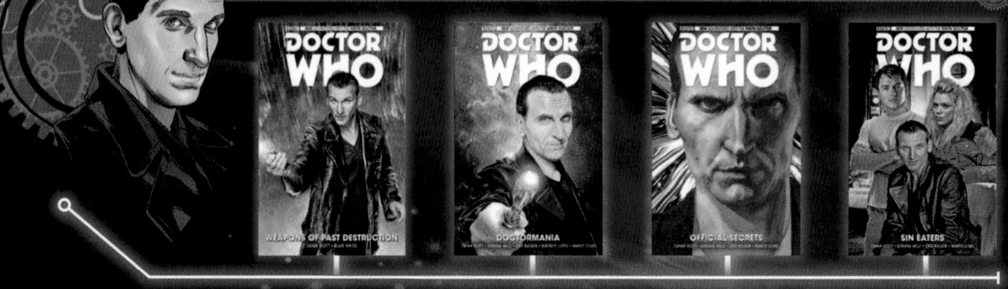

VOL. 1: WEAPONS OF PAST DESTRUCTION

VOL. 2: DOCTORMANIA

VOL. 3: OFFICIAL SECRETS

VOL. 4: SIN EATERS

ach comic series is entirely self-contained and focused on one Doctor, so you can follow one, two, or all
f your favorite Doctors, as you wish! The series are arranged in TV season-like Years, collected into roughly
ıree collections per Year. Feel free to start at Volume 1 of any series, or jump straight to the volumes
ıbelled in blue! Each book, and every comic, features a catch-up and character guide at the beginning,
ıaking it easy to jump on board – and each comic series has a very different flavor, representative of that
octor's era on screen. If in doubt, set the TARDIS Randomizer and dive in wherever you land!

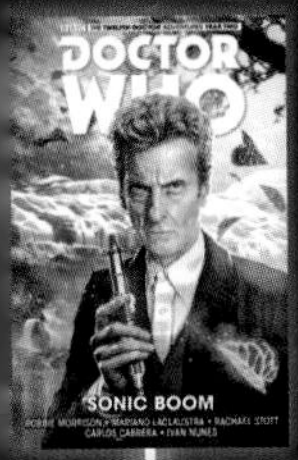
DOCTOR WHO
SONIC BOOM
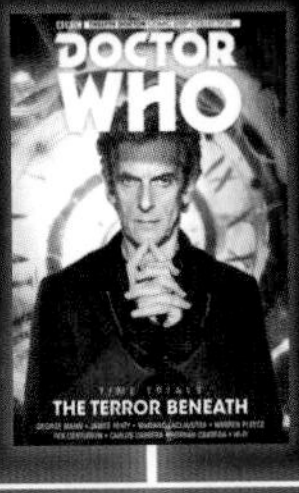
DOCTOR WHO
THE TERROR BENEATH
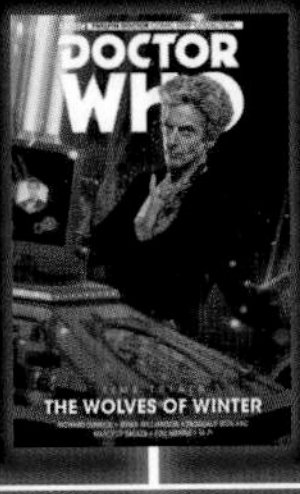
DOCTOR WHO
THE WOLVES OF WINTER
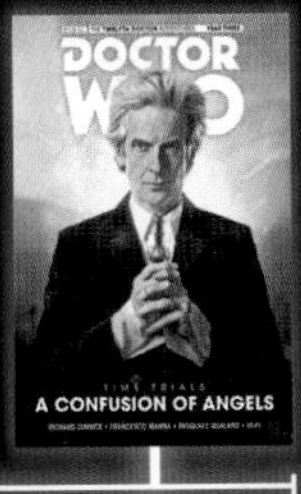
DOCTOR WHO
A CONFUSION OF ANGELS

VOL. 6:
SONIC BOOM

YEAR THREE BEGINS!
TIME TRIALS VOL. 1:
THE TERROR BENEATH

TIME TRIALS VOL. 2:
THE WOLVES
OF WINTER

TIME TRIALS VOL. 3:
A CONFUSION OF
ANGELS

THE THIRTEENTH DOCTOR

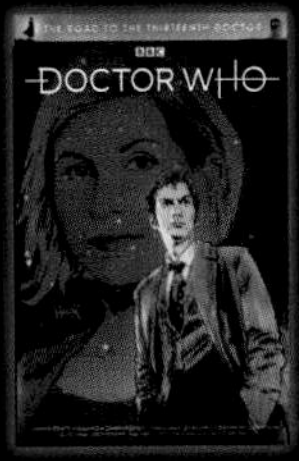
DOCTOR WHO

THE ROAD TO THE
THIRTEENTH DOCTOR

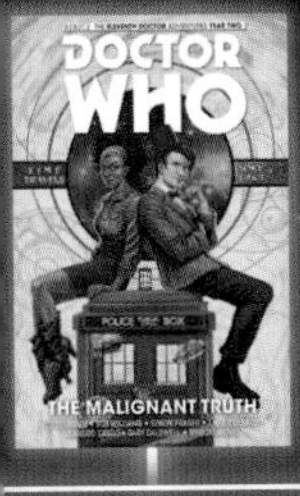
DOCTOR WHO
THE MALIGNANT TRUTH
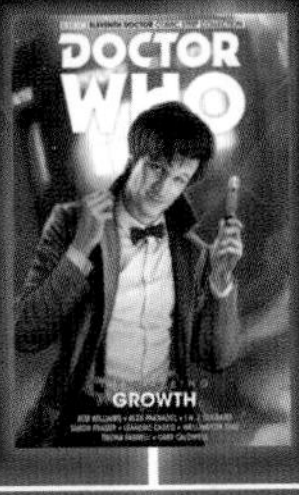
DOCTOR WHO
GROWTH
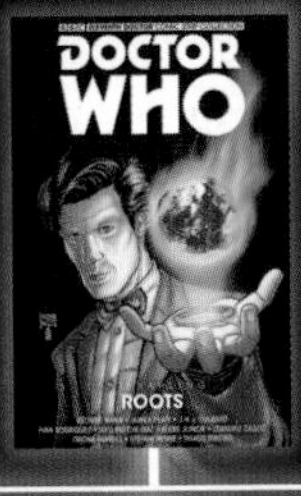
DOCTOR WHO
ROOTS
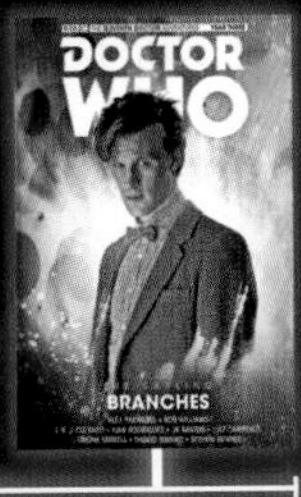
DOCTOR WHO
BRANCHES

VOL. 6:
'HE MALIGNANT TRUTH

YEAR THREE BEGINS!
THE SAPLING VOL. 1:
GROWTH

THE SAPLING VOL. 2:
ROOTS

THE SAPLING VOL. 3:
BRANCHES

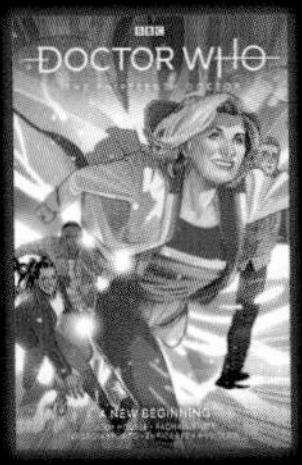
DOCTOR WHO
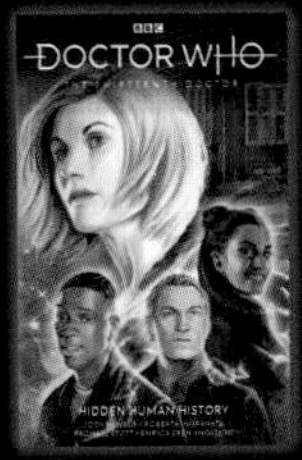
DOCTOR WHO

VOL. 1:
A NEW
BEGINNING

VOL. 2:
HIDDEN HUMAN
HISTORY

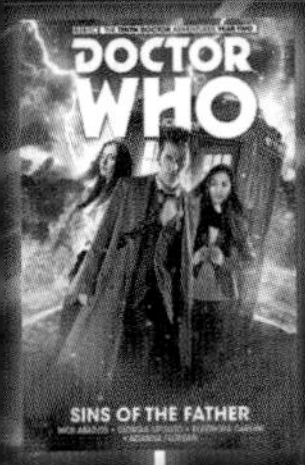
DOCTOR WHO
SINS OF THE FATHER
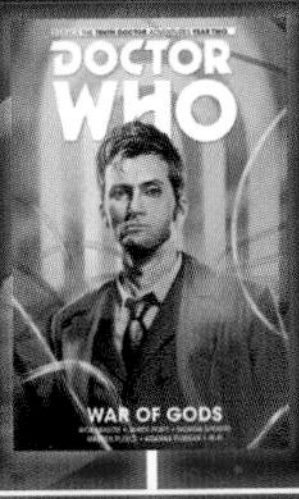
DOCTOR WHO
WAR OF GODS
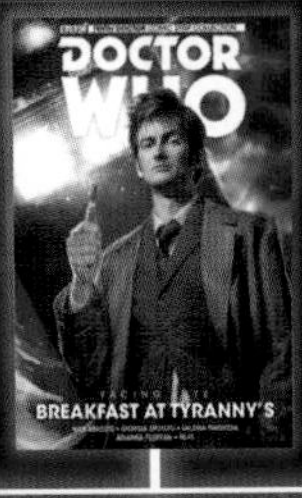
DOCTOR WHO
BREAKFAST AT TYRANNY'S
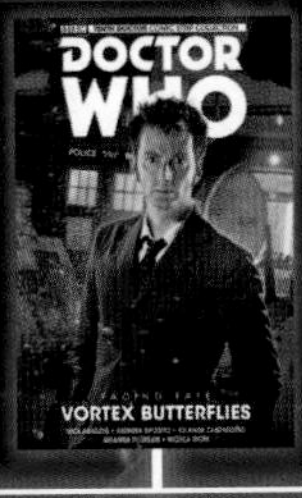
DOCTOR WHO
VORTEX BUTTERFLIES
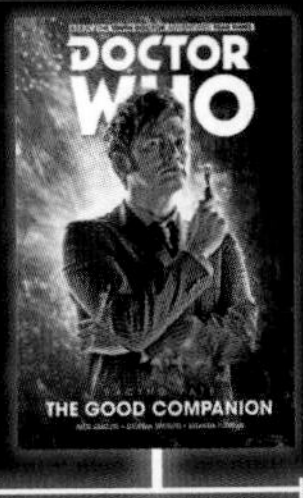
DOCTOR WHO
THE GOOD COMPANION

VOL. 6:
SINS OF THE FATHER

VOL. 7:
WAR OF GODS

YEAR THREE BEGINS!
FACING FATE VOL. 1:
BREAKFAST AT TYRANNY'S

FACING FATE VOL. 2:
VORTEX BUTTERFLIES

FACING FATE VOL. 3:
THE GOOD COMPANION

CLASSIC DOCTORS

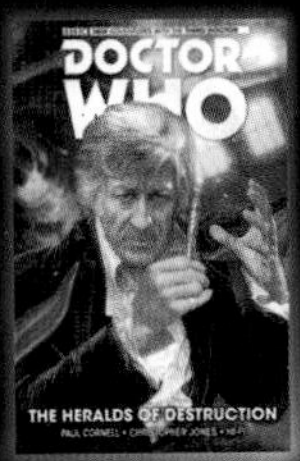
DOCTOR WHO
THE HERALDS OF DESTRUCTION
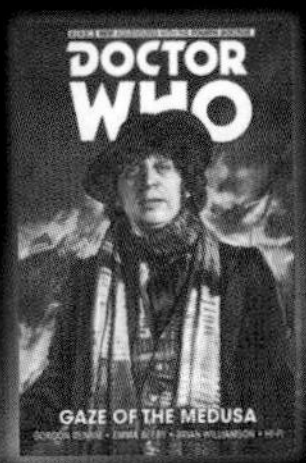
DOCTOR WHO
GAZE OF THE MEDUSA
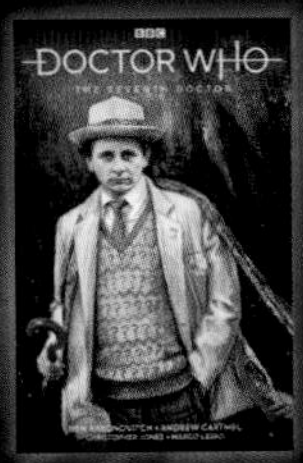
DOCTOR WHO
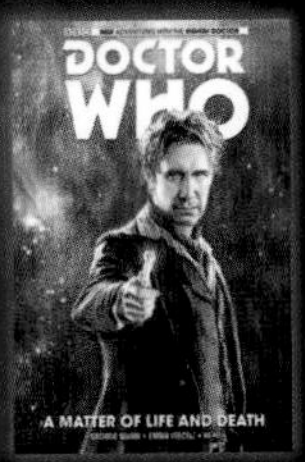
DOCTOR WHO
A MATTER OF LIFE AND DEATH

THIRD DOCTOR:
THE HERALDS OF

FOURTH DOCTOR:
GAZE OF THE

SEVENTH DOCTOR:
OPERATION

EIGHTH DOCTOR:
A MATTER OF LIFE
AND DEATH

MULTI-DOCTOR EVENTS

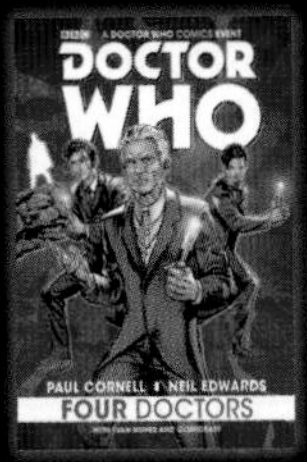
DOCTOR WHO
PAUL CORNELL NEIL EDWARDS
FOUR DOCTORS
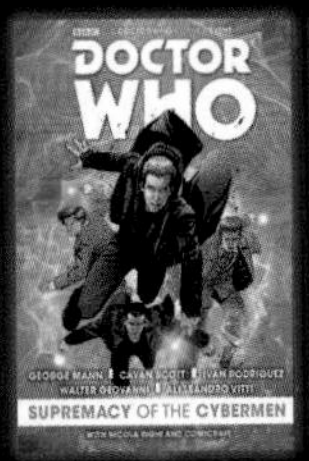
DOCTOR WHO
SUPREMACY OF THE CYBERMEN
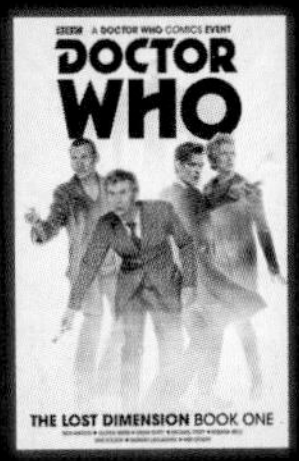
DOCTOR WHO
THE LOST DIMENSION BOOK ONE

FOUR
DOCTORS

SUPREMACY OF
THE CYBERMEN

THE LOST
DIMENSION
(BOOKS ONE & TWO)

The Many Lives of Doctor Who

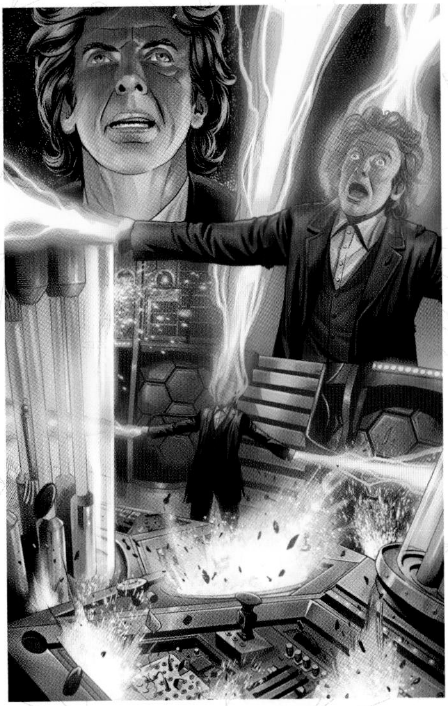

As the Twelfth Doctor regenerates into the Thirteenth, they flash back across their many lives and multiple incarnations – revealing brand-new stories from every era and face of the Doctor to date!

Written by **Richard Dinnick** (*The Twelfth Doctor*) and illustrated by a fantastic selection of mind-blowing artistic talents, this is the perfect introduction to *Doctor Who* for new readers, and the ultimate celebration of the series for long-term fans!

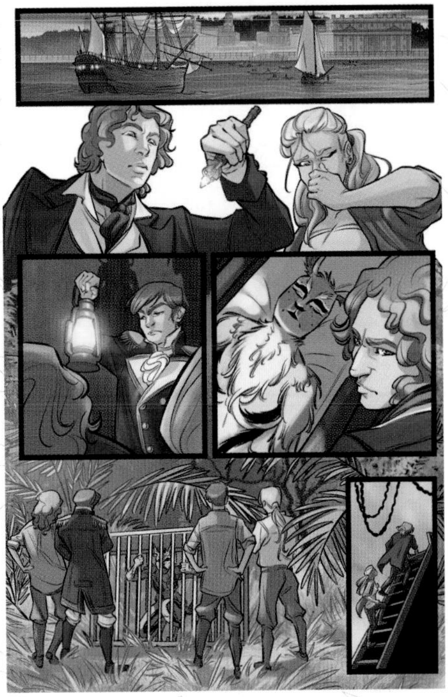

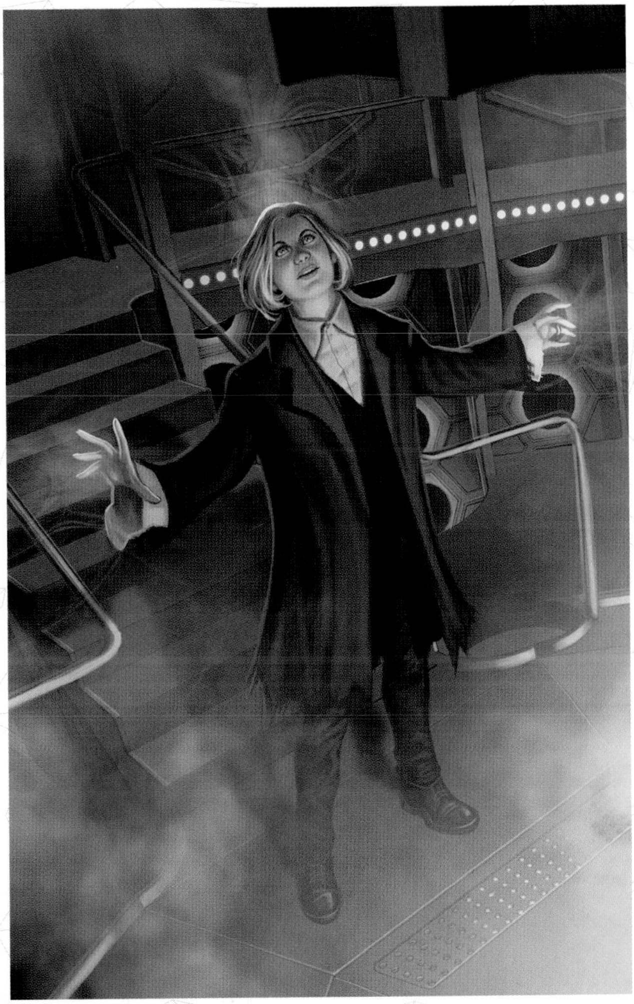

NEIL EDWARDS • PASQUALE QUALANO • CLAUDIA IANNICIELLO
RACHAEL STOTT • CARLOS CABRERA • ADELE MATERA • DIJJO LIMA

The Thirteenth Doctor's first amazing comic adventure with Yaz, Rian and Graham

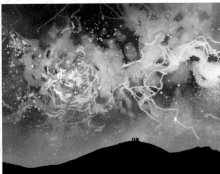

For the **Thirteenth Doctor**'s first adventure in comics, she is joined by fan favourites Yaz, Rian and Graham for a thrilling new adventure.

Trail-blazing through time tackling vile villains, avoiding an intergalactic alien civil war, uncovering the truth behind a secret human time travel experiment, and doing battle with an alien hoarder obsessed with amassing the greatest treasure in the history of the universe – with this new Doctor in charge, one thing's for certain: there's never a dull moment or a second to spare, even if you are a Time Lord!

Writer **Jody Houser**, artist **Rachael Stott,** and colorist **Enrica Eren Angiolini** deliver a stunning series!

BBC

DOCTOR WHO

THE THIRTEENTH DOCTOR

Biographies

Jody Houser

is a prolific writer of comics, perhaps best known for her work on *Faith* for Valiant, and *Mother Panic* for the Young Animal imprint at DC Comics. She has also written *Star Wars: Rogue One, Star Wars: Age of Republic, Amazing Spider-Man: Renew Your Vows*, and *Spider-Girls* for Marvel, *The X-Files: Origins* and *Orphan Black* for IDW, and *Stranger Things, StarCraft*, and *Halo* for Dark Horse.

Roberta Ingranata

is an Italian comic artist. Born in Milan in 1986, she worked for various Italian publishers before making the leap to US comics. Titles she has leant her considerable talents to include the highly acclaimed *Witchblade* series, *Robyn Hood*, and *Van Helsing*.

Rachael Stott

is a British artist who has worked on some of the most high-profile titles in comics, including *Star Trek, Planet of the Apes, Ghostbusters*, and *Doctor Who*. She has also worked on comics covers for titles like *Archie Comics*. A past winner of the Best Newcomer Award at the British Comics Awards, Rachael continues to enjoy critical acclaim for her brilliant work.

Enrica Eren Angiolini

is a colorist and illustrator from Italy. Enrica's rich colors go from strength to strength, as demonstrated by her work on *Warhammer 40,000, Shades of Magic: The Steel Prince*, and her cover work for Titan Comics, Dark Horse, and Aspen Comics.

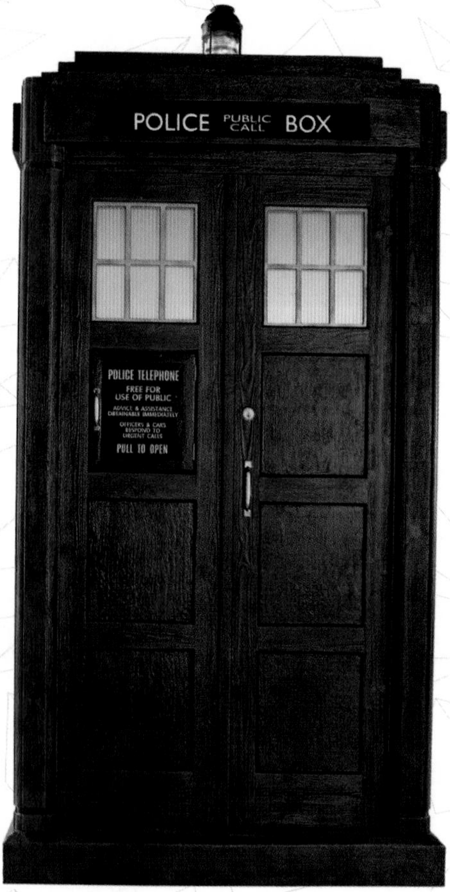
POLICE PUBLIC CALL BOX
POLICE TELEPHONE
FREE FOR USE OF PUBLIC
PULL TO OPEN